Echoes Down the Corridor

Echoes Down the Corridor

Edited by
Patrick Lonergan and
Riana O'Dwyer

Carysfort Press

A Carysfort Press Book in association with Peter Lang

Echoes Down the Corridor
Edited by Patrick Lonergan and Riana O'Dwyer

First published in Ireland in 2007 as a paperback original
by Carysfort Press, 58 Woodfield, Scholarstown Road
Dublin 16, Ireland
ISBN 978-1-78874-942-8

© 2007 Copyright remains with the authors

Typeset by Carysfort Press
Cover design by Alan Bennis

This book is published with the financial assistance of
The Arts Council (An Chomhairle Ealaíon), Dublin, Ireland

Caution: All rights reserved. No part of this book may be
printed or reproduced or utilized in any form or by any
electronic, mechanical, or other means, now known or
hereafter invented including photocopying and recording,
or in any information storage or retrieval system without
permission in writing from the publishers.

Contents

Acknowledgements		ix
Introduction **Patrick Lonergan and Riana O'Dwyer**		1
1	'Echoes Down the Corridor': The Abbey Theatre 1904-2004 **Christopher Murray**	13
2	A Synge for Our Times? Yeats's enquiring man revisited **Mary C. King**	29
3	Staging the Aesthetic: The Vagrant Artists of Padraic Colum and Seumas O'Kelly **Joan FitzPatrick Dean**	41
4	Shoyo Matsui, A Japanese Lennox Robinson: The Irish National Theatre and Japanese New Drama **Chiaki Kojima**	47
5	Wessex to Geesala: Hardy and Synge **Irina Ruppo**	59
6	Sean O'Casey and The Abbey Theatre: A Conflicted Relationship **Paul O'Brien**	69
7	*Observe the Sons of Ulster*: Historical Stages **Helen Lojek**	81

8	'Am I a con man?': Brian Friel's idea of the self-reflective artist, viewed in the light of Adorno's aesthetic theory **Christa Velten-Mrowka**	95
9	'A Voice and little else': talking, writing and singing in *The Gigli Concert* **Alexandra Poulain**	107
10	Spatializing the Renewal of Female Subjectivity in Marie Jones's *Women on the Verge of HRT* **Mária Kurdi**	117
11	The Present through the Prism of the Past: Frank McGuinness's *Dolly West's Kitchen* **Donal E. Morse**	129
12	'Grow a Mermaid': A Subtext for Marina Carr's Dramatic Works **Mika Funahashi**	141
13	Beyond Ryanga: The Image of Africa in Contemporary Irish Theatre **Jason King**	153
14	Nation and Myth in the Age of the Celtic Tiger: Muide Éire? **Lisa Fitzpatrick**	169

Bibliography	181
Contributors	193
Index	197

Acknowledgements

The papers published in this book were originally delivered at the 2004 Conference of the International Association for the Study of Irish Literatures (IASIL), which took place at National University of Ireland, Galway. The editors wish to thank their fellow conference organizers, Kirry O'Brien and Lesa Ní Mhunghaile, for their assistance with this project. Thanks are also due to our colleagues in the English Department of NUI Galway, and to the executive membership of IASIL. We wish to thank our panel of independent peer reviewers, whose advice on all of the papers submitted was invaluable. Finally, we wish to express our gratitude to Lilian Chambers, Dan Farrelly, and Eamonn Jordan of Carysfort Press, who supported this publication from an early stage.

Introduction
Patrick Lonergan and Riana O'Dwyer

This collection of fourteen new essays on Irish drama arises from the 2004 conference of the International Association for the Study of Irish Literatures, held at National University of Ireland, Galway. As we prepared for the conference during 2003, we became increasingly aware that the following year would be the occasion of a remarkably large number of Irish literary anniversaries: the hundredth Bloomsday, the centenary of the birth of Patrick Kavanagh, the centenary of the foundation of the Abbey Theatre in December 1904, and countless others. While the conference was on a broad theme related to all aspects of Irish literature, we felt it might be useful if IASIL 2004 provided a forum for our members to celebrate and interrogate these anniversaries; we also hoped that participants would use their explorations of the past as a way of pointing us towards new methods of studying, producing, and enjoying Irish literature in the future. In particular, we encouraged participants to reconsider the story of the Abbey Theatre's first hundred years.

Although we were aware of the recent growth in scholarship on Irish drama, we were surprised by the positive response to this call: of the 230 papers delivered at the conference, more than half were on Irish theatre, with papers being offered not only from scholars based in Ireland, but also by IASIL members from Australia, Japan, Korea, Poland, the Czech Republic, France, Italy, the UK, the United States, South Africa, and many other countries. We saw this enthusiasm and geographical spread as evidence of the way in which Irish drama is widely known throughout the world – and of the extent to which the study of Irish drama can be deeply enriched by the inclusion of voices from different theatrical and academic cultures.

Equally surprising, however, was that while the conference was underway, the Abbey Theatre's centenary programme appeared to be experiencing both a financial and artistic crisis – one that seemed at odds with the conference delegates' interest in the theatre and its repertoire. Throughout the year, the theatre had failed to generate sufficient levels of enthusiasm for its centenary programme amongst audiences, prospective sponsors, or the media; and two productions planned for the final quarter of the year (Paul Mercier's *Smokescreen* and a revival of Lennox Robinson's *Drama at Inish*) were cancelled due to financial problems. Attendance figures from January to May 2004 were considerably lower than the theatre's management had expected, and its fundraising committee had, according to some commentators, failed to meet its targets. The resulting sense of crisis led to an announcement one month after the IASIL conference that up to one-third of the Abbey's staff were to be made redundant, while there were many calls for the dismissal of the theatre's Artistic Director Ben Barnes from his post. Crisis threatened to become catastrophe with the leaking of an email from Barnes to his international colleagues, criticizing the Theatre's Board.

Key to this problem was the perception of many commentators that the 'abbeyonehundred' programme was decidedly conservative, placing too much 'emphasis on large-scale productions of existing Irish plays'.[1] Certainly, considered as a statement by the Abbey of its achievements during the previous century, the programme sent out confusing messages. Although it included acknowledged Irish classics such as *Portia Coughlan* (Carr, 1996), *Purgatory* (Yeats, 1937), *The Playboy of the Western World* (Synge, 1907), *The Gigli Concert* (Murphy, 1985) and *Observe the Sons of Ulster* (McGuinness, 1985), the programme also featured *I Do Not Like Thee Doctor Fell* (1979), the first play of former Abbey Board Member Bernard Farrell, whose works, while popular, would not generally be regarded as among the best Irish plays of the twentieth century. Also notable was the theatre's unwillingness to risk new drama on its main stage during 2004, which seemed disappointing for an institution that prides itself on a tradition of nurturing new Irish writers.

The messages conveyed by the theatre's omissions were also criticized. Only two of the full productions in the abbeyonehundred programme – Paula Meehan's Christmas play for children *The Wolf of Winter* and a revival of Marina Carr's *Portia Coughlan* – were by female authors, both of whom were being produced on the Abbey's Peacock stage, a smaller space used for experimental work and new writing. Although full productions by Yeats and Synge featured, the only work in the programme from the theatre's third figurehead Augusta Gregory was a once-off staged reading of *Spreading the News* in September 2004. Commentators also noted that only three of the year's full productions were directed by women. Also criticized was the theatre's omission of plays in the Irish language, its failure to undertake meaningful Irish tours, and many other features of its artistic policy. Finally, the theatre's management of the centenary programme itself was criticized, both during the summer of

2004 when it was forced into a number of unplanned rearrangements of its line-up, and from September 2004 onwards, when the theatre's management structures were subjected to intense media scrutiny.

Most of these criticisms of the Abbey seem to have been grounded in a belief that, as a national institution, the theatre confers value on dramatists and their works by including them in the national repertoire. Thus, the abbeyonehundred programme was not seen simply as a collection of plays, but as an act of public memory: a statement of what Ireland, as a nation in 2004, valued from its past. This explains the disappointment many felt about the lack of work in Irish or by women writers from the centenary programme. It should be noted that the Abbey produced three plays by women in 2003,[2] and produced four well-regarded plays in the Irish language under the Artistic Directorship of Patrick Mason.[3] Media commentary implied that the exclusion of both from the centenary programme was, however, a serious oversight that both reveals and reinforces many of the prejudices of Irish society. These criticisms appear to be derived from the belief that the power of a national institution to confer value is a responsibility that was neglected in the construction of the abbeyonehundred programme.

The construction of that programme might have implied that the theatre's immediate priority was simple financial survival, rather than national self-representation: the Abbey entered its centenary year with an operating deficit of €800,000, which, by the end of 2004, had risen to more than €2 million. Financial necessity may also explain the one controversy that seemed genuinely to surprise management at the Abbey: the media's sceptical response to Barnes's decision to produce Dion Boucicault's *The Shaughraun*, directed by John McColgan, as its major summer offering. In part, this scepticism was because McColgan had never before directed a professional piece of theatre, though he had been responsible for *Riverdance*. Commentators noted that he was chair of the Abbey's fundraising committee, and that he had himself donated large amounts of money to the theatre (believed to be in the region of €500,000). McColgan vigorously defended himself against the accusation that there was anything odd about a first-time director being given a mainstage summer production on the stage of the Abbey – notably in a *Late Late Show* special about the Abbey broadcast on Irish television on 16 January 2004, and in other public interviews.

Even without the controversy about McColgan, the inclusion of Boucicault in the Abbey's centenary programme reveals much about the theatre's current situation. The inclusion of a play reviled by the Abbey's founders in the centenary programme appears to ignore the foundational ethos of the theatre, and in particular its relationship to the production of melodrama. When the Abbey was established, melodrama was very popular in Dublin: the week before the Abbey's inaugural production on 27 December 1904, Dublin's Queen's Theatre had staged *The*

Shaughraun. And, as Christopher Morash points out, 'on the same December night' as the Abbey's first performances, 'across the Liffey almost two thousand people were howling for the informer's blood' in another Irish melodrama, J.W. Whitbread's *Sarsfield*, which was also staged at the Queen's.[4] Dublin audiences in 1904 were familiar with, and fond of, Boucicault: *The Shaughraun*, *The Colleen Bawn*, and *Arrah-na-Pogue* had been revived every year in Dublin during the 1890s[5], and were the most popular of the many Irish melodramas produced at that time. The foundation of the Irish Literary Theatre in 1898 and of the Abbey in 1904 was an attempt to offer Irish audiences something different from, and better than, these melodramas. 'We will show', wrote Yeats, 'that Ireland is not the home of buffoonery and of easy sentiment, as it has been represented, but the home of an ancient idealism.' The Irish people are 'weary of misrepresentation' by writers such as Boucicault, Yeats claimed.[6] This early hostility to melodrama persisted throughout the theatre's earliest years: for example, Sean O'Casey states that he 'instinctively kept firm silence about Dion Boucicault, whose works he knew as well as Shakespeare's', when he first began working for the Abbey, almost twenty years after its foundation.[7]

Stephen Watt points out that nineteenth-century melodrama has been undeservedly neglected, while Nicholas Grene reminds us that the authenticity of the Abbey's representations of Irish life would soon become as controversial as Boucicault's.[8] O'Casey was not the only Irish writer to have been influenced by Boucicault, whose works were admired by Synge, Beckett, and others. Furthermore, although some Abbey personnel continued to express distaste for Irish melodrama, it became a part of the theatre's repertoire from the 1940s onwards, notably in the work of Louis D'Alton. *The Shaughraun* was itself produced at the theatre for the first time in 1967, and revived in 1975, and 1990[9], and a production of *The Colleen Bawn* directed by Conall Morrison in 1998 was one of the Abbey's greatest successes under Patrick Mason. There was therefore a tradition of Abbey productions of Boucicault before 2004, many of which combined popular appeal with critical success.

Accordingly, it is not necessarily a problem that the Abbey included Boucicault in its centenary programme. It is after all desirable for any institution to move beyond the ideals of its founders, and the Abbey could not have survived for a century without doing so; indeed, many of the Abbey's most popular and admired plays would not necessarily have been approved of by Yeats, Gregory, or Synge. However, the historical significance of the Abbey is not that it provided an alternative to Irish melodrama, but that it sought to build upon that form to enrich and broaden the range of Irish drama. It did so institutionally: by contesting the Irishness of Boucicault's characters, the Abbey reinvested 'authority in new and different versions of Irishness', which became the basis for the theatre's subsequent output.[10] The return of Boucicault to the Abbey's repertoire in the 1960s should thus be seen as evidence of progression: the theatre was not abandoning its principles, but building on them to find new ways of performing and staging Irish work. The Abbey seemed aware of the continuities in Irish dramatic history in its construction of the abbeyonehundred programme. While *The Shaughraun* was performed on its mainstage, Stewart Parker's play about Boucicault, *Heavenly Bodies* (1986), was produced in The Peacock, and following both was a revival of *The Playboy of the Western World*. This programming established a relationship between Synge and Boucicault and, with the production of Parker's play, the theatre showed the relevance of that relationship to the contemporary tradition. This was an important statement by the Abbey of a sense of its place in Irish dramatic history. It was, as a national theatre, reaching back to a tradition that predated its own foundation, while also bringing into its own repertoire Parker's play, which had never before been produced in Ireland.

These continuities, however, were more apparent in the theatre's programming than in the production of the play itself: McColgan's *Shaughraun* seemed to have been conceived without any reference to the previous century's work at the Abbey. Twentieth-century productions of Boucicault at the Abbey tended to be notable for directors' employment of such distancing devices as music, tableaux, and the utilization of frames in stage design, all of which were used to emphasize the notion that Boucicault's claim to represent an authentic Ireland had been superseded. McColgan's production was, however, conceived without any apparent sense of historical distance between the source material and its performance. Audiences were instead encouraged to view the material from an ironic or perhaps nostalgic perspective: they were, for instance, told to boo and cheer at the action by a pre-performance announcement, which meant that part of the attraction of *The Shaughraun* was that it reproduced the ethos of a nineteenth-century melodramatic performance: thus, the production from 27 December 1904 being commemorated at the Abbey that summer was not *Cathleen Ní Houlihan*, but the Queen Theatre's *Sarsfield*. Furthermore, McColgan imported into the production many contemporary mass mediated images of Irishness that do purport to authenticity, including scenes of traditional Irish dancing taken directly from his own *Riverdance*, a show that is regarded as emblematic of contemporary mass Irish culture. The blend of a play from 1874 with the sensibility of *Riverdance* implied that, for McColgan, there was no difference between Boucicault's representation of Irish culture and his own, making the two men seem like contemporaries. The positioning of *Riverdance* beside Boucicault used the international popularity of the former to validate the revival of the latter's play: McColgan used the *Riverdance* brand to re-authenticate *The Shaughraun*. It is strange that the Abbey, during its centenary year, played host to a confluence that seemed to bypass its contribution to Irish culture during the previous hundred years.

The success of the production surprised and alarmed some commentators: Helen Meany, for instance, queried the production's presentation of 'ersatz Irishry'.[11] In an interview with RTE Radio's *Rattlebag* McColgan dismissed these criticisms as 'academic snobbery,'[12] pointing out that the production was selling-out most of its performances, and that it was likely to transfer abroad. McColgan's view of the *Shaughraun* appears to have been shared by the management of the Abbey. The consensus appears to have been that financial success and international exposure should be the sole determinants of the production's success. The production generated the theatre's 'highest box office returns in fourteen years', reports Fiona Ness, which is a substantial achievement.[13] However, it is unfortunate that criticisms of the play on the grounds of aesthetics and authenticity were not only ignored, but also dismissed as irrelevant. 'I never had a doubt in my mind that John McColgan was the right person to direct *The Shaughraun*,' said Ben Barnes, referring only to the commercial success of the play. 'The theatre has been vindicated and I have been vindicated.'

Should the Abbey have produced *The Shaughraun*? It would be wrong to suggest otherwise: the problem is not that the Abbey achieved great commercial success with a Boucicault play, but that it was incapable of drawing upon its own century-long repertoire to achieve a similar or greater commercial and critical success. The manifesto of the Irish Literary Theatre seems relevant when this situation is considered. The Abbey now competes in a theatrical marketplace in which commercial success and international endorsement are as important as – and sometimes more important than – artistic achievement, while a community of critics expresses alarm at the misrepresentation of Irishness, both at home and abroad. Although these issues have been part of Irish theatre throughout the twentieth century, their resurgence at a time when the Abbey ought to have been asserting its role as Ireland's national theatre is surprising. It seemed strange to us that, as the IASIL conference got underway in July 2004, the issues that had so dominated the foundation of the Abbey one hundred years previously were once again arising.

In part, this situation is a result of a growing tension between canon and repertoire in Irish theatre. The canon is an institutionalized collection of dramatic texts, which is underpinned by the 'national' status granted by production at the Abbey, and closely related to publishing and the formation of university courses on Irish drama. The repertoire is the theatre produced by Irish companies, and enjoyed by Irish audiences, year by year: it is constantly being reinvented and renewed and, at present, is moving away from canonical Irish themes and preoccupations to explore new modes of representation, new writing, and new ideas.

Yet despite this sense of crisis, Irish theatre enjoyed a particularly lively and creative year in 2004. Galway's Druid Theatre re-imagined *The Playboy of the Western World* for a celebrity-obsessed Ireland, drawing interesting parallels between the Mayo villagers' adulation of Christy Mahon in the play, and the media frenzy caused by the casting of rising Irish filmstar Cillian Murphy in Druid's production. Rough Magic gave us *Improbable Frequency*, an Irish musical set during the Second World War, which blended the absurdism of Flann O'Brien with the savvy humour of *Father Ted* to satirise an Ireland that feigns neutrality while international conflict rages – a theme that seemed pertinent in the light of debates at that time about the use by the US Military of Shannon Airport. In London, work by Conor McPherson and Sebastian Barry premiered, while Owen McCafferty and Martin McDonagh continued to achieve success. And exciting new drama was produced throughout Ireland, from Belfast to Ballymun, and from Limerick to Louth. At a time when the national theatre was (once again) in a state of crisis, the theatre of the nation was thriving, busily laying the foundations for the next hundred years of Irish drama. It seemed to us, therefore, that while there was a need to locate the Abbey's problems in a historical and critical context, it was also essential for scholars to broaden their perspective on Irish theatre – to become more aware of and responsive to the wealth of work appearing in all parts of Ireland.

This book is offered as a response to this situation. It sets out to explore some of the issues raised by the 2004 abbeyonehundred programme, placing particular emphasis on the issue of how staged acts of public memory – such as the Abbey's 2004 repertoire – are accurate reflections of our theatrical past. The papers collected in this book offer perspectives on Irish drama that aim to trouble this issue, inviting us to ask a number of important questions. Has the canonization of certain writers caused us to lose sight of their achievements and their power? Why have some writers fallen from the repertoire when their work is of a high quality – better, in some cases, than many of the plays that are regularly produced? Does the construction of Irish drama as distinctively 'national' cause us to overlook the local and international elements of our theatre? And, as the Abbey's celebration of its hundredth anniversary itself becomes part of our shared memories of Irish theatre, where are we going from here?

We begin with a consideration of these issues by Christopher Murray, who sees the Abbey's history not in terms of linear development, but as a series of 'echoes' that resound in different ways throughout the twentieth century: in that history, he writes, 'there is [a] frequent doubling back, recapitulation, slowing up of pace, followed by surges forward, to be again followed by what look like recapitulations once more of earlier patterns.' The subsequent essays set out to explore and reveal some of these patterns.

Along the way, we aim to give attention to voices that are frequently missing from considerations of Irish drama. Joan Dean shows how the plays of Padraic Colum and Seumas O'Kelly were an important part of the theatrical culture that produced such writers as Synge and O'Casey; while, at the other end of the twentieth century, Marie Jones's *Women on the Verge of HRT* is considered by Maria Kurdi. Colum and O'Kelly, as Dean shows, are unjustly neglected in studies of Irish theatrical history; their work might also deserve a place on the contemporary Irish stage. In contrast, Jones does not lack an Irish – or an international – audience: her plays have been among the most successful Irish theatrical exports ever. Yet her work rarely receives sustained critical attention: no book-length study of her plays or her relationship with Charabanc theatre exists, and there have been few critical articles about her work. We see these pieces by Dean and Kurdi as an attempt to redress absences from critical discourse about the past and present of Irish theatre.

Also an important issue in this book is the extent to which Irish drama can be seen in an international context, something that Christopher Murray explores in relation to the history of the Abbey Theatre. We are delighted therefore to be able to present essays that consider canonical Irish figures outside of the contexts in which they are normally understood. Irina Ruppo's consideration of the relationship between Synge and Thomas Hardy usefully broadens our understanding of the impact of anthropology and ethnography in Ireland during the late nineteenth century. Ruppo shows that Synge's work can be seen in the context of imperial discourse that aimed to present the Irish as 'Other'; however, she also shows that Hardy's presentation of the Wessex peasantry reveals the impact of a similar anthropological discourse within England itself. 'The idealization of the past legends that was such an important feature of the Irish Revival was also present in nineteenth century England,' writes Ruppo, arguing that 'England was subjected to the same pan-European trends as Ireland.' Her suggestion that scholarship on the Irish Revival may allow students of English literature to form a better understanding of their own national literary tradition is a fine example of how an international dimension may enrich our understanding of Irish theatre.

In a similar fashion, Chiaki Kojima explores the correspondences between the Irish National Theatre and the development of westernized theatre in Japan. Her case study is the adaptation by Japanese playwright Shoyo Matsui of Lennox Robinson's *Harvest* (1910). The two dramatists were near contemporaries, Matsui living from 1870 to 1933 and Robinson from 1886 to 1956. Both were involved in the production as well as the writing of plays; both engaged in the development of a new style of drama in their respective countries. Matsui had a background in the popular Japanese Kabuki theatre, and while he retained the basic plot of *Harvest*, his adaptation favoured traditional stereotypes rather than the complex characterization of Robinson's play. Kojima also explores the thematic concerns of the play, and argues that Robinson's satire on the false romanticization of the countryside by middle-class urbanites is absent from Matsui's version. While there was an urban pastoral movement in Japan at this time, Matsui, a countryman himself, was not sympathetic to it. His theatre reforms sought to make the theatre accessible to a broader social group, and he avoided the 'intellectual' label. For this reason, his contribution to the development of 'New Drama' in Japan has been neglected until recently. His adaptation of *Harvest* was one of his more successful contributions to this process, and should be seen as an important example of the impact of Irish drama internationally – and one that ought to stimulate a greater sense of the interrelationship of Irish and Japanese theatrical cultures.

Moving from the issue of literary influence to international reception, Helen Lojek's article on the critical history of *Observe the Sons of Ulster* makes clear that, while Irish theatre travels widely throughout the world, it can mean different things for audiences within and outside Ireland. Although McGuinness's play is a relatively recent addition to the canon (being premiered in 1985), Lojek shows how it has been transformed throughout its history, to address a variety of individual, local, and international concerns – from the Troubles, to gay rights in Ireland, to the US-led invasion of Iraq in 2003. Conversely, Donald Morse reveals in a study of *Dolly West's Kitchen* how Ireland's awareness of its own changing place in the world affects the reception and reputation of McGuinness's play which, as Morse shows, was considerably better received outside Ireland than in it.

If Irish dramatists move freely across national boundaries, so too do they cross generic and formal barriers. Mika Funahashi reads Marina Carr's short story 'To Grow A Mermaid' as an alternative treatment of issues that are also developed in her plays, and explores the different perspectives which emerge in a narrative, as opposed to a dramatic, form. The focus of the story and of the essay is the relationship between a daughter of about ten years of age and her abusive mother, told from the point of view of the child. Actual physical abuse is described in three episodes of the story, but the child endures it by immersing herself in a powerful imaginative relationship with a mermaid. The essay compares the technique of the story to a jigsaw, whose colourful but disconnected sections only make sense when they have all been fitted into their correct place at the end. Consideration of the psychology of torture and the endurance of pain illuminates this study of a dysfunctional parental relationship, while sensitivity to the literary tropes which pervade the short story facilitates the transference of these insights to Carr's family dramas, especially *The Mai* and *By the Bog of Cats*....

Christa Velten-Mrowka's essay gives us another form of border crossing, considering Brian Friel's artist surrogates in the light of Theodor

Adorno's aesthetic theory. The prime example is Frank Hardy the faith healer, although the essay also connects to *Give Me Your Answer, Do!* Synge's playboy also exemplifies the central characteristic of this aesthetic, central to which is the premise that apparent truths may be false, and that human reality is marked by delusion. A character whose relationship to reality is sceptical, such as Frank Hardy, is closest to the related insight that art, by telling lies, enables us to apprehend the truth. Velten-Mrowka was a student of Adorno's at Frankfurt, and a detailed knowledge of his thought and texts, and the work of his predecessor Nietzsche, underlies the argument of her essay. Considering the centuries-old debate on the relationship of imitation to life, Adorno developed a complex dialectic of mimesis, which forms the basis of the argument in this essay. The relationship of artistic creation to the perception of reality develops out of this dialectic, exploring the question posed by the faith healer and by the dramatist himself: am I a con man?

Alexandra Poulain likewise explores the relationship between music and theatre in Tom Murphy's *The Gigli Concert*. 'Murphy's characters are all in search of meaning, but they sometimes find that what they are seeking to apprehend is beyond the reach of words,' she writes: 'the dimension of the sacred, the *mysterium tremendum* which can be experienced intuitively but ultimately remains unknowable.' This raises the difficult issue of how scholars and critics can interrogate this 'unknowable' quality of Murphy's work, a task Poulain achieves by exploring the play's religious, musical, and psychological elements.

Murphy and Friel are of course canonical Irish dramatists, but as both produce new work, their reputations continue to develop. This is not the case with O'Casey and Synge, two writers whose secure reputation is now the subject of increased reconsideration – in the case of O'Casey, thanks to Christopher Murray's 2004 biography, and of Synge, because of Druid Theatre's astonishing re-staging of his plays in the *DruidSynge* cycle. We include with this book two essays that aim to add to this process. Paul O'Brien considers 'what might have been' in his exploration of O'Casey's early collaborations with the Abbey, showing how his involvement in that theatre's life aided the processes of composition; by doing so, O'Brien also calls for a reappraisal of O'Casey's later works. Mary C. King's essay on Synge shows how his reputation was constructed both by Yeats and, to a certain extent, by Synge's own attempts to construct a sense of himself. She draws attention to the divergences between both men, suggesting that 'Synge, had he lived, would scarcely have travelled the high road to Unity of Being' undertaken by Yeats. Exploring a range of Synge's dramatic and other writings, King concludes that 'in [Synge's] questing and questioning openness to the other and his interrogation of absolutes and fundamentalisms, that enquiring man is an exemplary writer and dramatist for today.'

The book concludes with essays that consider the preoccupations of other 'writers and dramatists for today', asking where Irish theatre might be going tomorrow. Jason King shows that Irish drama has moved 'Beyond Ryanga', drawing on voices coming from a diverse range of backgrounds and cultures. As the essays throughout this book show, Irish theatre has always tended to be international in character, often to an extent underappreciated by scholars and audiences. King shows however that the increased multiculturalism and globalization of Ireland makes it all the more important that this international element is acknowledged, and that it is supported as Irish society moves forward.

Lisa Fitzpatrick draws attention to similar issues, considering how the recent changes to Irish society affect our conception of what an Irish 'national' theatre might be in a postnational Ireland. Her essay is a call for Irish dramatists to explore a space that is:

> neither here nor there, but some space in between: in between endlessly self-selecting micro-communities and the great, global marketplace; between the conjoining of local legends and classical mythology in productions that look out past the boundaries of Ireland or seek to stage specific localities, and somewhere in between the endlessly contested yet secure Irish identity of the past and the threatening chaos of an increasingly globalised world.

It is our hope that this book will pick up some of the echoes that recur in Irish theatre history, pointing us towards new ways of understanding both Irish drama (or the canon) and Irish theatre (or the repertoire) to allow us to continue to support and enjoy Irish writers', practitioners', and critics' exploration of Ireland's in-between spaces.

---

[1] Karen Fricker, 'The Abbey has lost touch with its people', *The Guardian* 4 February 2004, http://www.guardian.co.uk/arts/theatre.

[2] These were Marina Carr's contribution to *Sons and Daughters*, Hilary Fannin's *Doldrum Bay*, and Stella Feehily's *Duck*, all of which were presented on the Peacock stage. Since 2000, the only other plays by women at the Abbey were Elizabeth Kuti's *Treehouses* (2000) and Marina Carr's *Ariel* (2002). The latter play appeared on the Abbey's mainstage, in a production that was critically and commercially unsuccessful (Source: Abbey Theatre Archive).

[3] These included Tom McIntyre's *Caoineadh Airt Uí Laoghaire* (1998) and *Cúirt an Mhéan Oíche* (1999), Antoine O'Flaharta's *An Suas Dearc* (1995) and Eilis Ní Dhuibhne's *Dún na mBan Trí Thine* (1994) (Source: Abbey Archive) .

[4] Chris Morash, *A History of Irish Theatre 1601-2000* (Cambridge: Cambridge University Press, 2002): 129.

[5] Cf. Stephen Watt, *Joyce, O'Casey and the Irish Popular Theatre* (New York: Syracuse University Press, 1991).

[6] Augusta Gregory, *Our Irish Theatre* 2nd ed. (Gerrards Cross: Colin Smythe, 1972): 19.

[7] Sean O'Casey, *Autobiographies 2* (London: Macmillan, 1963): 105.
[8] Nicholas Grene, *The Politics of Irish Drama* (Cambridge: Cambridge University Press, 1999): 5-50.
[9] Cf. Christopher Fitz-Simon, *The Abbey Theatre* (London: Thames and Hudson, 2003): 123, 203. Information also taken from National Theatre Archive.
[10] Stephen Watt, 'Late Nineteenth-Century Irish Theatre – Before the Abbey and Beyond', *The Cambridge Companion to Twentieth-Century Irish Drama*, ed. Shaun Richards (Cambridge: Cambridge University Press): 18-32; Grene, *The Politics of Irish Drama*, ibid, 8.
[11] Helen Meany, 'Review of *The Shaughraun*', *The Irish Times* 4 June 2004: 12.
[12] *Rattlebag*, broadcast on RTE Radio, 9 July 2004.
[13] Fiona Ness. 'Artistic Director to Quit Abbey Next Year', *The Sunday Business Post* 4 July 2004, http://archives.tcm.ie/businesspost/2004/07/04/story89912768.aspc 1 August 2004.

1 | 'Echoes Down the Corridor': The Abbey Theatre 1904-2004

Christopher Murray

'Our retrospection is all to the future' – R.B. Sheridan, *The Rivals*

There are many ways one might approach this wide topic, most of them involving lengthy historical narrative and lists of plays and players, dates and details of productions and audience reception. The more I thought about it, the less wise it seemed to make a précis of theatre and dramatic history: on every side, the pitfalls lay of over-simplification and banality. The main difficulty is that while the story of the Abbey over the past hundred years appears to offer a continuous narrative which can be broken up for convenience into three or four main periods before and after O'Casey, it may be more instructive to inspect the ways the narrative winds back upon itself as often as it moves forward. In the history itself there is this frequent doubling back, recapitulation, slowing up of pace, followed by surges forward, to be again followed by what look like recapitulations once more of earlier patterns. In that regard there is a series of 'echoes', though 'series' too is a suspect term in this context. I borrow the quotation in my title from Arthur Miller's epilogue to *The Crucible* (1953), not to suggest that witch-hunts lie behind the history of the Abbey—though an interesting study might disclose this to be the case—but rather to make the argument that history, including theatre history, is a living current whereby foundational moments are transmitted in new forms through reaction, revolution and change which always contain energies from preceding formations. There is indeed nothing new under the sun. For Arthur Miller, that great exemplar of American genius who will be sorely missed, time was linear, a relentless progress towards the disclosure of repressed or unacknowledged truth. We Irish think differently. For us the circle is more appropriate as image of time's meaning – Yeats's gyres, Joyce's Anna Livia, Beckett's circular plays – and even today we are not altogether convinced believers in progress. We expect a return to the bad old days. The ghosts that haunt us from the past are not ones that can ever be laid. We are not a great people for 'moving on' in the modern sense. We strongly suspect that the echoes we hear from the past are not so much warnings of recurrence, as in Miller's liberal imaginings of consequence, as sacred testimony that all is 'rounded' like beads on a string, separate but somehow connected.

As a key to this narrative, or 'circumbendibus' as Goldsmith's Tony Lumpkin might call it, I would put forward the titles of two recent Abbey plays: *That Was Then* (2002), by Gerard Stembridge, a satire on contemporary Ireland-England relations, and *Defender of the Faith* (2004), by Stuart Carolan, set on the border between Louth and south Armagh in 1986 and concerning betrayal and retaliation within the IRA. There are those who would say in relation to the whole question of tradition within the Irish cultural narrative, 'that was then', a topic modernity has swept aside. There are others who will respond that a true analysis necessarily implies maintaining faith, not as a matter of choice but of conviction and of moral compulsion. Each phrase is a cliché; each is a shibboleth; each is politically ambivalent. (Stembridge's play is all about turning the tables; though a play about republican loyalism, Carolan's *Defender of the Faith* harks back to Henry VIII's proud title, still stamped on British coinage.) Each phrase offers a particular historiography, whether liberal or conservative. These are the Scylla and Charybdis of current Irish literary criticism. The reader must act as helmsman.

The theatre programme for the year-long commemoration in 2004 known as abbeyonehundred was, among other things, a blend of the national and the international.[1] On the one hand, *The Playboy* and *The Plough*, on the other Chekhov, Sophocles, and Polish, Slovenian and Hungarian plays with surtitles. The broad division between Irish and foreign work was a good arrangement because it was present at the conception of the Irish Literary Theatre (1897), precursor of the Irish National Theatre Society Ltd, popularly known (until August 2005[2]) as the Abbey from the street where it is located. But this interaction also contains the seeds of contradiction, of wheat and tares, one might say, which grew together and in some hostility at times. When Joyce attacked the drift towards the national in 1901, he termed it 'The Day of the Rabblement' of 'the most belated race in Europe'.[3] Nearly eighty years later Katharine Worth entitled her book *The Irish Drama of Europe from Yeats to Beckett,* arguing against the conventional view most eloquently presented up to that time by Una Ellis-Fermor in *The Irish Dramatic Movement* and firmly reinserting the Abbey into the European dramatic movement after Ibsen. But if the Abbey was both national and international in style and repertory, how is it that with the founding of the Dublin Gate in 1928 a division was made so that the Gate walked off with the international spoils? In turn, if that is the case, how is it that Joe Dowling's famous production of *Juno and the Paycock*, with two such outstanding Abbey players, Donal McCann and John Kavanagh, took place at the Gate and not the Abbey in 1986? How is that in 2004 Friel's *Dancing at Lughnasa* played at the Gate while *The Burial at Thebes* played at the Abbey? Is it possible to see the answers in the history of the Abbey as cultural formation, governed by personalities as diverse as Yeats, Ernest Blythe, Hugh Hunt, Tomás Mac Anna, Joe Dowling, Garry Hynes, Patrick Mason and Ben Barnes?

***

The idea for the Irish Literary Theatre came from the international little theatre movement born in Paris in 1887 with André Antoine's pioneering *Théâtre Libre* and spreading to London with Dutchman J.T. Grein's founding of the Independent Theatre in 1891. The new theatrical creed known as naturalism inherent in Antoine's experiment initiated a movement which spread to Berlin and then to Moscow, where Stanislavski and Nemirovich-Danchenko were inspired to create a new art theatre for the production of Chekhov's plays. Yeats's interest in the huge implications of this new movement was limited, as he hated naturalism and was out of sympathy with most modern drama except for the French symbolists. Happily, Edward Martyn, who along with George Moore and Bernard Shaw also supported the London Independent Theatre, was an ardent Ibsenist. Disabled though Martyn was, in the young James Joyce's phrase, 'by an incorrigible style' (Joyce, 71) his enthusiasm for the new European drama was profound and he was to go on enthusing at venues other than the Abbey until his death in 1923. The repertory agreed on for the three seasons during which the ILT existed was a compromise between naturalized Ibsenism and Yeats's denaturalized symbolism. Lady Gregory was at this stage no more than a useful supporter of a shaky venture, as she knew nothing of contemporary drama and less about production styles. She was to teach herself mainly through patching up Yeats's dull dialogue and by translating Molière. Whereas the plays went reasonably well, after the slight hitch over *The Countess Cathleen* in 1899, having to use English professional actors showed up a glaring contradiction in the Society's manifesto regarding 'a high ambition [...] to build up a Celtic and Irish school of dramatic literature'.[4] The problem with the ethos of the ILT lay in Yeats's ignorance of what Antoine was after in Paris. In his press releases in 1899 he constantly mentioned Ibsen and Hauptmann as models for the new theatre while at the same time declaring, 'All literature and all art is national.'[5] Nothing could be further from the French idea. Further, as is well known, it was the afterpiece for Yeats and Moore's *Diarmuid and Grania* in the final season of ILT plays in October 1901 which altered the whole future. This was Douglas Hyde's one-act play in Irish, *Casadh an tSúgáin*. Hence Joyce's impatience: 'the Irish Literary

Theatre must now be considered the property of the rabblement of the most belated race in Europe' (Joyce, 70). But Synge, reviewing for the appropriately named *L'Européen,* was much more aware of the significance of seeing a play in Irish, the first to be produced in a major Dublin theatre (the Gaiety), where, Synge declared, one could sense for an instant the soul of a nation ('l'âme d'un people'[6]).

Working with members of the Gaelic League, unlisted in the programme, Willie Fay as director apparently managed to create 'an unqualified success',[7] which turned the whole project of an Irish theatre around. George Moore began to call for an all-Gaelic theatre, and while he was, as he put it, 'taking the Irish language under his protection,'[8] Edward Martyn took himself off. Yeats, cautious about drama in Irish since he himself knew none and never learned any, could nevertheless see the appeal and poetry in Hyde's work and with Lady Gregory's help wrote *Cathleen Ní Houlihan* for the Fay brothers to stage, using the amateurs they so obviously could train into proficiency. It was the players as much as, if not more than, the writers who were about to create the Irish National Theatre Society following the Fays' outstanding production of *Cathleen Ní Houlihan* and AE's *Deirdre* in 1902. Before this event, as one of the actresses was later to say, 'there was little to indicate that our first appearance as a company of amateur players, producing two Irish plays in a small Dublin concert-hall, would begin a movement which would change in many ways the course of theatrical history.'[9] It is important to note that these players were passionately nationalist. As far as they were concerned, the INTS was their Society. When it evolved into the INTS Ltd in 1905, following Annie Horniman's gift of a theatre, many of these players were outraged that the amateur ethos was to be altered to professional and that a new undemocratic managerial system was to replace the cooperative venture they had embraced. The majority of the actors walked out. Again, Máire Nic Shiubhlaigh speaks for many when she says in *The Splendid Years*: 'In those days I never thought of the National Theatre Society as a purely theatrical enterprise. It was merely a part of the larger national movement in which most of us were then participating.' (73) The point has been elaborated in recent times by several scholars writing on the Irish revival and the dramatic movement, notably Mary Trotter, P.J. Mathews, Lionel Pilkington, and Ben Levitas. In a different vein, Adrian Frazier has in *Behind the Scenes* described the sequel, as Yeats, Lady Gregory and Synge, the three directors who had assumed control over the Abbey, worked with Annie Horniman to create the kind of theatre they preferred. It was at the Abbey that the uncreated conscience of the race was to be forged, after all, and it was to be an Anglo-Irish conscience, necessarily at odds with the majority. Its ethos is summed up in Yeats's frank admission many years later in *On the Boiler*: 'The success of the Abbey Theatre has grown out of a single conviction of its founders: I was the spokesman because I was born arrogant and had learnt an artist's arrogance – "Not what you want but what we want" – and we were the first modern theatre that said it.'[10] But matters were not quite as simple at the Abbey as this motto implies.

There was continual unease among the members at the emerging ambitions of Yeats and Miss Horniman. By 1906, Yeats did not quite know how to handle the question of the relationship between the traditional / national and the foreign/international but he knew it had to be reformulated. His own work, to put it crudely, turned mythic with *The Shadowy Waters* (1903) and *On Baile's Strand* (1904), the one esoteric and the other derivative from Lady Gregory's translation of the tales from the Red Branch Knights, *Cuchulain of Muirthemne* (1902), which Yeats praised with all the extravagance of the uninitiated. But in the first issue of *The Arrow*, the Abbey in-house newssheet, in 1906 he saw that so far as the general repertory was concerned it was time to look a little further than the form of peasant drama now firmly established by Gregory, Synge and Padraic Colum:

> We are now fairly satisfied with the representation of peasant life, and we can afford to give the greater part of our attention to other expressions of our art and of our life. Our romantic work and poetical work once reasonably good, we can, if but the dramatist arrive, take up the life of our drawingrooms, and see if there is something characteristic there [...] and so create plays of that life and means to play them as truthful as a play of Hauptmann's or of Ibsen's upon the German or Scandinavian stage. I am not myself interested in this kind of work, and do not believe it to be as important as contemporary critics think it is, but a theatre, such as we project, should give a reasonably complete expression to the imaginative interests of its country.[11]

There was a clause in the Abbey patent, which was in Lady Gregory's name only, granting the theatre permission to stage in addition to plays in Irish or English by Irish writers 'such dramatic works of foreign authors as would tend to educate and interest the Irish public in the higher aspects of dramatic art'.[12] Annie Horniman felt that the time had come to do just that. Accepting that the Abbey had reached a turning point at the end of 1906, since it was 'extremely accomplished in the performance of Irish peasant comedy and in nothing else', Yeats tried to get his other two directors to agree to broaden the repertory. 'We should keep before our minds the final object which is to create in this country a National Theatre something after the Continental pattern. This Theatre should be capable of showing its audience examples of all great schools of drama. [...] Such a National Theatre would perforce keep in mind its educational as well as its artistic side.'[13] Over six pages long (in print), Yeats's memorandum was a blueprint to revolutionize the Abbey. He could depend on Lady Gregory to back him, but Synge was the stumbling block. Yeats might have known that citing Miss Horniman as a reference was hardly likely to move that rooted man, yet in a postscript marked 'private' wrote: 'Miss Horniman I know has always had before her the German Municipal Theatre as an ideal. She has stated to one or two people and almost in so many words to myself, that she has £25,000 for the development of the Company under certain circumstances' (175). There were just over four years to go before the Abbey patent would have to be renewed and Yeats did not think Horniman would continue the subsidy beyond that time if the company went on as it did. Synge's view was surprisingly forthright: 'I think we should be mistaken in taking the continental Municipal Theatre as the pattern of what we wish to attain as our "final object" even in a faintly remote future.' A dramatic movement, he argued, was either the creation of a new dramatic literature or the pursuit of 'perfect interpretation of works that are already received as classics'. The Abbey had chosen the creative path and to turn to the other would be disastrous. Synge instanced Goethe's conviction at the end of his life that he and Schiller had failed in Weimar in the late eighteenth century 'because they had confused the public mind by giving one day Shakespeare, one day Calderon, one day Sophocles and so on' (177-78). Synge thought it preferable to break with Horniman – 'because I have no confidence in her ideals' (179, n.2) – if necessary in order to pursue a purely Irish theatre. His view, offered just weeks before *The Playboy* riots, prevailed. Apart from three translations of Molière by Lady Gregory there was to be no international dimension to the repertory in Synge's lifetime. When soon after that, Horniman withdrew her subsidy and the Abbey had to look to popular means to keep the box office going, there was nothing to be done but try to honour Synge's commitment. To his credit, Yeats backed him to the hilt.

Referring to Synge's *Playboy* Ben Levitas subtitles the conclusion to his book *The Theatre of Nation* 'Mahon and the Echo'. His point is that the *Playboy*, as much as *Cathleen Ni Houlihan* and as much again as other representations of revolt at this time when currents ran in many channels towards the one broad sea of liberation, predicted and projected forward the idea of revolution through what he calls 'an explosion of possibility' (242). The 1916 Rising, by his reading, was in some measure an 'echo' of Christy Mahon's 'cry freedom'. There is a problem with this view in as much as the *Playboy* so upset nationalists of various shades of green that audiences at the Abbey were minimal at least until Shaw's *Blanco Posnet* supplied 'another trophy for the freedom of the theatre' in 1909.[14] The Gaelic League asked its members to boycott the Abbey. But in any event, the man and the echo I have in mind here relate more closely to what happened in 1918 and what the future consequences were to be.

***

Lennox Robinson, playwright and Abbey manager after 1909, was unusually interested in contemporary drama. His own work being influenced by Ibsen and his sojourns in the United States with the first

Abbey tours (1911-1914) opening his eyes to new ideas in theatre production, he began to think of expanding the repertory at home, 'and Yeats and I had a public discussion on the subject'.[15] The date was around 1918. Robinson argued that without the competition of 'the drama of the world' too many third-rate plays would continue to be accepted by the Abbey. Yeats replied: 'I had all this out with Synge years ago. I was of your opinion, and he convinced me that I was wrong.' (118) He then rehearsed Synge's argument in detail before elaborating on his own neo-conservatism. The novels of Balzac and Dostoevsky, it seems, made better models for the aspiring playwright than any modern dramatist:

> The modern novel is perfectly achieved in its form, and the modern play – even when Ibsen is the writer – remains still an inadequate form [...] because the men who have made it study each other in translation, just as they study paintings from photographs. A photograph leaves out the colour, and a translation leaves out the style. I doubt if Ibsen can have a style in the original, he has certainly none in the English translation. I would far sooner our dramatists learnt dramatic expression from our own people who have almost all a sense of dialogue and of dialogue where vivid words, where picturesque phrasing count for more than dry logic (120-21).

It seems odd that Yeats would have felt obliged to stay faithful to Synge's dogged preference for a purely Irish repertory. That was then. The fact that 'now' was a sensitive time on the cusp of the Anglo-Irish War may have had something to do with it. It could be dangerous to be too European. Robinson was courageous in promoting the Dublin Drama League, announcing: 'Here in Ireland we are isolated, cut off from the thought of the world, except the English world [...]. Seeing foreign plays will not divorce our minds from Ireland.'[16] Yeats then consented to be president of the League and allowed it to use the Abbey stage on Sunday and Monday evenings to put on non-Irish, mainly European, plays. The defender of the faith could also bend the rules.

In its ten most active years the League introduced Dublin to the work of Andreyev, Benavente, Chekhov, O'Neill, Pirandello, Strindberg, Toller and others: 66 plays in 11 languages by 36 authors from 15 countries.[17] When Hilton Edwards and Micheál MacLiammóir arrived on the scene in 1928, the League had prepared a path for them.'[18] In short, Robinson's splinter group at the Abbey became the Gate Theatre.

Robinson's venture needs to be re-inserted into the history of the Abbey, for which a complete study of the Dublin Drama League is badly needed. During the years 1919 to 1929 the Abbey's aesthetic was expanded, to the benefit of actors, audiences and new writers alike, O'Casey being a noteworthy beneficiary. At the same time, the Abbey's fortunes were suddenly repaired through the outstanding success of O'Casey's own plays, *The Shadow of a Gunman* (1923), *Juno and the*

Paycock (1924) and *The Plough and the Stars* (1926). In 1925, the Abbey was officially recognized by the new Free State government as Ireland's national theatre, worthy of a small annual subsidy. This was a mixed blessing, since a government appointee on the board of directors implied the arrival of state censorship, something Yeats and Gregory both lived to oppose. In addition, not fully integrating the enterprising Dublin Drama League was a mistake. The Gate proposed a new and more dangerous rivalry than Edward Martyn – no small pioneer – had ever been able to establish with his Irish Theatre, Hardwicke Street, from 1914 to 1923. It is one of the great 'what ifs' of Irish theatre history to speculate what shape the Abbey's repertory and style might have assumed had the Gate not succeeded as it did. The Gate became the Abbey's 'other', eventually (in 1969) to be awarded an annual government subsidy as if to reinforce the point.

In allowing Edwards and MacLiammóir into the Peacock, the Abbey's annex opened in 1927, Yeats had ironically condemned the Abbey to a narrow Irish repertory and a limited style of acting and production. Ironically, too, Yeats was responsible for rejecting O'Casey's most experimental play to date, *The Silver Tassie* (1928), thereby bringing about O'Casey's permanent exile in England, a huge loss to the Abbey. Too late, in the mid-1930s, Yeats saw that he had steered the Abbey onto the rocks. Ireland since independence was no longer biddable to his imagination.[19] Lady Gregory was dead, Robinson, too long sidelined, had taken to drink, and the ageing Yeats could do no more than fight off opposition to a belated production of *The Silver Tassie* in 1935 and then offer the young English director Hugh Hunt the job of enlivening the Abbey repertory once again. It was too late. When Yeats died in January 1939, it has been said, the Abbey died too. 'It was his creation and he took it with him.'[20]

***

As fate would have it, the building itself burned down the year after Kavanagh made this pronouncement. To understand what happened under the general management of Yeats's successor Ernest Blythe from 1941 until 1967 it is necessary now to return to the question of Gaelic drama, last heard of when George Moore seemed about to dedicate what remained of his life to it in 1901. Nothing happened. Yeats believed that one wrote best in one's mother-language and there an end. Synge's disdain for the Gaelic League disqualified him from attempting a drama in Irish himself, and while Lady Gregory was content to translate Douglas Hyde's plays Hyde himself was never invited to participate in the NTS. So the whole question of drama in Irish was quietly sidelined.

In a symposium held at the Abbey in 2004 on language, theatre and identity, the playwright Paul Mercier argued that the success of Synge's plays made any attempt at a Gaelic drama redundant at the Abbey. For here was a drama in Irish: it was a language that to English audiences seemed exotic as well as charming and to them this was 'Irish'. The Abbey had no need to cultivate the real thing when the ersatz was internationally acceptable. Thus was Irish drama upstaged. The poet Thomas MacDonagh, mourning in *Literature in Ireland* (1916) the failure of the Gaelic League, in this regard thought a folk movement in the Gaeltacht the answer, 'a movement coming from the West eastward'.[21] The idea was to see fruition twelve years after MacDonagh's execution when the Taibhdhearc was founded in Galway, a foundation that got the Abbey off the hook.

The Abbey had just received an extra government subsidy for the production of drama in Irish, following an extraordinary appeal by Yeats and Gregory in 1922: 'The Directors know that the Government desire to build on a Gaelic civilisation. They therefore intend, if the Government will assist them, to engage a Gaelic-speaking producer of plays and to form a Gaelic company of players.' Writers would then be encouraged to provide new plays in Irish. Yeats and Gregory pointed out that the Gaelic plays 'would not be mixed with the English ones' but be given a week in the schedule every five or six weeks. The Abbey might, in fact, eventually be turned into 'the Gaelic Theatre' should the government plan be to create a 'great National Theatre' of a different kind.[22] This crazy idea was replaced by the equally daft one of presenting the Abbey to the government as a gift. Ernest Blythe, then Minister for Finance, saw the offer as 'more tactical than serious' but Lennox Robinson states that it was 'a perfectly serious offer'.[23] What happened was that after the directors (again three in number, Robinson having been awarded Synge's place in 1923) received the Abbey subsidy they allowed a group of Irish actors, Aisteoirí Átha Cliath, to use the Abbey on Monday evenings, thereby making the point that Gaelic drama was to be on a footing similar to that of foreign drama as staged by the Dublin Drama League. It was not until Ernest Blythe, out of a political job once Fianna Fáil took office, was also made a director on the expanded board in 1935 that what Yeats and Gregory had agreed to was put into effect. Thus, speaking at the Abbey Festival in 1938, Blythe could say: '[T]he work we are now undertaking for the Irish language will bring us back into the full stream of national life and effort, and will link to the theatre the enthusiasm and support of those who today, in a new field, carry on the work of the Young Irelanders, of the Fenians, of the Land Leaguers, of the early Gaelic Leaguers, of the men of Easter Week.'[24] Within six months, Yeats was dead and not long afterwards, Blythe had his job. Thereby hangs the tale of the Abbey until the later 1960s. One of Blythe's catch-cries was, 'The Abbey is not an art theatre but an instrument of national defence!'[25] with the Irish language in the vanguard. All actors were required to be bilingual, audiences were forcibly fed with one-act plays in Irish tagged on to plays in English, and pantomimes in Irish were the main events in the calendar (that they lost heavily was never a factor[26]).

Very few foreign or classical plays were staged after Blythe's accession in 1941 until *The Cherry Orchard*, directed by Maria Knebel from the Moscow Art Theatre, sounded a relieving note in 1968, the year after Blythe's retirement. *The Cherry Orchard* may perhaps be taken as symbolic of what Blythe as Lopakhin achieved in chopping down Ascendancy ideology. Foreign plays did not interest Blythe unless they were translations into Irish, including his own.

There was an Experimental Theatre in place in the Peacock when Blythe became manager which was essentially an actors' training school: nobody much minded what they did until Ria Mooney took over in 1948. One of the first things she did was to invite Eric Bentley to direct *The House of Bernarda Alba,* about which he wrote an interesting essay in 1950. 'I was told by Frenchmen and Italians that Lorca resembled Synge, and would therefore be no problem in Dublin. [...] None the less, Synge himself was always a big problem in Dublin: the manager [Blythe] told me he emptied the theater for five years.'[27] The bemused Bentley had to battle against entrenched traditions of acting style and scene design in order to find a way past complacency into creativity. When in 2003 the Abbey staged a new version of *Bernarda Alba* by Sebastian Barry, whose mother Joan O'Hara had played in the Bentley production in 1950 and who played the mother Maria Josefa in Martin Drury's production in 2003, there was continuity of a kind on view. But it was 'the radical discontinuity of the Abbey's history' which Bentley noticed and found frustrating. 'Habits are sanctified as traditions. Departures from tradition are permitted, if at all, with the sulks and much mumbling of "What the hell does he think he's doing?" A director [...] will ask an actress to wear her shawl like this and be refused with the declaration that Sara Allgood (who never appeared in the play in question) wore it like that.'[28] The Blythe spirit encouraged all that.

The Experimental Theatre did not survive the fire which destroyed the Abbey in July 1951. Things then went from bad to worse. During what Michael J. O'Neill in his book on the Abbey at the Queen's Theatre (now demolished) euphemistically calls the 'Interregnum Years' from 1951 to 1966 only seven foreign plays were staged, including two by Eugene O'Neill, while sixteen translations into Irish were offered, some of these now being translations into Irish of one-acts by Yeats, Synge and Lady Gregory, no doubt intended to instruct neophytes in the craft. The contrast with present arrangements is striking. Although Blythe's final achievement was to insist that the new Peacock, opened in 1967, should mainly be for the production of plays in Irish this policy is now more honoured in the breach than the observance, and a compromise is sometimes used whereby a play is presented in Irish and in English on alternate nights. No play in Irish, whether original or a translation, has reached the main stage since Blythe's time. The Abbey has delegated its responsibility in this area to Taibhdhearc na Gaillimhe. And the Taibhdhearc has found that, 'With Irish-language theatre we're always on the fringe and are constantly asked to prove ourselves. There still exists a cultural apartheid that views an Irish-language play as merely a vehicle to secure a grant.'[29]

Instead, foreign plays in English became increasingly frequent at the new Abbey after 1966, and Pinter, Bond, Stoppard, on the one hand, O'Neill, Miller, Williams, Shepard and Mamet on the other have all been staged. Translations or versions or adaptations – the terms are interchangeable – seem attractive to Irish playwrights, including Brian Friel, Tom Murphy, Thomas Kilroy, Brendan Kennelly, Frank McGuinness, Michael West, Sebastian Barry and Seamus Heaney. There is almost always an Irish inflection in these translations, never so pronounced, of course, as in Lady Gregory's early work but nevertheless searching as she did to find approximations in Irish speech for foreign idiom as well as echoes between what was 'then' and 'there' and Ireland's here and now.

To Tom Murphy, a 'version' is 'more subjective and more interpretively open' than a translation: 'it is speculative in its considerations of the "spirit" of the original and seeks to translate that "spirit" into a language and movement that have their own dynamic; the ordering in the version attempts to recreate what was alive, musical and vibrant in the original. A version, of itself, wants to avoid looking like the back of the tapestry.'[30] In a sense, this is to bring the past into the present without overtly modernizing. In a programme note for *The Burial at Thebes* Heaney said that he could get nowhere with the rhythms of his translation from Sophocles until the opening lines of an Irish elegy came to mind, *Caoine Airt Ó Laoghaire*. Then, Heaney says, 'Theme and tune coalesced'.[31] In a very tenuous way, this intertextuality relates back to Blythe's hopes. For most Irish playwrights who translate classics, however, the contact is less with Gaelic than with Hiberno-English rhythms and possibly with dialect as a means of solving the problem of style Yeats thought bedevilled translation. In that regard, it is possible to see in the work of Marina Carr, who does not do translations or versions, a concern to stay faithful with tradition. Her assimilation of Greek myth into an Irish context and idiom is very much a two-way estrangement strategy to create a distance from conventional Abbey realism while interpreting modern Irish experience under the rubric of classical associations.[32] So, as Tom Kilroy remarked in his review of Heaney's *The Burial at Thebes* (the text), 'The history of theatre (and cinema) is a history of adaptations. This endless recycling is, perhaps, part of the very art of imitation itself.'[33] Hence the attraction for Irish writers. The process allows the postcolonial to dialogue with the postmodern along a tightrope which is the present.

***

Indisputably, Yeats's dream of a modern poetic drama faded with the flames of the Abbey fire. Austin Clarke, his only true successor, lost his Lyric Theatre in that fire. At the Queen's the policy was undisguisedly populist and realism in its most accessible form governed the repertory. Here as in all matters Blythe kept some kind of contact with the past. Accepting after 1910 that though popular realism was the only way for the ailing Abbey to survive, Yeats had issued 'Advice to Playwrights' in which he stipulated that a play 'should contain some criticism of life, founded on the experience or personal observation of the writer'.[34] The phrase 'a criticism of life' comes from Matthew Arnold's definition of poetry. Realism or not, drama should in that sense be poetic. By 1919, Yeats had mournfully to accept that 'a people's theatre' in a sense he could no longer approve had triumphed: 'we did not set out to create this sort of theatre, and its success has been to me a discouragement and a defeat.'[35] By 1922, when one of O'Casey's early, harsh, working-class pieces of realism was under discussion and Yeats was against it, he finished off his reader's report with the bitter words, 'If [Lennox] Robinson wants to produce it let him do so by all means & be damned to him. My fashion has gone out.'[36] And so it had. Thirty years on, Blythe's home-baked aesthetic was a combination of so-called realistic drama as criticism of life plus a means of progressing the national ideals. Abbey plays should deal with controversial issues but in such a manner that they were 'combed out' and 'rendered innocuous' on the stage.[37] 'Defusing utopias' is Chris Morash's telling gloss on this policy, 'and this could only be done by creating a theatrical style which eschewed theatricality.'[38]

Since 1966, and the opening of the new theatre on the old site, theatricalism has gradually transformed what the Abbey stands for. The gap between the Gate and the Abbey has now disappeared. The Abbey's permanent company has been disbanded. The Abbey is a modern repertory company like that of any major modern city, except that it is specially subsidized as a national theatre and has what one might call a heritage remit. It was the artistic directors who fought with a conservative Abbey board to bring about the changes which render the Abbey now artistically much more sophisticated and international in outlook than it has ever been. But ironically, it has been the artistic directors who have embroiled the Abbey in controversy and brought it to the brink of collapse. Although this topic awaits full analysis and can be properly explored only when the records of the Abbey board are available for inspection by theatre historians, it seems reasonably clear that the recurring crises have their origin in a conflict between the radical, progressive views of artistic directors from Joe Dowling to Ben Barnes and the cautious, sometimes reactionary, attitude of successive management boards. In short, the 'defenders of the faith' have seen it as their duty to restrain and eventually to disable the visionaries whose chant necessarily is, 'that was then'.

As I write, the Abbey is enjoying a calm just after the major storm with which abbeyonehundred came to a close. Such calms, in the natural, social (some would say the real) world provide opportunities for new planning and rebuilding. In the post-tsunami and post-New Orleans real world, finances are being found to redesign, to rebuild, and, as the cant phrase is, to move on. In Ireland, things are never so simple. It is not quite clear what the new plans for the Abbey are. It has lost the artistic director, not just in the person of Ben Barnes but the office itself. This is a major change in administration, for it was only when Hugh Hunt insisted on the title and powers of artistic director in 1969 that he agreed to accept the Abbey's invitation to become 'artistic manager'. Hunt was a link with the past; in particular, he was a link with Yeats's idea of a theatre, for it was Yeats who first summoned him to counter the Gate's success in 1935. By 1969, Hunt was both an academic (being Professor of Drama at Manchester University) and internationally experienced as a director: the combination served to raise standards and to create an attitude towards experimentalism which paved the way for a new kind of Abbey. Decades of important new writing and exciting productions by liberated directors such as Tomás Mac Anna, his protégé Joe Dowling, and by Hunt's protégé Patrick Mason followed. The centenary programme attempted to do honour to this comparatively recent theatrical revolution by displaying the range of work the Abbey is now capable of producing. It succeeded admirably if unevenly in this aim (the production of *The Shaughraun* tended to rob the artistic policy of credibility during its long run). The financial crisis which hit the Abbey in August 2004 destroyed any real chance of Barnes's programme being evaluated fairly. One year afterwards, the Peacock was dark, there was no artistic director, only one new play had been staged (Vincent Woods's *A Cry from Heaven*), and a government minister was calling all the shots. He promised a new theatre building to replace the old. The echoes fade down the corridor and in some purgatorial dream life, Yeats undergoes a fresh pang of remorse, while Miss Horniman whispers, 'I told you so.'

---

[1] The complicated, year-long programme comprised five divisions: the Abbey and Europe (translations, etc); the Abbey and new writing (Paula Meehan, Peter Sheridan, Eugene O'Brien, Colm Tóibín, while a new play by Paul Mercier was cancelled); summer at the Abbey (mainly *The Shaughraun* and Parker's *Heavenly Bodies*); the Abbey and Ireland (eight plays from the repertory plus ten rehearsed readings); the Abbey on tour (*The Playboy, The Gigli Concert* and *The Plough*). There were also lectures, discussions, etc.

[2] All was changed at a meeting called by the Minister for Arts on 20 August 2005 to resolve the latest crisis at the Abbey, as a result of which the National Theatre Society Ltd. became the Abbey Theatre Ltd. under a new board. See Fintan O'Toole, 'O'Donoghue proposes radical reform at Abbey' *The Irish Times* 16 August 2005: 1, and 'How the show will go on', 11. See also Chris

Dooley, 'National Theatre: historic decision likely at today's extraordinary meeting: Advisory council of Abbey likely to make way for new entity', *The Irish Times* 20 August 2005: 3, and editorial, 'Abbey's future'.

[3] *The Critical Writings of James Joyce*, eds Ellsworth Mason and Richard Ellmann (London: Faber and Faber, 1959): 70.

[4] Augusta Gregory, *Our Irish Theatre*, 2nd ed. (Gerrards Cross: Colin Smythe, 1972): 20.

[5] *Uncollected Prose by W.B. Yeats*, eds John P. Frayne and Colton Johnson, 2 vols (London: Macmillan, 1970, 1975): Vol. 2, 141.

[6] *The Collected Works of J.M. Synge*, 4 vols. (Gerrards Cross: Colin Smythe, 1984): Vol. 2, , 382.

[7] Lennox Robinson, *Ireland's Abbey Theatre: A History, 1899-1951* (London: Sidgwick and Jackson, 1951): 22 citing the *Daily Independent*.

[8] Adrian Frazier, *George Moore, 1852-1933* (New Haven and London: Yale University Press, 2000): 284.

[9] Máire Nic Shiubhlaigh, *The Splendid Years* (Dublin: James Duffy, 1955): 1.

[10] W.B. Yeats, *Explorations* (London: Macmillan, 1962): 414.

[11] Yeats, *Uncollected Prose*, 2, 345-46.

[12] Peter Kavanagh, *The Story of the Abbey Theatre* (New York: Devin-Adair, 1950; repr. Orono, ME: National Poetry Foundation/University of Maine at Orono, 1984), Appendix D: 214.

[13] Yeats to Lady Gregory, 2 December 1906, *Theatre Business: The Correspondence of the First Abbey Theatre Directors*, ed. Ann Saddlemyer (Gerrards Cross: Colin Smythe, 1982): 169-70. Gregory was to pass the letter on to Synge. The following quotations are also from *Theatre Business*, to which page numbers refer.

[14] Joan FitzPatrick Dean, *Stage Censorship in Twentieth-Century Ireland* (Madison, WI: University of Wisconsin Press, 2004): 96. Lady Gregory tells the story in *Our Irish Theatre*. See also Lucy McDiarmid, *The Irish Art of Controversy* (Dublin: Lilliput Press, 2005): 87-122.

[15] Lennox Robinson, *Curtain Up: An Autobiography* (London: Michael Joseph, 1942): 118. The following quotations are from this source and are referenced by page numbers.

[16] Brenna Katz Clarke and Harold Ferrar, *The Dublin Drama League 1918-1941* (Dublin: Dolmen Press, 1979): 12-13.

[17] Ibid., 14.

[18] Robinson, *Ireland's Abbey Theatre*, 121.

[19] For details, see Terence Brown, *Ireland: A Social and Cultural History 1922-2002* (London: Harper Perennial, 2004): 129-58, and R.F. Foster, *W.B. Yeats: A Life: 2: The Arch-Poet 1915-1939* (Oxford: Oxford University Press, 2003): 515-26.

[20] Kavanagh, *The Story of the Abbey Theatre*, 184.

[21] Thomas McDonagh, *Literature in Ireland* (Dublin: Talbot Press, 1916; Nenagh: Relay Books, 1996): 111.

[22] Robert Hogan and Richard Burnham, *The Years of O'Casey, 1921-1926: A Documentary History, The Modern Irish Drama* (Newark: University of Delaware Press; Gerrards Cross: Colin Smythe, 1992): Vol. 6, 97.
[23] Robinson, *Ireland's Abbey Theatre*, 126.
[24] Ernest Blythe, 'Gaelic Drama', in *The Irish Theatre: Lectures Delivered during the Abbey Theatre Festival Held in Dublin in August 1938*, ed. Lennox Robinson (London: Macmillan, 1939): 191-2.
[25] Vincent Dowling, *Astride the Moon: A Theatrical Life* (Dublin: Wolfhound Press, 2000): 247.
[26] Box office receipts, Abbey Theatre Archives, show that the annual pantomimes consistently lost money from 1945 through the 1950s.
[27] Eric Bentley, 'The Poet in Dublin', *In Search of Theater* (New York: Vintage Books, 1954): 215.
[28] Bentley, 'Heroic Wantonness' (1951), *In Search of Theater*, 309. The preceding quotation is from p. 314.
[29] Ray Yeates, referring to the place of Irish-language plays in the Dublin Fringe Festival. See Seán Tadhg Ó Gairbhí, 'Thirsty for good stout and bad company', *The Irish Times*, 27 September 2004: 12.
[30] Tom Murphy, *The Cherry Orchard* (London: Methuen, 2004): n.p., originally a programme note, 17 February 2004. Oddly, the title page reads: 'adapted by Tom Murphy'.
[31] 'A Note by Seamus Heaney', Abbey programme for *The Burial at Thebes*, 31 March-1 May 2004.
[32] 'I wonder what Marina Carr believes? I can't say for certain, but I am certain in this play she writes in Greek.' Frank McGuinness, programme note, *By the Bog of Cats...* , in *The Theatre of Marina Carr: 'before rules was made'*, eds Cathy Leeney and Anna McMullan (Dublin: Carysfort Press, 2003): 88.
[33] Thomas Kilroy, 'A young girl before the king: Seamus Heaney takes possession of a classic and in the process gives us a play for our time', *The Irish Times* 10 April 2004, 'Review', 10.
[34] Lady Gregory, *Our Irish Theatre*, 62.
[35] W.B. Yeats, *Explorations*, 250.
[36] *The Letters of Sean O'Casey, Vol. 1, 1910-1941* ed. David Krause (New York: Macmillan, 1975): 103.
[37] Ernest Blythe, *The Abbey Theatre* (Dublin: National Theatre Society, n.d. [1963]): n.p.
[38] Chris Morash, '"Something's Missing": Theatre and the Republic of Ireland Act', in *Writing in the Irish Republic: Literature, Culture, Politics 1949-1999*, ed. Ray Ryan (Basingstoke: Macmillan, 2000): 76.

2 | A Synge for Our Times? Yeats's enquiring man revisited

Mary C. King

In his critical biographies, *Fool of the Family* and *The Silence of Barbara Synge*, W.J. McCormack offers a radical anatomy of generations of the Synge family. Using the disciplines of literary history and interpretative biography, these contextualizations of John Millington Synge further advance the deconstruction of W.B. Yeats's magisterial, still influential, hermetic invention of the dramatist as a rooted Ascendancy genius. In 1982, in my introduction to the first publication of the complete two-act version of Synge's Nietzschean and post-Ibsen drama, *When the Moon Has Set*, I interrogated Yeats's version of Synge. Somewhat controversially at the time, I pursued the issue of his social, political and aesthetic interests and their influence on his writings in *The Drama of JM Synge*. Since then, the process of re-evaluation has been ably developed in major literary critical and historical studies of Irish drama and the Irish Revival. More recently, these include works by Christopher Morash, Lionel Pilkington, Ronan McDonald, Fiona MacIntosh, Gregory Castle and Ben Levitas. On-stage, the epic *DruidSynge* cycle of six of Synge's plays, directed by Garry Hynes, has continued the process where it matters most: in the theatre.

Yeats famously or notoriously created for Synge the *post mortem* persona of a man of genius engaged in a political communion with an antique peasantry, sympathetically recovering their endangered culture, and speaking powerfully on their behalf through his plays. Opportunely, perhaps, for his ideological purposes, Synge departed this life to join the shades of the living dead in 1909. Dogged by chronic ill-health and preoccupied in his final physically debilitated years with the urgency of completing his last two plays, his early death facilitated the Arch-Mage's conjuring up of this partial version of his spirit. Ghosts are not in a position to defend themselves against appropriation to a cause, but biography and literature can be helped to speak from beyond marble and gilded monuments. Getting down to the difficult and detailed business of documentation, McCormack pursues, in their often murky contexts, the elisions and aporia in versions of Ascendancy history and sociology that Yeats strategically deployed and manipulated, and that Synge began fearfully to recover, negotiate, and mediate in his early autobiographical writings, in *When the Moon Has Set*, in *The Aran Islands*, and in his Wicklow essays. He would later translate these into the great enquiring art of his mature plays. Yeats's version of the dramatist and his work may now be read productively as partly a tribute to a fellow genius, partly a compulsive censorship of a shared troublesome history in favour of a myth of Unity of Being. Intriguingly, what is expressed in these new accounts of Synge's life, times, and writings is often what is repressed in Yeats.

Given the compromised social status of the Ascendancy Anglo-Irish, and their diverse, often conflicting, national and nationalist ambitions and anxieties, any attempt 'to speak for a primitive or savage people other than themselves ... and to use them in order to establish a new national culture' generated specific crises of identity and peculiar pathologies, shaping and shaped by external contradictions and strains.[1] These pathologies manifested themselves early in Synge's artistic development. They can be traced in the autobiographical sketches and the fictional autobiographical essays, the 'Vita Vecchia' and the 'Étude Morbide', as well as in his apprentice play, *When the Moon Has Set*. The autobiographical prose writings are all deeply traumatized by versions and perversions of Darwinism that haunted the nineteenth century bourgeois Victorian imagination, challenging and contaminating its rhetoric of high cultural humanism. In the Irish context, Darwinism and socio-Darwinism articulated with varieties of Celticism and dogged their complex political and aesthetic negotiations with philology, anthropology and ethnography. As evolutionary science engaged in increasingly dangerous liaisons with socio-biology and began disastrous flirtations with eugenics and anti-Semitism, Synge, who recorded how he had been at once terrified and inspired by his youthful reading of Darwin, further discovered in Ibsen and his drama, and particularly in Ibsen's play *Ghosts*, the *sinthome* that Lacan identified in Joyce. According to Jean-Michel Rabaté, the *sinthome* is the writer in whom the interlocking of the Real, the Imaginary, and the Symbolic depends on the function of the Sigma or Symptom – the ability or willingness to derive *jouissance* from an artifice of writing which enables the ego to become atoned, not with Yeatsian Unity of Being, but 'with the Symptom', producing 'a literature of supplementary chains, bypasses, ducts and prosthetic devices'.[2]

Proving that the human species evolved from common ancestors through environmentally selected chance mutations – through a series of randomly occurring but environmentally beneficial supplementary chains and ducts, as it were – Darwin's science of evolution undermined any scientific basis for all possible claims to racial essentialism. Ironically, but inevitably, given the nascent eugenicist phobias of empire, his theories were appropriated and distorted by Herbert Spencer and his successors, to legitimate various brands of imperialist racism. Indeed, in 1850, before Darwin dared publish his *Origin of Species*, Spencer's first book, *Social Statistics*, had appeared. This argued the case for the destruction of the decrepit and the infirm as part of nature's stern but kind discipline. It was Spencer, not Darwin, who coined the notorious phrase, 'the survival of the fittest'. Like many of his compatriots, he regarded the native Irish as an unfit race destined to be demographically controlled by the rigours of famine and disease that visited the unfortunate population during the black 1840s and into the end of the nineteenth century. The rise of Irish nationalism, in its Catholic and its Ascendancy manifestations, took place in the context of this great and disastrous hunger and in the midst of scandalously unrelieved mortality.

Yet another great Victorian, Matthew Arnold, championed what appeared on the surface to be a more kindly, humane and promising myth for the Celts. Somewhat hybrid himself – he was the son of a mother with Cornish ancestry and of a famous Celt-despising, Teuton-loving English public school headmaster – Arnold promoted assiduously, and with great rhetorical skill and cultural and pedagogical influence, the ideal of the artistic, primitively pure Celt, whose poetic and mystic qualities complemented the strength and the steady-going habit of the Saxon. According to this theory, however, only the patriarchal Saxon possessed the political qualities needed to dominate the world through science, technology, and the industry and commerce of the British Empire; that is, through burgeoning monopoly capitalism. Arnold seemed to offer those beleaguered, alienated Anglo-Irish, who had begun in the nineteenth century to seek an identity through reclaiming Celtic roots, an answer to fears of impotence, degeneracy and inferiority, but at a price. His aesthetic variety of Celticism entailed final abdication of the political power that had long been their *raison d'être* in Ireland to the pragmatic masculine Saxon, in return for what was at best psychologically castrating. Their consolation prize was to exercise a feminized cultural influence in a body politic where 'the Celtic genius' could never 'hold its own against them as a political and social counter-power, as the soul of a hostile nationality'.[3] Yeats assiduously dedicated himself to appropriating Arnold's aesthetic thesis and deploying his own subversive Machiavellian critical, aesthetic, and political genius to turning the unequal and gendered deal on its head. Throughout his long life, he played brilliantly with numerous and numinous variations on the perilous theme of aesthetic and cultural ascendancy conflated with purity of bloodline and legitimized as a political force by appeals to art, to older civilizations and to traditional ancestral authority.

Considering Charles Darwin's notoriety by the mid-nineteenth century, Synge came to the theory of godless evolution belatedly. The very young

Synge developed a pious childhood interest in a strictly deistic biblical natural history that persisted in modified, still theologically orthodox, form into adolescence. In a juvenile diary shared with his first cousin, Florence Ross, the childhood sweethearts recorded nature excursions in a format that is a beguilingly naive imitation of the seven days of Creation schema of the *Book of Genesis*. The children name places, plants, and animals as Adam, when called upon by God to exercise his authority over creation, named the flora and fauna in the Garden of Eden. Recalling these excursions in his fragmentary 'Autobiography', Synge links the Edenic experience with an infantile Celticism that is troubled by repressed fears about sexuality. 'We were always primitive. We both understood all the facts of life and spoke of them without much hesitation but a certain propriety that was decidedly wholesome. We talked of sexual matters with an indifferent and sometimes amused frankness that was identical with the attitude of folktales'.[4] It is difficult to imagine circulation of any non-scriptural literature in the Synge household, where maternal instruction in the Word of God and moralistic admonitions from John's pious brother Samuel were a daily event, and daily events were interpreted as witnessing the power and literal truth of God's Word. Yet in this evangelical *Tir na n-Óg*, serpents also lurked, ready to inflict symptom-inducing wounds on young psyches. The neglected and moth-eaten libraries in the various Synge houses and holiday lodging-places had their books and documents relating to legal matters. Families had their whispered secrets and story-telling retainers, servants and tenants, and local trampers and peasants, recounted oral versions of events that were not always either flattering or wholesome in their versions of ancestral Synge antics and intrigues. Terror of damnation, tantalizing intimations of sexual pleasures, and guilt reminiscent of Dante's *Inferno* and its denizens, and fears of illegitimacy and madness also tormented the often-sickly, almost posthumous youngest son, fatefully named John after another infant who had died at birth. As the maturing young man explored the family archives and gathered information about Synge origins and exploits, theological qualms and doubts were compounded with anxieties about class, identity and race.

The disjointed semi-autobiographical jottings dating from around 1898 and edited and compiled by Alan Price still comprise the only published fictionalized reprise of the future playwright's childhood and adolescent memories. Much scattered material relating to Synge's dissolute *bildungsroman* still remains to be explored amongst the Synge papers in Trinity College Dublin. This includes aborted attempts at a novel that takes up some of the themes of his first play as well as introducing trade union matters in relation to nursing, and the first chapter of an earlier projected novel provisionally entitled 'Flowers and Footsteps'. Several manuscripts contain intriguing verbal and graphic marginalia and there is much unpublished adolescent verse, some of which expresses the young poet's commitment to science and wrestles with the challenge of atheism. Early interests in nature, music and science provoked and alleviated in the struggling young artist appalling gothic terrors and ecstasies. These mingle uneasily with accounts of attraction towards, and sectarian and tribal shrinking from, local peasant types and Dublin slum children. The jottings include one brilliantly crafted, predictive paragraph that anticipates Synge's diagnostic essay, 'A Landlord's Garden in County Wicklow', and his great modernist prose work, *The Aran Islands*. It also exercises verbal ambiguities and metonymic strategies related to those that structure and inform his mature plays. Synge recalls how he began,

> when still very young to live in my imagination in enchanted premises that had high walls with glass upon the top where I sat and drank ginger beer in a sort of perpetual summer with one companion, usually some small schoolfellow I hardly knew. One day the course of my class put me for a moment beside my temporary god, and before I could find a fit term of adulation, he whispered an obscene banality, which shattered my illusions.[5]

Here, Synge juxtaposes and plays skilfully with variations on elements from a kind of naive faerie Celticism and imperial *Boys' Own* adventure, interwoven with intimations of darker intrigues and experiences worthy of an Ibsen play. Sexual and linguistic trauma and related verbal ambiguities disturb the surface innocence, betraying the instability and guilt-ridden origins of enchanted but viciously defended property and the folly of ignorant adulation of members of his class. The glass on the top of the wall, recalling, perhaps, the thorny enclosure of roses surrounding Sleeping Beauty, is in reality broken glass that has been viciously embedded in cement on the top of an estate wall: a fortified mini-pale installed on Synge real estate to exclude unwelcome peasants or deter native Irish intruders or rebels.

The discovery and realization that sex, sin, and guilt were of more than solipsistic personal origins and spiritual consequence came, nevertheless, as some relief to Synge, whose childhood was passed smothered in the bosom of an extended but close, intensely religious, matriarchal family. If his wrestling with Darwin filled him with fears of incest and parricide, it also awakened the desire to become scientist, writer, or musician. Before and during his frequent European sojourns and travels once he managed to escape from oppressive domesticity, Synge acquainted himself with an eclectic range of European writings, including the works of Schiller, Goethe, Wagner, Nietzsche, and Marx. Having seriously studied music in Dublin and then in Würzburg, he abandoned ambitions to compose and chose instead to become a writer and to study Celticism and philology at the Sorbonne. There he attended lectures in 1895 by Passy and de Julleville, whose lecture notes he took with him on his second visit to the Aran Islands in 1899. He also studied under the famous Professor Henri d'Arbois de Jubainville, with whom he rapidly established a personal and professional friendship. Synge immersed himself in aesthetics and philosophy and explored the literature of France, Germany and Italy, moving quickly from translations to originals, and including the works of Taine, Heine, Herder, Gautier, Loti, Baudelaire, and Huysmans. Unlike Yeats, he found that foreign languages presented little difficulty, as is evidenced by his easy switching between them in his journals, jottings, and lists of books read. He first read Ibsen when in Oberwerth at the end of the 1880s, in German translation, not in William Archer's joyless and pallid English version.

Synge's Italian travels and readings are still largely neglected, but they undoubtedly changed his attitude towards the Roman Catholic religion, regarded in family circles as the superstitious heresy of an ignorant peasantry. In 1907, at the height of his powers as a playwright, he translated some of Petrarch's sonnets on Laura into Irish peasant dialect. Long before that, however, he became a keen reader of Dante, a passion shared with James Joyce along with mutual admiration of Ibsen. The 'Vita Vecchia' takes its title and its genre from Dante's poetic autobiography, the *Vita Nuova*. This, and its more Pateresque companion piece, the 'Etude Morbide', are marked by a morosely indulgent absence of self, a reluctance to enquire too deeply into what is disturbing the subject, and by a rootless vagueness about place, that debilitate the attempts at creativity. The marginalia of some of the biographical manuscripts are decorated with Darwinian drawings of a bird's wing metamorphosing into the membrane of a bat's wing, a monkey's paw, a human hand, and a violin or cello. At times, Kafkaesque insects made from Rorschach-like blots and smudges crawl over and between words and lines and Janus-like heads, half human, half canine, peer out. Convinced he was unhealthy and would produce unhealthy offspring, Synge resolved early in his career never to bring into the world children to suffer as he had suffered. This fearful conviction is reformulated in one of the 'Vita Vecchia's' fourteen poems as a life-denying and self-denying ascetic vow to live celibate but clean. For Synge at this time, or for his class, there seemed to be little or no prospect of a Vita Nuova here or hereafter.

The companion fictional autobiography, the neurasthenic 'Étude Morbide', is somewhat less solipsistic than the 'Vita Vecchia'. While he was writing it, Synge was reading Walter Pater's *Imaginary Portraits* and studying Nietzsche and Schopenhauer. In the 'Etude', he introduces traumas and tropes of social as opposed to exclusively solipsistic insanity, as if he is beginning to come to grips with his personal nightmare as part of the nightmare of history, and specifically in its Euro-Irish manifestations. Green-robed musical doppelgangers and dissolute female personae, later translated into characters and props in *When the Moon Has Set*, haunt the pages, in which the speaker, an aspiring musician and writer, wrestles with theories of aesthetics and with the relationship of the arts with life. Mediated through Herbert Spencer, the Darwinian nightmare of incest and parricide is rewritten as symptomatic of the diseases of Western civilization, as a social and economic pathology. The angst-ridden narrator refers from time to time to newspaper accounts of men who have slain their kindred and review articles about socio-somatic nerve decay. One wonders if, perhaps, these were reviews of Freud's widely publicized, scandalous gender-bending lecture, 'Male Hysteria', given to the Vienna Institute on 5 October 1886. The fictional anti-hero also writes about 'falling in on the streets with wretched beings on the brink of total alienation'.[6] The theme of male hysteria emerges with the comic force of a mature dramatic imagination in *The Playboy of the Western World*, when Old Mahon alleges that his puny son 'was taken with contortions till I had to send him in the ass cart to the females' nurse'[7].

Throughout Synge's autobiographical writings, essays, journalism, reviews and drama, one can detect oscillations between aesthetic attraction towards versions of primitivism and elitist Celticism and realization that history and science destabilized the idealism and essentialisms implicit in them and betrayed their elisions of class. As I established in *The Drama of JM Synge*, as well as reading Weber and Spencer, Synge studied *Das Kapital* in German and English, making notes as he did so. He also read *The Communist Manifesto*. From Ibsen in particular he learned how to mediate through drama the psychic pathologies of socially imbricated bourgeois repression. The man who landed on Aran Mór in 1898 did so almost two years later than Yeats somewhat opportunistically claimed to have despatched him from unproductive European decadence to redemptive study of the unspoilt way of life of the west of Ireland. Still a prey at times on the islands, and during his wanderings in the Wicklow countryside, to nightmares of psychic dissolution, by 1898 Synge was in possession of a well-stocked enquiring mind. His studies had inoculated him against simplistic subscription to the prophylactic Celtic primitivism Yeats prescribed. In 'A Little Cloud' Joyce famously deconstructs a Catholic nationalist version of this Arnoldian dream turned nightmare. As part of his dream of becoming a Celtic Twilight artist, Little Chandler indulges and falls victim to a collusive febrile stereotyping that issues in the violent behaviour of a frustrated father towards a resented infant. Father figures are almost always problematic repressed presences in Synge's dramatic world: figures such as Daniel Burke in *In the Shadow of the Glen*, the ineffectual young priest in *Riders to the Sea*, and perhaps the Saint in *The Well of the Saints*, until the blood-boltered Old Mahon erupts onto the stage to be willingly mastered by his son in *The Playboy of the Western World*.

The three distinct Aran entities that Yeats synecdochically merged into one 'wild island off the Galway coast' in his Nobel Prize evocation of Synge may have been remote geographically from Paris and Yeats deliberately chose to underscore their immunity from European modernity.[8] Synge knew, however, that the Aran Islands and their people were economically and culturally an integral part of a changing Europe. He discovered that this supposedly primitive outcrop of the western world also looked nervously towards and depended economically on the United States and he returns repeatedly to this theme in *The Aran Islands*. The islanders possessed a repository of folk tales, but they and the stories they tell are obsessively preoccupied with money, with the price of everything, as their subsistence economy crumbles under the combined pressures of dissolute landlordism and nascent capitalism. Most of them depended on dollars from America for consumer goods. Politically, these story-telling people were on the verge of a mass move towards Dublin, preparing to throw in their lot with Catholic nationalist Ireland's 'Ivy Day in the Committee Room' travesty of Parnellism. Synge portrays this ideological movement physically in the powerful vignette of the train-journey that concludes Part II of *The Aran Islands*. He also knew, however, that, armed with the King James Bible translated into Gaelic, his proselytizing uncle, the Reverend Alexander Synge, had both fished for Catholic souls on the islands and had a go at more worldly entrepreneurship. Much to the anger of local fishermen, he ran a modern trawler that threatened their livelihood and he thriftily asked for old legal documents from Glanmore Castle in Wicklow, to cut up for labels for his fish-boxes. In Synge's day, the family still derived useful if diminishing rent income from property in Galway and elsewhere. Such income kept Synge at least marginally above the wonderfully pure, politically innocent, utter poverty Yeats ascribes to him in 'Synge and the Ireland of his Time'.

Before turning to Synge's wrestling with dubious matters of property and inheritance in *When the Moon Has Set*, it is worth recalling that the late nineteenth century Ascendancy Irish had become notoriously inbred as they consolidated property and power. Like Darwin, who, after careful and detailed financial, social and genealogical calculation married his well-heeled pious Wedgwood first cousin, Emma, they desired and feared the consanguineous marital practices that material interests and genetic prejudice dictated. Darwin mused whether a woman was 'better than a dog anyhow?' and speculated that it were better if his wife 'was an angel and had money'.[9] Although legal endogamy was expediently practised, extramarital liaisons and miscegenation with Catholic peasant others were inevitable. As Ibsen knew, when miscegenation and extramarital affairs are proscribed yet indulged, incest and the dread of incest lie in wait. Plagued by lumps on what his widowed mother circumspectly called poor Johnny's groin, Synge seems to have feared that his dead father, reputedly a victim of smallpox, might not have been as saintly as his God-fearing mother made out. He wrote that his reading of Darwin filled him with fears of incest and parricide as well as religious doubts. It 'was a terrible experience. By it I laid a chasm between my present and my past and between myself and my kindred and friends'.[10] It is not always observed that in Old Mahon, the mature Synge has created a dissolute patriarch of noted and scheming misbehaviour with females old and young. This sex-mad father's sons and daughters walk the four corners of the earth cursing their progenitor.

Throughout his life, Synge certainly entertained and dreaded the possibility that his own afflictions replicated the transgenerational fate visited on the syphilitic antihero of *Ghosts*. His delving amongst family documents and attentiveness to local history alerted him to unsavoury goings-on amongst his not-so-remote ancestors and avatars. *When the Moon Has Set* associates this fear with political guilt and tries through its plot to cancel both out. In the two-act version, the artist hero, Columb Sweeny, has returned from France to the Wicklow home of his recently dead uncle. He receives a letter from Paris from a friend with the Old Irish Catholic name, O'Neill. Anticipating the *Heart of Darkness* collection of skulls displayed in Dublin's Museum of Natural History that erupts into *The Playboy of the Western World* via Liverpool: 'White skulls and black skulls and yellow skulls, and some with full teeth and some haven't only but one.'[11] O'Neill keeps human skulls lined up on his Paris mantelpiece. In his letter to the gravely troubled heir, who has begun to unearth skeletons in his own family cupboard, O'Neill ironically congratulates Columb on inheriting the Sweenys' ill-gotten wealth. He writes in a language that looks back to the 1798 revolution and deploys stereotypes of the native Irish that evoke and blackly ironize contemporary racist slurs: 'Et ton héritage? Mes têtes de mort te saluent. My compliments to the little Irish pigs that eat filth all their lives that you may prosper.'[12] As Stephen Howe points out, both in the medieval period and in the French Revolution, for the English, France and all things French were 'a more significant Other than the Irish Celts or, indeed, any other conquered peoples'.[13] In their search for identity and difference, the radical Anglo-Irish committed, like Yeats and Synge, to Irish nationalism were compelled both to assimilate to and to reject that dangerous legacy. Moreover, and more insidiously and attractively, perhaps, French writers on race, including Gobineau and Georges Vacher de La Pouge, had already initiated an assimilation of the continental Celt into the Aryan race, while inveighing against miscegenation and even polyglottism as slippery slopes towards decadence and extinction.

Synge's first play does not remain silent about the repressed ground of its protagonists' bad faith. In it, dead ancestors whisper acts of violence, murder, expropriation, bastardy and infanticide. The one-act version brings on-stage Mary Costello, a wronged peasant woman of noble Castillian stock, to weep for her born yet unborn children. Mary was to have been married to Columb's landlord uncle. She has lost her reason and is confined to the asylum that reappears, in *In the Shadow of the Glen*, as the fine Union below in Rathdrum. Attempting to reverse the fate of the doomed heir in *Ghosts* while retaining the uncle-father's ill-gotten inheritance, Synge's earlier shaky and obfuscating plot compulsively expresses what it seeks to repress. Striving to restore primitive innocence and aristocratic legitimacy to a tainted blood-kindred line, the play concludes with a naïve, pseudo-Nietzschean leap out of Darwinian complexities into music, unconvincingly reversing as it does so the transgenerational doom of Oswald in *Ghosts*. In a pagan ceremony, Columb symbolically cancels out – but compounds – the wrong done to Mary, by wedding his Catholic convert cousin, Sister Eileen. Literary cousin of the Chouska and the Celliniani in the 'Vita Vecchia' and the 'Etude Morbide', Eileen is a fictionalized version, also, of the cousin who shared the innocent pursuit of the biblical origin of species in Synge's childhood, and an icon for Ireland. Renouncing her vows of celibacy, Eileen dresses in the green bridal dress destined for Mary Costello. She plays the Irish harp to Columb, who is recovering from a revenge shooting in his right (writing) arm. Mary's rebel brother has mistaken him for the uncle-father. The play's final aestheticization of life as a symphony colludes with the silencing of Sister Eileen. This act of silencing the subaltern woman resonates painfully with the real-life historical silence of Barbara Synge, about whose allusive and elusive life McCormack has written so hauntingly. But even as Synge wrote his dramas, music itself was moving into as great a turmoil of imminent transformation as any of the arts. Like the eponymous Daphne in Strauss's opera of 1937, who metamorphoses into a vegetable, Sister Eileen's achievement of ecstasy, harmony with nature is achieved at the price of relief from the burden of self-knowledge. 'I know nothing' would be the motto of her fulfilment.[14] There is much, also, in *When the Moon Has Set* that bears the traces of modernist traumas, and of related traumas of our post-modern, neo-fundamentalist era. That the play, with all its imperfections, has begun to resonate with the troubled spirit of the twenty-first century may perhaps be evidenced by its movement from being virtually unknown to having had several recent performances in Ireland, including one in the Samuel Beckett Theatre at Trinity College and another more ambitious venture by a local North Dublin amateur group, The Ballymun Players. These players staged an Irish translation of *When the Moon Has Set* for the 2004 Dublin Theatre Festival Fringe Programme. Unfortunately, the projected production by Garry Hynes, as part of the *DruidSynge* cycle was abandoned, although the company got as far as printing flyers that included the intention to present it. Playwright and critic Frank McGuinness greatly lamented this decision when he opened the Synge Summer School in Wicklow in July 2005.

If Synge's uneven but fascinating apprentice play partially succumbs to the dubious consolation of entropic repression, this outcome is vigorously contested in each of his mature dramas, from *In the Shadow of the Glen* to his unfinished final tragedy, *Deirdre of the Sorrows*. Yeats's dramatic career virtually terminates with the anguished interrogation, in *Purgatory*, of his desire for Unity of Being. What that project flirts with, and mediates into the world of real politick, is suggested by the play's contemporaneity with 'On the Boiler'. That sinister essay notoriously gestures towards unnamed – and unspeakable – acts, half-silenced racist measures, to support the rights of old families to go on living where they always have done. Having read *The Descent of Man*, Synge, by contrast, wryly noted that implicated in the word 'ascendancy' was its gravitational antonym: that what goes up highest descends furthest. Against the odds, perhaps, and through the exercise of great personal courage and integrity, Synge's imagination and sensibility became committed to openness and remained painfully but courageously open to material history, even if that history condemned his class to extinction. Accepting, like Maurya in *Riders to the Sea*, that no man at all can be living for ever, and we must be satisfied, he celebrated life in its imperfections and accepted, even welcomed, his own mortality and that of his class. By making possible the celebration of a workable if flawed future for mankind, his works have more in common with James Joyce's celebration of hybridity than with quests for an antique past that might legitimate dubious blood kindred claims to superiority over or elitist leadership of a collective Other. Yeats perceptively called Synge an enquiring man and showed his own artistic integrity and critical acumen by continuing to champion him even though, one suspects – or perhaps even because – he knew deep down that their paths diverged radically. Synge, had he lived, would scarcely have travelled the high road to Unity of Being. In his questing and questioning openness to the other and his interrogation of absolutes and fundamentalisms, that enquiring man is an exemplary writer and dramatist for today.

---

[1] Gregory Castle, *Modernism and the Celtic Revival* (Cambridge: Cambridge University Press, 2001): 44-5.

[2] Jean-Michel Rabaté, *James Joyce and the Politics of Egoism* (Cambridge: Cambridge University Press, 2001): 7.

[3] Matthew Arnold, *Lectures and Essays in Criticism,* ed. R.H. Super (Ann Arbour: University of Michigan, 1962): 298.

[4] John Millington Synge, 'Autobiography' in J. M. Synge, *Collected Works, Vol. II: Prose*, ed. Alan Price (London: Oxford University Press, 1966): 7.

[5] Ibid., 6.

[6] Synge, 'Etude Morbide', *Prose*, 29.

[7] Synge, *The Playboy of the Western World*, in J. M. Synge, *Collected Works, Vol. IV: Plays*, Book II, ed. Ann Saddlemyer (London: Oxford University Press, 1968): 123.

[8] William Butler Yeats, *The Collected Works of W.B. Yeats Vol. III, Autobiographies*, eds William H. O'Donnell and Douglas N. Archibald (New York: Scribner, 1999): 416.

[9] Adrian Desmond and James Moore, *Darwin* (London: Michael Joseph, 1991): 257.
[10] Synge, 'Autobiography', *Prose*, 11.
[11] Synge, *Playboy*, 135.
[12] John Millington Synge, 'When the Moon Has Set', *Long Room: Bulletin of the Friends of the Library, Trinity College Dublin*, ed. Mary C. King, Double Number 24-25 (Spring-Autumn 1982): 21.
[13] Stephen Howe, *Ireland and Empire: Colonial Legacies in Irish History and Culture* (Oxford: Oxford University Press, 2000): 121.
[14] Michael P. Steinberg, 'Myth and Mediocrity' *Richard Strauss and his World*, ed. Bryan Gilliam (Princeton: Princeton University Press, 1992): 181.

3 | Staging the Aesthetic: The Vagrant Artists of Padraic Colum and Seumas O'Kelly

Joan FitzPatrick Dean

As the nineteenth century turned to the twentieth, the possibility of a distinctly Irish culture was no longer abstract but increasingly real. In the proliferation of arts-sensitive periodicals, as in the Irish Literary Theatre, the Irish National Theatre Society, and the theatre companies sponsored by organizations like Inghinidhe na hÉireann (the Daughters of Erin) and Cumann na nGaedheal, Irish writers, activists and actors interrogated what it was to be Irish and what it was to be an artist. Who these artists were, what they did, what the culture owed them, and they the culture, were deeply contested questions.

On 8 October 1903, the Irish National Theatre Society, already dogged by controversy and rivalled by original plays performed by *Inghinidhe na hÉireann*, the National Literary Society and the Celtic Literary Society, presented a double-bill of Yeats's *The King's Threshold* and Synge's *In the Shadow of the Glen*. Famously, the debut of these plays provoked protests in and outside the theatre. Maud Gonne, Dudley Digges, and Marie T. Quinn sat through Yeats's play and then walked out of Synge's. Less famously, these plays by Yeats and Synge initiated a string of theatrical responses by Padraic Colum, Seumas O'Kelly, and others that addressed questions of artistic privilege, the relationship of artists to their community and culture, and the linkage of artists and outcasts.[1] Like the 1903 double-bill by Yeats and Synge, Colum's *The Fiddler's House* (1907) and O'Kelly's *The Shuiler's Child* (1909) also examined what it was to be an Irish artist. In more realistic and prosaic contexts, Colum and O'Kelly positioned the Irish artist in a less abstract and, hence, more problematic relation to community.

In lectures, in-house publications like *Beltaine* and *Samhain*, prefaces, and public letters, Yeats and to a lesser extent Synge addressed the place, privileges, and responsibilities of the artist. *The King's Threshold* and *In the Shadow of the Glen* suggest a national theatre and heroic model peopled with outcasts who chose rebellion, freedom or even death as release from strictures of society. Artist and outcast, Yeats's Seanchan chooses his liminal status in *The King's Threshold* to protest King Guaire's denial of the ancient bardic privileges by a conspicuously public hunger strike. Rendered un- or semi-conscious by his hunger on the palace steps, 'speaking as if in a dream',[2] 'Yeats/Seanchan', in Adrian Frazier's description, 'makes ever more absolute claims for art, passing from powerful assertion through hyperbole to delirious megalomania'.[3]

Structurally, *The King's Threshold* depicts a procession of supplicants – king, pupils, mayor, cripples, emissaries from his family, beautiful princesses, and his lover Fidelm – who urge Seanchan to compromise by taking food and accepting Guaire's offers. Several of them discuss or rehearse their appeals to Seanchan before they speak directly to him, which heightens the theatricality and irony of their speeches.

Although not fully of this world, Seanchan is wholly sincere and single-minded in his devotion to his art. He reminds the oldest pupil that poetry is 'One of the fragile, mighty things of God/That die at an insult',[4] a death that imperils the entire community. Art's affect on the health of the culture imagistically appears in the thrice-repeated trope of the pregnant woman whose child transmits and reflects what the culture makes available as art. The Oldest Pupil asserts, 'the poets hung images of the life that was in Eden/about the child-bed of the world, that it, looking upon those images, might bear/triumphant children', but should 'the Arts perish,/the world that lacked them would be like a woman/That, looking on the cloven lips of a hare, /Brings forth a hare-lipped child' (73). Later, Seanchan will ask the cripples: 'But why were you born crooked?/What bad poet did your mothers listen to/That you were born so crooked?' (88) If the culture is to be triumphant, if it is to avoid the crippled, deformed, and crooked, the community must afford the artist a privileged centrality so that the poet can create salutary art for that community.

Seanchan's defiant, even triumphant, death at the end of Yeats's play was perhaps less shocking than Nora's departure at the end of Synge's. Of all Irish playwrights in the early dramatic revival, Synge is the best known for his portrayal of outcasts and vagrants in Irish rural life. A tramp seduces and takes to the roads with the woman of the house in *In the Shadow of the Glen*. Two blind travellers briefly enter and then reject the settled, sighted life in *The Well of the Saints*. A desolate Mayo village embraces the enigmatic Christy Mahon before he upsets its tedium in *The Playboy of the Western World*. *The Tinker's Wedding*, which Synge balked at publishing in his lifetime, ends with the choric exhortation: 'Run, run. Run for your lives.'[5] Synge's protagonists are free-spirited, independent individuals, unfettered by social conformism or religious piety or even the artistic responsibilities of Yeats's Seanchan.

Synge's fascination with life outside settled communities dates from at least 1898 when he wrote that 'man is naturally a nomad and all wanderers have finer intellectual and physical perceptions than men who are condemned to local habitations'.[6] Synge privileged the vagrant throughout his writing. In *Modern Irish Literature,* Vivian Mercier describes the choice the author and his characters make in a section entitled 'Tramp or Bourgeois?'[7] Mercier traces that choice to Synge's essay 'The Vagrants of Wicklow', written in 1901-1902 and published in the autumn 1906 issue of *The Shanachie.* There Synge self-consciously iterated the construction of the romanticized wanderer: 'In all the circumstance of this tramp life there is a certain wildness that gives it romance and a peculiar value for those who look at life in Ireland with an eye that is aware of the arts also.'[8] Not only did Synge recurrently connect, as he does here, the tramp and the artist, but also he was conscious of his own tendency to fuse and to romanticize the tramp/artist. Even if they do not include artists, Synge's plays dwell on the complexities of reconciling the individual to the community.

The response to *In the Shadow of the Glen* is the subject of extensive analysis by Frazier, Hogan and Kilroy, and others.[9] The response to *The King's Threshold* was buffered but nearly unanimous. The advanced nationalists at *Sinn Fein* deliberately twisted Yeats's play to suggest sympathy not with Seanchan, but with those who dismiss him as effete, irrelevant and heartless. Arthur Griffith, for instance, wrote: 'We are firm believers in the freedom of art …[but] our sympathy went out to the honest soldier who wished to put his sword into the selfish old man who lay on the King's steps intimidating where he could not convince….We hold it a pity that King Guaire did not hang Seanchan. Had he done so, Art would have been for all time his debtor.'[10] In extracting a commitment from Standish O'Grady to comment on *The King's Threshold*, Yeats could not have anticipated the candour of O'Grady's response, which appeared in *The All-Ireland Review*: 'I did not like your play. The incredibility of a man abstaining from food or drink until he died, died before our eyes, was so contrary to nature, so unhuman, that of itself it was enough to make the whole play unreal, unaffecting. Add to this the preposterous notion that the poet, the true poet, can ever demand honour and recognition from the average man, even when typified as the King.'[11]

Like the critics in the advanced nationalist press, playwrights like Colum and O'Kelly felt that a national dramatic repertory ought to present a more truthful, even if less poetic, picture of Irish life. Colum and O'Kelly soon explored the same issues, but moved the artist from the threshold of a palace to far humbler sites: to public houses and fairs and to the open road. They also moved their own plays out of the Abbey and onto the far humbler stages of the Theatre of Ireland.

By December of 1905 Colum and O'Kelly, along with Máire Nic Shuibhlaigh, Honor Lavelle, Emma Vernon, Maire Garvey, Frank Walker,

Seamus O'Sullivan, and George Roberts broke with the Abbey, just a year after the patent for the theatre had been issued. They gathered around them the support of George Russell (AE), James Cousins, Thomas Kettle, H.F. Norman (editor of the *Irish Homestead*), Stephen Gwynn, and Thomas Keohler [Keller]. Several of the central figures in this second secession, perhaps not coincidentally, were on the 1903 Yeats/Synge double-bill: Seamus O'Sullivan played the Lord High Chamberlain; Honor Lavelle, Aileen; George Roberts, Senias; and Frank Walker as P. MacShuibhlaigh, Cian in Yeats's play. Maire Nic Shuibhlaigh, who played Fedelm in *The King's Threshold* and Nora Burke in *In the Shadow of the Glen*, would prove the most popular actor in the Theatre of Ireland company. Padraic Colum, who played a Cripple in Yeats's play, premiered both *The Fiddler's House* and *The Miracle of the Corn* (1908) under the auspices of the Theatre of Ireland. In 1909 O'Kelly's *The Shuiler's Child*, which was inspired by and dedicated to Maire Nic Shuibhlaigh, followed his plays *The Matchmakers* (1907) *and The Flame on the Hearth* (1907) in the Theatre of Ireland repertory.

On these lesser-known stages of the Irish revival, these younger playwrights opted for a nuanced, realistic portrayal of vagrants and artists. In *The Fiddler's House* and *The Shuiler's Child*, the protagonist chooses a travelling existence over the pressures and responsibilities of 'settled' life, regular labour or societal structures, but this choice comes easily for neither Con Hourican nor Moll Woods. Colum and O'Kelly problematized the portrayal of vagrants by depicting domestic as well as artistic entanglements. Colum's *The Fiddler's House* (the three [and later four] act revision of *Broken Soil)* portrays the artist not as a poet but as a fiddler; as a (single-parent) father, not a privileged sage; as a rural wanderer and failed farmer, not as a court advisor. Colum's contemporary domestic setting exposed the constructed fantasy of Yeats's Celtic Twilight in *The King's Threshold*. Colum's dramaturgy sought to engage a mass audience, rather than a well-cultivated elite by portraying the artist not as court poet but as fiddler and by employing not chanted verse, but an accessible colloquial speech.

Both Yeats and Colum underscore the artist's freedom as a prerequisite for art, and depict that the artist exists in (very different) symbiotic relationships with his audience. Colum's fiddler, Conn Hourican, stands in stark contrast to Seanchan. Whereas Yeats emphasized the culture's need for the artist, Conn stresses the artist's need for an audience: 'The man of art must have his listeners....Many's the day I put in with the scythe in Ireland, and in England too; I did more than stroll with the fiddle, and I saw more places than where fiddling brought me' (9, 5). The land can sustain only some of the community's needs: 'God help them that are depending on the land and the weather for the bit they put into their heads. It's no wonder that the people here are, [sic] harassed, anxious people.' (7) Moreover, Colum asserts the importance of an audience for a fiddler like Conn: 'I could never play my best in this place.' (42)

Unlike the single-minded Seanchan, Conn has mixed feelings about his artistic and domestic responsibilities, about the demands of his musical and paternal roles. His daughters worry about his age, his health, his drinking, especially when he is on the roads. The selfless Maire is similarly torn about returning to the roads with her father, but finally decides to do just that. Conn is hardly idealized: his ego, his pride and his drinking all figure in his assertion of freedom seen in both his breaking his promise to Maire by going to play at Flynn's pub and in his choice to return to the travelling life. Ultimately, the title of the play has an oxymoronic quality: the road, we are repeatedly told, for the fiddler. Confined to his house, the fiddler has no audience. Whereas Yeats foregrounded the society's need for the artist, Colum underscores the artist's need for society.

In O'Kelly's *The Shuiler's Child,* the artist, if she can indeed be considered that, is a woman criminalized, reduced to subsistence, dependent on her singing for handouts. Moll Wood's song is her claim to life outside society's strictures and its prescribed place for her: the workhouse. There is little, if any, romance associated with Moll's freedom and mobility on the open road. Several characters fear that if Moll Woods were to take her child from the O'Heas (or the workhouse) and bring him with her on the road, he would suffer terribly, as terribly as she herself suffers. Recognizing the realities rather than the romance of a wandering life, Moll has almost nothing positive to say about life on the road – only that it is a less undesirable place than the workhouse or gaol. Although Moll's standing as an artist is barely recognized, only in her songs does she retain any of her much-discussed 'pride'; only in song can she begin to express the injustices she has endured.

If the artistic status of the Tramp in *In the Shadow of the Glen* and Moll Woods in *The Shuiler's Child* is not as heavily emphasized as Seanchan's privileged role as poet, the significance of place is even more important. Moll Woods recalls the workhouse with horror: there they 'put me on a level with women from the lanes of the town – strange, bad women ... They swore I was insubordinate: so I was ... Do you know the scent you would get between the potato ridges a year the blight would come heavy upon them? ... A scent of wasting and withering. Well, that's the way it is in the wards of the workhouse'.[12] As in Yeats, issues of health and vitality are closely identified with specific place. Likewise, the centrality of place is found in the fact that she takes her son to see the now-derelict home that her husband, 'a wild reckless man' (12), let go to ruin. For her, although a settled life might be her first choice, life as a shuiler on the roads is the only alternative left to gaol or the workhouse.

The contrast between the portrait of the artist staged by Yeats and Synge on the one hand and Colum and O'Kelly on the other is marked by geographical, linguistic, class, and cultural differences. Although many of the plays written by Colum and O'Kelly employed a humble domestic setting familiar to Abbey audiences, there is a marked difference in the 'peasant quality' or 'PQ' in works like *The Fiddler's House* and *The Shuiler's Child* and the plays of the Abbey triumvirate. This contrasting 'PQ' appears in other works that portray the indigenous Irish artist such as Rutherford Mayne's *The Turn of the Road* (1906) and is indicative of the contrast between the early Abbey and its alternatives such as the Theatre of Ireland and the Ulster Literary Theatre.

To trace the linkage of the artist and vagrant in the twentieth century is to follow an increasingly well-trod path. As the century progressed not only virtually all autobiographical works, but also seminal works by Joyce and Heaney examined questions of artistic responsibility and privilege and the artist's relation to the community. On stage, the path leads from Colum and O'Kelly through Samuel Beckett's *Krapp's Last Tape* (1958), to Stewart Parker's *Heavenly Bodies* (1986), Frank McGuinness's *Innocence* (1987) and Martin McDonagh's *The Pillowman* (2003).

---

[1] The nomenclature and lexicon are vexing when it comes to individuals who stand apart from their societies and communities: outcasts, vagrants, tramps, travellers, nomads, tinkers, vagabonds, fugitives, wanderers, the displaced, the homeless, and the dispossessed, strangers, and exiles are only a sampling of the linguistic alternatives in English.

[2] W.B. Yeats, *The Collected Plays of W.B. Yeats* (New York: Macmillan, 1952): 72.

[3] Adrian Frazier, *Behind the Scenes: Yeats, Horniman, and the struggle for the Abbey Theatre* (Berkeley: University of California Press, 1990): 69.

[4] Yeats, 74.

[5] J.M. Synge, *Plays II*, 1968: 49.

[6] Synge, *Prose*, 1962: 24.

[7] Vivian Mercier, *Modern Irish literature: Sources and founders*, ed. Eilis Dillon (Oxford: Clarendon, 1994): 207.

[8] Synge, *Prose*, 1962: 48.

[9] See Frazier, *Behind the Scenes* 64-92; Hogan and Kilroy, 69-83.

[10] Arthur Griffith, 'All Ireland', *The United Irishman* 17 October 1903: 1.

[11] Standish O'Grady, 'On The King's Threshold' in *Laying the foundations 1902-1904*, eds Robert Hogan, and James Kilroy (Dublin: Dolmen Press, 1976): 73.

[12] Seumas O'Kelly, *The Shuiler's Child: A Tragedy in Two Acts* (Chicago: DePaul UP, 1971): 24.

4 | Shoyo Matsui, A Japanese Lennox Robinson: The Irish National Theatre and Japanese New Drama

Chiaki Kojima

> 'It was no coincidence that the Japanese New Drama movement used the basis of the Irish Theatrical Renaissance' – Kaoru Osanai

The years 1906 and 1909 are the two main turning points in the history of Japanese theatre. The Literature Association (文芸協会, Bungei-Kyokai) was established in 1906 by Shoyo Tsubouchi and Hogetsu Shimamura. The Liberal Theatre (自由劇場, Jiyu-Gekijo) was then founded in 1909 by Kaoru Osanai and Sadanji Ichikawa. New Drama (新劇, Shingeki) aimed to create new realistic plays different from the Japanese traditional performing arts: Noh, Kyogen and Kabuki plays. Because theatre arts have great potential to influence people, intellectuals concerned with theatre considered New Drama important, as it was conceptually equivalent to drama in western countries. A large number of western plays were translated, adapted and performed. Along with English, French, German, Norwegian, and Russian plays, Irish drama had a great influence on Japanese New Drama.

At that time, the emergence of Irish theatre had a lot in common with the start of realistic plays in Japan. Because the two countries began to establish modern original theatre at about the same time, Japanese playwrights of the period were particularly interested in Irish plays. It is not surprising, therefore, to find that the Japanese playwright Shoyo Matsui, and his Irish contemporary Lennox Robinson, had much in common since both worked to develop indigenous theatres that had been established by an earlier group of activists. Although almost forgotten now, Matsui was known as a prolific writer at that time: among those he has written, 147 scripts were produced for the stage. Lennox Robinson deserves special mention for his career as a director of the Abbey Theatre for more than forty years. The second generation of these theatrical movements has attracted less attention than the first generation in both countries, yet this was the period when the new initiatives were developed and enabled to settle. At the time, the New Drama movement in Japan was interested in producing and adapting foreign plays, including Irish plays. However, the influence of Irish theatre on Japanese playwrights has not been much studied. Focusing on Matsui and Robinson, this paper will introduce the theatrical activity of these two playwrights in the first section. The second and third sections provide an analysis of the adaptation process from Robinson's *Harvest* to Shoyo's *Tea Making House* (『茶を作る家』, *Cha wo Tsukuru Ie*) from the point of view of the characters and background atmosphere. Lastly, the paper reviews Matsui's ideas and the reform of Japanese new theatre.

Shoyo Matsui and Lennox Robinson

Shoyo Matsui (1870-1933) was a dramatist who knew an enormous amount about theatre, energetically produced a large number of scripts, and conducted various theatrical reforms. Under his autonym, Masaharu Matsui, Matsui was born in Shiogama, Miyagi prefecture, Japan. *Akugenta* (『悪源太』, *Akugenta*), one of his early works, was phenomenal at that time as it was the first script used by a Kabuki theatrical company which was not written by a Kyogen playwright who belonged to a theatre company. He travelled to America and Europe between 1906 and 1907 to learn about Western theatre. After returning to Japan, Matsui introduced a substantial number of theatrical reforms ranging from new performance skills to modern theatrical systems. His ambitious improvements caused fierce opposition from the conservative theatre establishment, leading him to retire to Shizuoka. However, because Shoyo Tsubouchi, a doyen of Japanese theatre, had a high opinion of him, Matsui was persuaded to go back to Tokyo in 1909. From then on, he was an extremely prolific writer, producing a substantial amount of translated, adapted, and original plays. His second visit to Europe in 1919 enriched his work as a dramatist. His translation of *The Twentieth Century* by George Bernard Shaw, which premiered in 1922, earned a high reputation amongst various theatre and literary magazines.

His Irish counterpart, Lennox Robinson (1886-1958), gained recognition in Dublin for his first play, *The Clancy Name* in 1908. He became manager and producer of the Abbey in 1909, and was sent to London by Yeats in order to learn stage management. Although he was there only for six weeks, he learned a great deal, attending all of Shaw's rehearsals, among other events. However, very soon afterwards Robinson was almost fired from his post as manager because the Abbey failed to close its doors on the day following King Edward VII's death in May 1910.

This incurred the rage of Miss Annie Horniman, who subsidized the theatre. Yeats supported him, so he did not have to resign. Nevertheless, he was obliged to leave the Abbey for five years between 1914 and 1919 because the second Abbey tour to the US did not make money. He returned to the theatre in 1919 as manager and director of production and remained in this position until his death in 1958.

Matsui and Robinson's accomplishments in establishing a new national drama at that time paralleled each other; both went abroad to learn a modern theatre system, introduced the system to the national theatre and were supported by a significant literary doyen (Tsubouchi and Yeats). While Matsui was in Europe from 1906 to 1907, he studied European new theatre systems. Robinson also went to London three years later to learn theatre management. Matsui sent Sadanji Ichikawa II, a Kabuki actor, over to Europe and let him acquire western style acting and theatrical expressions including voice training. In order to introduce modern European and American plays to Dublin, Robinson and Yeats founded the Dublin Drama League and some productions took place in the Peacock, which had been opened in 1927. This, as Christopher Fitz-Simon has pointed out, became the basis of the Abbey School of Acting.[1] However, the path both Matsui and Robinson had to tread was thorny. Matsui's controversial play, *Kesa and Morito* (『袈裟と盛遠』, *Kesa to Morito*) aroused the antipathy of conservative theatre people and he had to retire for two years. Similarly, Robinson had been obliged to quit his managerial position for a number of years.

Matsui was one of the first people to be intrigued by the Abbey Theatre movement and my research has led me to find that at least four of his plays are based on Irish ones. Irish dramas attracted Matsui's attention while he stayed in England, and after he returned to Japan, he started to order the new Irish plays from Maunsel as they were published. He eventually became instrumental in making Irish plays fashionable in Japan. *Tea Making House*, an adaptation of Robinson's *Harvest*, earned a good reputation in contemporary literary magazines and it is probably one of his best-adapted works.

Characters in *Harvest* and *Tea Making House*

Premiering in 1910, *Harvest*, Robinson's first full-length play, was severely criticized when it was put on the stage of the Abbey Theatre. The audience was offended by the play. The correspondent for *The Evening Telegraph* was most critical:

> It out-Synges Synge. It gives us all the suggestiveness of the malodorous problem play without any intelligible problem. It is clever of its kind. It is intellectual — so are many things that are intolerable, some that are unspeakable. But as a product of what is alleged to be an Irish National Theatre it is repellent, repulsive, abhorrent. The last Act especially is a

mere seething pot of vice, filth, meanness, dishonour, dishonesty, depravity and duplicity.²

As if excusing the play, Robinson himself later wrote that *Harvest* was not one of his best.³ However, Yeats responded favourably in the *Cambridge Daily News*: 'Then we have *Harvest*, by S.L. Robinson, a powerful play, in which is shown the struggle of the farming classes to bring up their children in the professions, thereby ruining their farms.'⁴ In addition, after accepting the play for production but before it appeared, Yeats wrote a letter to Robinson to arrange a meeting in Dublin: the young Cork playwright impressed Lady Gregory and Yeats. Although the public did not appreciate the play's sense of disillusionment with the Irish countryside, *Harvest* was the springboard for Robinson's career. As Yeats suggested, it powerfully depicts the complexity of the emotional struggle of each character and describes the contradictions that provincial Ireland was facing at the time.

The first act of *Harvest* unfolds with an episode in which Jack, the fifth son of the Hurley family, and his new wife, Mildred, arrive home to Knockmalgloss. Jack, whose marriage has left him in financial difficulties, asks for money from the eldest brother Maurice but he is told that their family is on the brink of bankruptcy due to the expensive education that all of the brothers, including Jack, have received. In Act II, a letter arrives from another brother in which he refuses to send any money. Timothy, their father, commits arson in order to receive compensation and clear the debt. Maurice says that both he and Jack should pretend that they do not know about their father's crime in order to save their house, but Jack insists that it would be dishonest for the family to accept the compensation. Jack decides to work on the farm with Mildred leaving Dublin and selling his furniture. Act III, however, shows the failure of this plan. Mildred, from a middle-class background, becomes sick and tired of farm work while Jack is physically unable for the heavy duties. Mary, the Hurleys' only daughter, having decided to make a break with her life as a courtesan, also comes home. However, she has asked a lover for money, and brings money for the family, pretending that Patrick, the second brother, sent it to them.

Tea Making House, the Japanese adaptation of *Harvest*, premiered a short time after the original production. The play ran for twenty days from 1 October 1918, as one of the programs of the Public Theatre (公衆劇団, Koshu Gekidan). The basic storyline is the same in the adaptation; however, it modifies the personalities of the original characters, substituting stereotypes typically seen in traditional Kabuki plays. The adaptation is also restructured into a two-act play by omitting the first half of Act I and inserting the last half into Acts I and II. These alterations give a different nuance to the storyline of the play and they were probably the result of considering the preferences of an audience of ordinary people in Japan.

The change of the character of Jack to Hakuzo is one of the interesting modifications. Jack, a chemist in Dublin, is portrayed as a simple and straightforward person typical of a youngest son. Unlike Hakuzo, Jack cannot guess the problems of his own family; he has not realized the fact that his family had to spend a large sum of money for education, so he repeatedly asks Maurice the reason why the family became penniless; he cannot immediately infer who set the fire either, although his father hints at what he did several times. On the other hand, Hakuzo in *Tea Making House* is described as an intuitive moral person: an educator. Although asking for five thousand yen from his family, he has a stronger reason: to establish a school for girls. Hakuzo, judging from his attitude, guesses that his father set the fire, and questions him. Both Jack and Hakuzo oppose accepting compensation but they do so from different motivations. Jack opposes it because of his honest straightforward personality, while Hakuzo does so because it is against his sense of morality as an educator. Robinson's Jack, the youngest son of the family, is portrayed with an emphasis on his naivety, unaware of the seriousness of the monetary situation in the family, especially in the first act. The way Matsui describes Hakuzo accentuates his moralistic rationalism that is later contrasted with his sister's selfless and instinctive sacrifice, particularly towards the end.

Substantial character changes are made from Mary to Ohana. Both of them make money by selling themselves to save the family, yet Mary is more willing to go back to the city. Recognizing the family's financial distress, she asked her lover for fifty pounds and told her family that it was from Patrick. Though she had grown tired of life in London and returned to her old home, she decides to go back to her life as a prostitute because she found she could not forget about the vivid life she led in the city. She describes this to Jack, who found out what she was doing in London:

> But, Jack, the dreadful thing is I want to go back … You weren't at home, you don't see how father — because he loved me — kept me here against my will … almost strangled me. Well, I broke out when I got away, I threw all the old things overboard. I've had a splendid time. I can't give it up. I'm longing for that life, and its excitement and splendour and colour. I want a big city and crowds of people and bright lights and lovely costly clothes, and — and — oh, Jack, I want it all, all that dreadful, splendid life.[5]

Her contradictory expression, 'dreadful, splendid life', conveys her mixed feelings. She does not return to London simply because she is sacrificing herself for her family. As she gets used to city life, she notices that she can no longer bear the 'the roughness and the hard living and the coarse food' (49). She realized that she cannot give up the flamboyant life in the city; therefore, she goes back there, in spite of her misgivings.

In the adaptation, Ohana is the character that corresponds to Mary. However, she is quite different from Mary because she completely sacrifices herself for her family. She argues with Hakuzo who severely criticizes the Geisha for being such a derogatory profession and explains their inescapable situation, revealing her own disconsolate feelings:

> Brother Hakuzo, you said that to be a Geisha is ever such a menial profession, but their backgrounds are absolutely various ... Most of them are not selling their virtue by their wish. They did not make themselves playthings of men. All of them are covering their tears putting powder on their face and force their bitter tears down their throat with sake. What seem like easy lyrics are actually coming from the voices of oppressed women cursing themselves. What sounds like the jovial tune of the Shamisen [three stringed instrument] is the counter resonance of the trembling minds of helpless women. Nevertheless, why do they keep doing such an awful profession? They have to do it for their parents, for the sake of duty, or because of their circumstances.[6]

The reason Ohana became a Geisha was that the man who promised to marry her needed three hundred yen. She did not sell herself for a luxurious life. Here, she sells herself again because she is anxious about her father. She is swayed by misgivings that her father himself is actually the one who set fire to the barns hearing the rumour in the village. She is in agony worrying about her father becoming a criminal. Her character is in marked contrast to Mary's who cannot stand the peasant's life. Ohana, whose actions are totally selfless, is a tragic figure full of sorrow typically bringing the audience to tears. She reminds Japanese audiences of the protagonists of Sewamono, a type of Kabuki drama dealing with the common people's life, whose theme centred on a girl who has to sell herself to help her family or loved ones out of severe poverty or the pain of sickness. Matsui's adaptation evokes scenes from traditional Japanese plays that were already established as dramatic patterns. Ohana's actions, disregarding her reputation, also sharply contrast to the 'moral ethics' represented by Hakuzo and Mieko. Hakuzo, who has lofty ideals, cannot save his family by his philosophy. Mieko, Hakuzo's wife, also quickly complained about the hard labour on the farm, and tries to persuade Hakuzo to return to Nagoya, saying that they have to devote themselves to education. Yet she also criticizes Ohana because of her moral philosophy. However, Hakuzo's faith wavers when he realizes the sincerity of Ohana who devotedly sacrifices herself for the family.

Though the basic story line is the same in both plays, the adaptation has its own theme different from the original. Matsui simplified the characters of the play, and made them more stereotypical, while the characterization is quite complicated in Robinson's *Harvest*. Matsui did not make an easy compromise regarding this adaptation but developed a contrast between the sense of 'morality' and 'affection' in a typical Japanese way, and successfully depicts the irony of 'morality'. The ultimate theme of *Tea Making House* resides in the irony of morals and tragic affections represented by Ohana. Taro Akiba, a critic and drama scholar, praised *Tea Making House* saying, 'While it is taken from a foreign play, I have no hesitation in saying that it is one of the best among Shoyo's.'[7]

The image of the 'country' and the 'soil'

Harvest faced unfortunate circumstances compared to its Japanese adaptation as regards its initial reception. Andrew Malone wrote, 'It [*Harvest*] is typical of Robinson's earlier plays, showing the evil consequences of applying to a rural population a type of education which unfits them for any but an urban life.'[8] He did not value the play highly as he thought the theme to be mere criticism of the educational system. Other critics were furious about the immorality of the characters as seen earlier in the review in *The Evening Telegraph*. At a time of high patriotic feeling in Ireland, most missed the aspects of Robinson's play that illustrate the irony of egocentric human psychology and the disillusionment of the countryside and instead saw criticism of education or the decay of a sense of morality.

The motif of the 'soil', representing Ireland, is present in various parts of the play and it contains two opposite ideas: illusion and reality. The illusion of Irish soil is well presented in the first half of Act I. This act begins as Jack brings his wife, Mildred, of Protestant middle-class background, back to his home village. Mildred has imaginative ideas towards so called 'Irish' things, such as 'soil' and 'country', and Jack also has the childish idea that the 'soil' can make money in no time. Mildred asks him if his father and Maurice, the eldest brother, are 'real, genuine peasants' (3). After hearing her husband say, 'Knockmalgloss is real peasant through and through', Mildred responds, '(with a sigh of ineffable content) That's what I love! I've always longed to know their lives, to get close to the soil, to get to know the great, eternal mother of us all.' (3) This line expresses her naïve illusions about 'soil' and 'country'. Brought up in the city, she also has an image that 'Irish' things are supposed to make her feel 'country'. When she notices that Jack's home has a slate roof, she says, 'But I thought it was a cottage ... a thatched cottage' almost with a wail (1). Jack even has to cheer her up saying 'I'm sure you'll find the inside all right and Irish enough to suit even you.' (1) Their conversation is heavy with Robinson's irony. He questions whether the illusion of the great 'country' and 'soil' of Ireland can be retained when Jack and Mildred face the reality.

Harvest depicts other characters embodying the corrupting illusion of the 'country' and the 'soil'. Mary's image of her father who is 'so simple, so innocent, so unspoiled' (56) is destroyed when she is told that he set fire to the buildings to receive compensation. She is shocked at the fact that she thought her father worked in ease and comfort but he is actually no different from her who sold herself. The character of the father implies that Irish 'soil' and 'country' are actually trampled down and covered with muddy disgrace.

The yearning after the country and rural life also started to appear in Japan though its disillusionment was rarely described. The intellectuals especially, who did not experience the hardships of life in rural areas, tend to long for the image of the country. In his essay 'On Country Literature' (「郷土文芸論」, 'Kyodo Bungei Ron'), Yoshihiro Kono describes the people's sense of loss in the modern city, Tokyo. Kono was one of the first people who contrasted the busy materialistic city life with the serenity of country life surrounded by nature. Influenced by the German idea of 'das Land' and 'die Heimat', he claimed the necessity of the birth of a 'country literature'.[9] After this essay, intellectuals' imaginative ideas about the country and rural areas developed and topics on the revival of the country began to be discussed a great deal. A half year later, the same magazine featured, 'The Issues of Country and City' (「田園と都市の問題」, 'Denen to Toshi no Mondai') written by five critics: Isoo Abe, Seiya Hasegawa, Ikuo Ooyama, Shin-ichiro Okada and Gyofu Soma. An article by Jituzo Shiraishi, 'People in the Tokyo Countryside and Their Projects' (「武蔵野の人々とその, 'Musashino no Hitobito to Sono Jigyo') also appeared in the same issue. Intellectuals, especially in the Tokyo area, started to compare and contrast the city and countryside and some idealized the beauty of nature and the serenity of rural areas.

Matsui himself, however, was not involved in this trend. Since he was born in Shiogama, Miyagi prefecture, which kept sending its people to Tokyo, he knew the reality of the country. In the back of his mind, he was haunted by the harsh life in provincial Japan and he recognized that the common people still cannot appreciate the idea of a 'beautiful' countryside. Therefore, the fantasy and illusion about the country are not precisely transferred to *Tea Making House* although some corrupted images of the country appears in Mieko's lines, 'I was deceived by the fantasy of life in the country. I was attracted by the soft name of Uji and admire it by my own image.' (21) He also considered that illusions about 'soil' and 'country' were not well established among his audience of ordinary people, since Japanese people do not have a strong attachment to the land, compared to Irish people. Thus, he did not wish to include a contrast between illusion and reality: soil and country.

Robinson's original, which apparently expresses the reality and irony of living in rural Ireland in the early days of the twentieth century, provoked a fierce response from the Irish audience. As a promising but fledgling playwright, Robinson had composed a script expressing a complex reality but might not have been able to think beyond the creation of the play to its reception.

Matsui, on the other hand, though he was sometimes criticized for flattering his audience to win its favour, always bore in mind the story tradition familiar to the ordinary people. The play ran not only in Tokyo but also went on tour to Nagoya, Kyoto and Osaka and was revived twice during the short era of Taisho (1912-1926). Amongst a large number of adapted plays, *Tea Making House* was one that transformed well into the Japanese style and was accepted by the Japanese public in that period.

Matsui's reforms and theatre for the public

The background of Robinson's *Harvest* reflects the situation of rural areas that people were leaving continuously; though Irish politics moved steadily along the path to independence and the land problem began to be solved by land purchase legislation, people still tried to escape from the country. The play mentions the brothers who received education, left their farm and never looked back. Even if they returned home, they might not be able to adapt themselves to the farmer's life anymore as seen in the case of Jack and Mary. A similar situation occurred in Japan: people headed to the city for a job and a better life. At the same time, a certain image of the 'country' was born along with the movement of the people from rural districts to the city of Tokyo. People began to recognize their 'country' from a distance. The dramatists also focused on the 'country' and 'country people' as if they had not been discovered yet.

During the revival period, Irish plays that emphasized the creation of the atmosphere of the 'country', and depicted 'rural people', were highlighted more than ever. Mainstream western playwrights were still portraying the upper social classes and exploring the inner ego of modern people: Ibsen shocked world theatres, but he did not particularly treat of people in rural areas; August Strindberg pursued a similar style to Ibsen by describing upper class characters; Chekhov portrayed the decaying Russian nobility. In the same period or soon after, Irish and German dramatists made the country and rural people appear on the stage. The depiction of country people in Irish plays reminded Japanese of their own. The vogue of Irish drama in Japan, therefore, synchronized with the period when the power of the 'people' was becoming evident, and it was a time when an increasing interest was taken in the 'country'.

Within this movement, some theatrical people believed that the audience of the plays should be not the upper class intellectuals but ordinary people and Matsui was one who believed this. As Yoshio Ohsasa points out, the name of the 'Public Theatre' set up by Matsui suggests, 'the fortnight of the debate on popular arts'.[10] In his essay 'Commonising Theatre', Matsui strongly insists that plays should be 'made for the people'. He states that unlike other countries where 'there aren't almost any plays which could develop under the care of the nation, aristocrats, or a well-off class', Japanese plays 'have been nourished by the common people for three hundred years and have grown up as popular'.[11] He regarded it as the most important factor of Japanese plays. What he referred to especially here is a type of traditional Japanese play that is popular among the common people: Kabuki. Matsui originally started his career as a Kabuki playwright and thus he knew the power of traditional plays to attract people. He applied the core of these traditional plays to New Plays as can be seen in the way he adapted *Harvest*. He maintained the basic story and character lines of *Harvest* but altered the central theme and nature of the characters to reflect the typical Kabuki and Joruri plays. The psychology of the characters in the adaptation is very traditional. Matsui did not try to supplant Japanese plays by western plays but he made good use of the various methods they employ.

As Robinson worked for and contributed to the Abbey, Matsui established and changed the system of Japanese New Theatre as a brave pioneer. Referring to western theatre direction and management, he appointed actresses to perform on the stage that used to be occupied by actors only, refurbished the stage setting and lighting, and eliminated the fees for programme, story pamphlet, tea, portable heating, cushion, and slippers which used to be services billed by the tea house attached to the theatre. He also banned the use of gratuities for the teahouse and usher. These reforms were also to encourage the people to come to the modern theatre. He kept in mind that people should be the centre of the New Play.

Matsui's achievement and contribution to the Japanese New Play has not been properly recognized until now. It is probably because in producing his work as he did, he identified himself as belonging to the common people instead of maintaining that he was an intellectual. He was generally considered a popular writer who was not often appreciated as 'artistic'. Such aspects of Matsui contribute to the comparison with Robinson, who was not paid much attention compared to his predecessors, although his works repeatedly appeared on the stage of the Abbey until the middle of twentieth century. The body of dramatic works of Matsui and Robinson cannot be said to be comparable, since Matsui produced an enormous number of plays with a variety of themes, including, for example, history plays. Still, the audience they targeted remained the same: the ordinary people. Inspired by the idea of a National Theatre as exemplified by the Abbey, Matsui tried to open up the well-made modern play to ordinary people in Japan and his efforts have now firmly taken root in the soil of Japanese New Play.

---

[1] Christopher Fitz-Simon, *The Abbey Theatre: Ireland's National Theatre, The First 100 Years* (London: Thames & Hudson, 2003): 59.

[2] 'An Outside Criticism', *The Evening Telegraph* 20 May 1910, quoted in Robert Hogan, Richard Burnham, and Daniel P. Poteet, *The Rise of the Realists: 1910-1915, The Modern Irish Drama: A Documentary History IV* (Dublin: The Dolmen Press, 1979): 34.

[3] Robinson wrote: '*Harvest*, my third play, was not a good one. It had a serious

theme with one or two fine dramatic scenes but the characters, except the small peasant ones, were lifeless, mere pegs on which to hang my ideas. It had some shocking faults of construction; the play began with a scene between two brothers who sit on the wall and tell each other facts about themselves and their family, facts perfectly well known to each of them. It was a beautifully easy way of putting the audience *au fait* with the situation but quite absurd'. Lennox Robinson, *Curtain Up: An Autobiography* (London: Michael Joseph, 1942): 33.

[4] W.B. Yeats, 'Irish National Drama', *Cambridge Daily News* 25 March 1910, quoted in Hogan et al., 72.

[5] Lennox Robinson, *Two Plays: Harvest; The Clancy Name* (Dublin: Maunsel & Company, Ltd., 1911): 49. Subsequent references will be taken from this edition, and included in the text.

[6] Matsui Shingen, ed., *Tea Making House, Selected Play Scripts by Shoyo*, (Tokyo: Kikuya Publisher, 1915): 1-85. Subsequent references will be taken from this edition, and included in the text.

[7] Taro Akiba, *History of Japanese New Drama,* 2 vols (Tokyo: Riso-sha, 1955): Vol. 1, 581.

[8] Andrew E. Malone, *The Irish Drama* (London: Constable, 1929): 177.

[9] Yoshihiro Kono, 'On Country Literature', *Waseda Literature* (February 1916): 39-50.

[10] Yoshio Ohsasa, *The History of Modern Japanese Drama: Taisho and Showa Era* (Tokyo: Hakusui-sha, 1986): 171.

[11] Shoyo Matsui, 'Commonising Theatre', *New Entertainment* (February 1920): 6.

5 | Wessex to Geesala: Hardy and Synge

Irina Ruppo

'Danged if our country down here is worth singing about like that' exclaims a glazier, as he listens to Farfrae's Scottish song in *The Mayor of Casterbridge*: 'When you take away from among us the fools and the rogues, and the lammigers, and the wanton hussies, and the slatterns, and such like, there's cust few left to ornament a song with in Casterbridge, or the country round'.[1] In *The Playboy of the Western World,* Pegeen Mike utters a similar opinion of her native town:

> I wouldn't bother with this place where you'll meet none but Red Linahan, has a squint in his eye, and Patcheen is lame in his heel, or the mad Mulrannies were driven from California and they lost their wits. We're a queer lot those times to go troubling the Holy father on his sacred seat.[2]

In both cases, the characters lament the incompatibility of their provincial society with their visions of romance. The utterances of Pegeen and the glazier are characterized by a two-fold incongruity. First, they speak of their native places as locations of unattractive banality, while at the same time unknowingly attesting to the peculiar grotesque attraction of these places. Second, due to the richness of their speech, Pegeen and the glazier contradict themselves by their very act of speaking. This incongruity, however, is not perceived by the characters' interlocutors but by the readers (or audience). Through their understanding of this inherent contradiction the readers/audience are implicated in the authors' view of the same locations. In both cases, the characters' sentiments are in direct opposition to those of the author. Hardy's novel and Synge's play are testaments to how much the glazier's country is 'worth singing about' and what joy it is to 'bother with' a place like Pegeen's village.

The similarities between the glazier's complaints and Pegeen's remonstrations point to the question of a larger context of correspondences between Hardy and Synge. So far, the subject has received very little critical attention. In a 1970 Italian article, Rosangela Barone has demonstrated several affinities between the two writers whom she considers to belong to two different literary traditions.[3] There are also a few telling observations in W.J. McCormack's recent biography of J.M. Synge.[4] However, Hardy and Synge share enough distinctive features to call for a further investigation. First, as McCormack observes, 'both writers exploited a geographical and cultural region with which they had enjoyed a personal intimacy'.[5] Second, as Barone notes, both Hardy and Synge are fascinated by the local dialect in their respective areas. Both writers turned the dialect into a poetical medium, experimenting with it and emphasizing its essential qualities to an extent that several contemporary reviewers questioned its authenticity and deplored the negative ways in which it seemed to reflect on the image of the country people. Thus RD Lang, writing in 1875, censured Hardy in a manner reminiscent of the well known criticisms of Synge:

> The author is telling clever people about unlettered people, and he adopts a sort of patronising voice ... The labourers are all humourists in their way, which is a very dreary and depressing way ... Shepherds may talk this way: we hope not; but if they do, it is a revelation; and if they don't it is nonsense, and not very amusing nonsense![6]

Further, both Hardy and Synge lament the threatening advance of civilization upon the communities which they see as last strongholds of the older primitive traditions. One thinks of Synge's *Aran Islands* in connection with Hardy's depiction of the Isle of Sligers in *Well Beloved* as

> home of a curious and well-nigh distinct people, cherishing strange beliefs and singular customs, now for the most part obsolescent .... In this last stronghold of the Pagan divinities, where Pagan customs lingered yet, Christianity had established itself precariously at best.[7]

While both writers are deeply interested in the traditions and superstitions of these communities, neither is satisfied with a mere description of these traditions. Hardy and Synge alike assimilate the local traditions and beliefs into their writing, turning them into structural devices of their works. This feature is particularly noticeable in *Riders to the Sea* and *The Return of the Native*. Moreover, both writers find the countryside a fit stage and rural characters fit actors for the enactment of classical tragedies (the classical nature of *The Mayor of Casterbridge* is as apparent as that of the *Riders to the Sea*, while the main protagonists of both 'tragedies' are low class characters). Finally, both writers have an ambivalent view of rural life. Its sublime, tragic, and beautiful facets are contrasted in the works of both with the prosaic, comic, and grotesque.

McCormack notes that Synge was only slightly familiar with Hardy's work. This case of literary affinity should therefore be studied within the reference to the similarities and interrelation between the respective social and literary contexts of Hardy and Synge. Indeed, several similarities between The *Playboy of the Western World* and *The Mayor of Casterbridge* are reflective of the authors' literary approach to the social concerns awakened by the contemporary emergence of anthropological studies.

In the opening scene of Act III of *The Playboy*, Jimmy and Philly speculate on the chances of Christy's crime being revealed. Jimmy believes that should Old Mahon's body be discovered it would probably be taken for 'an old Dane ... was drowned in the flood' (132). He tells the sceptical Philly of the Dubliners' interest in the prehistoric skulls: 'Did you never hear tell of the skulls they have in the city of Dublin, ranged out like blue jugs in a cabin of Connaught.' (34) A museum is a place of which Jimmy and Philly have heard only by hearsay; the tiny village in the Belmullet peninsula obviously does not possess one. The case is different with Casterbridge. In chapter twenty-two, Lucetta sends Elizabeth-Jane to the Museum. 'It's an old house in a back street,' explains Lucetta: 'and there are crowds of interesting things – skeletons, teeth, old pots and pans, ancient boots and shoes, birds' eggs – all charmingly instructive.' (173) Lucetta's hurried listing of the museum items bears a slight resemblance to Jimmy's description. In both cases jugs and skulls, skeletons and old pots are jumbled together. More importantly, the mention of a museum in *The Playboy* and *The Mayor of Casterbridge* indicates the authors' awareness of the significant interests of their time.

Both Hardy and Synge were writing in a period that saw the rise of archaeology and ethnography, along with the related disciplines of folklore studies and anthropology. The colonial encounters with cultures that were considered to be more primitive than the Europeans were among the chief catalysts of these developments; they also resulted in a change of the European self-perception. The four above-mentioned disciplines have a common underlying belief that a better understanding and evaluation of the present civilization depend upon the study of its primitive origins and its modern analogues in the 'primitive' societies. Indeed Jimmy's report of his acquaintance's experience at the Dublin museum, incongruous and comic as it is, points towards the connection between archaeology and ethnography: 'They have them there ... making a show of the great people there was one time walking the world. White skulls and black skulls and yellow skulls' (135). The contemporary interest in the study of different races is here conjoined with the interest in the prehistoric past.[2]

In *Modernism and the Celtic Revival*, Gregory Castle has shown the connection between the rise of anthropology and its related doctrines, and the Irish Literary Revival. Among other issues, Castle's study concentrates on the relationship between anthropology and literature, showing how the unofficial and unscientific nature of the literary form allowed the writers of the Irish Revival to unveil the anxieties and problems that were bound up with 'foundational theories of culture and some of its ... assumptions about primitive peoples'.[8] Castle's thesis can be extended to include English writers as well. The unofficial nature of a literary text allowed them to assess the psychological problems that the nineteenth century ethnographer faced as an outsider in the community that he was writing about. It enabled them to explore the fears and fantasies emerging from the situation in which the civilized and the primitive meet.

Peasant communities, Irish and English alike, were made the objects of such ethnographic enquiry. As McCormack notes, writing of a scientific expedition to the Aran Islands that took place in 1857, '[t]he allegedly primitive condition of the west of Ireland, its lying beyond the rim of civilization, was increasingly a theme which placed it at the centre of discontented civilization's concerns.'[9] Ireland's colonial status, the predominance of Catholicism among its peasant classes, the supposed racial differences between its inhabitants and those of England made it, as Declan Kiberd observes, 'England's Other'.[10] However, ethnographic studies of English rural communities were also affected by the spirit of primitivism. English villagers' way of life, their dialect, their customs, and their comparative lack of education distanced them from the upper classes. While living in the heart of the Empire, these people were studied by their compatriots with as much interest as the supposedly more 'primitive' peoples in the outer reaches of the Empire. One example is George Lawrence Gomme's study, *The Village Community*, published in 1890, which explores, among other issues, the persistence of 'savage customs', which the author considers to be survivals of earlier times, in the English village.[11] The issue of the survival of savage customs is also one of the central concerns of *The Mayor of Casterbridge* and *The Playboy*. But the unofficial nature of a literary text allows Hardy and Synge to take the line of enquiry further and to question the connection between the historical and the personal past, and between historical savagery and the latent criminality in the human heart.

While the plot of *The Mayor of Casterbridge* is more complex than that of *The Playboy*, both works adhere to the same formula. In both cases, the protagonist is an outsider in a community, where he achieves a temporary but incredible success. In both cases, the entry into the community is preceded by the protagonist's committing of a crime. The advent of the figures related to the protagonist's past (Old Mahon in *The Playboy*; the Furmity-Woman and Newson in *The Mayor*) results in his subsequent exposure as a liar and his castigation by the community. The protagonist's subsequent departure leaves the community in a state of serenity but is also accompanied by recognition of profound loss and failure. This structure allows the authors to conduct an investigation of a rural community through its interaction with an outsider. In both *The Playboy* and *The Mayor of Casterbridge* there is a sense that the protagonist-outsider awakens buried forces within the community, forces that are contained also within his personality, and that are related to the issue of his haunted past. Both Hardy and Synge explore the literary potential of the unscientific approach to history in rural areas to create a world in which personal and historical past are interconnected.

In the opening scene of *The Playboy*, Pegeen regrets the decline of her community:

> Where now will you meet the like of Daneen Sullivan knocked the eye from a peeler, or Marcus Quin, God rest him, got six months for maiming ewes, and he a great warrant to tell stories of holy Ireland till he'd have the old women shedding tears about their feet. (59)

Through her allusion to the late Quin's ability to tell stories of holy Ireland, Pegeen merges the image of the Irish heroic and holy past with her memories of the local criminals. History is misshaped. Pegeen does not fully understand history in terms of various periods; there is an indication that the past is perceived as a single temporal location populated by ancient heroes as well as modern criminals. This can be also noted when Jimmy mentions an 'old Dane … was drowned in the flood.' This remark indicates the Mayoites' inability to distinguish between different historic periods, or indeed, between fact and legend (scriptural and scientific history).

A similar conception of history is prevalent in Casterbridge. Note for instance Buzzford's remark: 'Casterbridge is a old, hoary place o'wickedness, by all account. 'Tis recorded in history that we rebelled against the King one or two hundred years ago, in the time of the Romans and that lots of us was hanged on Gallows Hill, and quartered and our different jints sent about the country like butcher's meat; and for my part I can well believe it.' (82) In both cases, the ancient past and the more recent violence and criminality are interwoven in the local imagination. Further, both works establish a connection between the violent past of the community and the criminal past of the protagonist.

In *The Mayor of Casterbridge,* this connection is established in the chapter in which Henchard first meets the woman that he had sold. Their meeting place is the Ring (an old Roman amphitheatre) whose description is preceded by a passage in which we are told that Casterbridge 'concealed dead men of Rome' and that

> It was impossible to dig more than a foot or two deep about the town fields and gardens without coming upon some tall soldier or other of the Empire, who had lain there in his silent unobtrusive rest for a space of fifteen hundred years. He was mostly found lying on his side, in an oval scoop in the chalk, like a chicken in its shell; his knees drawn up to his chest; sometimes with the remains of his spear against his arm … a bottle at his mouth; and mystified conjecture pouring down upon him from the eyes of Casterbridge street boys and men, who had turned a moment to gaze at the familiar spectacle as they passed by. (97)

Hardy explains that the inhabitants of Casterbridge were 'quite unmoved' by those shapes. 'They had lived so long ago, their time was so unlike the present, their hopes and motives so widely removed from ours, that between them and the living there seemed to stretch a gulf too wide for even a spirit to pass.' (96) The description of the Roman skeleton is peaceful, making this assertion ring true. However, the subsequent progression of the motif of the past relics subverts the initial assumption that the past whether historical or personal is too remote to interfere with the present.

Several statements, appearing almost immediately after this passage, challenge this notion. We are told that the Ring was mostly a spot for secret meetings and intrigues but hardly ever the meeting place of happy lovers. 'Perhaps', speculates the narrator, 'it was because its associations had about them something sinister. Its history proved that.' (98) This is followed by an account of a public execution of a woman who killed her husband, which took place in the location in the preceding century, and a grotesque anecdote that the heart of the victim leapt out of her chest as she was being burnt. In addition, we are also told that the amphitheatre was often a place of 'pugilistic encounters'. The associations between the ancient past and the present criminality are thus strengthened in this passage. The intimation that the violent Roman past is still alive is further literalized when we are told of a rumour that Roman soldiers occasionally appear in a vision to people visiting the Ring. The past is thus disturbingly and mysteriously alive. It survives in the local expressions of violence. And it is significant that this intimation should be made at the point when Henchard is confronted with his own past in the figure of the woman against whom he has committed a crime.

The connection thus established becomes more apparent in the episode of Henchard's discovery of Elizabeth-Jane's true parentage. As Henchard watches his sleeping step-daughter, we are told that 'in sleep came to the surface buried genealogical facts, ancestral curves, dead men's traits, which the mobility of daytime screens and overwhelms.' (147) This sentence is reminiscent of the earlier description of Casterbridge as concealing dead men of Rome. The narrator speaks of the face of the sleeping girl as if of a landscape, which like Casterbridge conceals behind its modernity the buried secrets and dead men of the past. Thus, Henchard's own past, and the past of the town and community in which he lives are blended, as the consequences of his past crime come to haunt him.

Finally, the description of the public reaction to the revelation of Henchard's selling of his wife by a furmity woman is evocative of the already quoted description of the Roman corpse: 'Had the incident been well known of old and always, it might by this time have grown to be lightly regarded ... But the act having lain as dead and buried ever since, the interspace of years was unperceived; and the black spot of his youth wore the aspect of a recent crime.' (229) This passage completely reverses the earlier statement that the Casterbridge folk do not fear the long buried body of a Roman soldier.

The idea of the connection between the historical past and the personal past is treated comically in *The Playboy*. It is observable in the interchange between Philly and Jimmy in the beginning of Act III, an episode noted above. Jimmy speaks of the skulls in the museum in Dublin and suggests that the body of Old Mahon, should it ever be found, would be taken for an old Dane. Thus, a connection is established between Christy's deed and the historic past. In response, Philly tells the following story:

> when I was a young lad there was a graveyard beyond the house with the remnants of a man who had thighs as long as your arm. He was a horrid man, I'm telling you, and there was many a fine Sunday I'd put him together for fun, and he with shiny bones, you wouldn't meet the like of these days in the cities of the world (135).

This grotesque interlude is interrupted by the appearance of Old Mahon, who retorts: 'You wouldn't, is it? Lay your eyes on the skull and tell me where and when there was another like it, is splintered only from the blow of a loy.' (56) By his absurd comparison of his own skull with the skeleton of the Dane, Mahon connects the historic past with Christy's personal past. In *The Playboy*, both personal and historical past are steeped in legend and in the aura of greatness ('you wouldn't meet the like of these days'). Mahon succeeds in destroying the two legends at once: that of the greatness of Christy's deed, and that of the wonder of the past ages. He challenges Philly's romantic vision of the antediluvian Danes by insisting that his own skull, split as it is by a blow of a loy, is worthy of comparison with that of the Dane.

Notably, both Christy and Pegeen initially assume that Old Mahon has literally risen from the dead. Christy exclaims, 'It's the walking spirit of my murdered da!' (119), while Pegeen upon hearing that Christy's assailant is his 'own father' asks: 'Is it rose from the dead?'(161) Taken in conjunction with Mahon's connecting himself with the dead Dane quoted above, these remarks constitute a level at which Mahon symbolizes the resurrection of the buried past: buried skeletons and buried secrets.

The connection between the personal past of the protagonist and the historic past of the community is thus conveyed similarly in *The Mayor of Casterbridge* and *The Playboy* (although the scale is much more limited in *The Playboy*). Both Hardy and Synge exploit the symbolic potential of the realistic fact that the soil of the English and Irish countryside contains actual ancient skeletons. The idea that both Henchard and Christy are trapped by the secret of their past is reinforced through its juxtaposition with the notion that the historic past of the community is still alive.

Another correspondence can be found in the way that Christy and Henchard attempt and fail to redeem the mistakes of their past.

Christy's second 'killing' of his father only further enrages the community. While the appearance of Mahon shows them that their legendary hero is a sham, the second killing exposes their legend as a sham as well. The Mayoites have envisioned the past as a repository of heroism; when the actual deed of the past is staged in their backyard they realize that their response to the past has been inadequate. Henchard tries to redeem his past mistakes throughout the novel, but the still living past subverts all such attempts. His decision to make amends to his daughter is subverted by the 'ancestral curves' and 'dead men traits' in her face. His decision to accept the love of his stepdaughter is upset by the arrival of Newson.

What makes Hardy and Synge's treatment of the theme of the domination of the past particularly relevant to contemporary concerns related to anthropological studies is the way in which the personal past of an outsider is related to the historical past of the rustic community. The barbarism of ancient times is shown to be still alive beneath the veneer of mundane reality of rustic life. It is equated in both works to the barbaric, criminal past of the protagonist. In *The Mayor of Casterbridge* and *The Playboy* the interaction between the criminal past of the protagonist and the primitive past of the community results in the dramatic revival of the past. This revival is culminated in both works by an outburst of popular violence. In *The Playboy*, this takes form in the mob binding and torturing of Christy; in *The Mayor*, this is manifested in the staging of the Skimmington ride, an archaic and illicit ritual. Henchard's dummy (and that of his old sweetheart) is mounted on a donkey and paraded in the street accompanied by the loud blowing of horns and the clang of the tambourines.

I would like to conclude by suggesting that a comparative critical neglect of the question of literary affinities between Hardy and Synge might be related to the canonization of Synge and Hardy as national writers of, respectively, Ireland and England. The Irish Literary Revivalists insisted on the unique national nature of their endeavour and their divergence from English tradition. However as Deborah Fleming demonstrates in *A Man Who Does Not Exist* the Irish Revival is indebted to the nineteenth century English Romantic movement. As Fleming points out:

> the cult of the Irish peasant as a repository of ancient wisdom and natural virtue found its origins in the English Romantic movement of the nineteenth century, an important aspect of romanticism being the return to nature – the desire to find the spiritual within the natural to achieve a union of real and unreal, tangible and mysterious.[12]

Moreover, while the Irish Revival did not succeed in shutting the door on the continuing influence of English literary tradition, it must also be noted that several literary and social trends of nineteenth century England paralleled on a minor scale the developments of the Irish Revival. Thus Stefan Collini argues that contrary to the generally held view, English cultural nationalism was a 'pervasive feature' in Victorian England that was 'not immune to all the forces and impulses that fuelled more explicitly nationalist movements elsewhere'.[13] Indeed, English cultural nationalism expressed itself by similar means to the Irish Revival. The idealization of the past legends that was such an important feature of the Irish Revival was also present in nineteenth-century England. Stephanie Barczewski, who traces English cultural nationalism in the nineteenth-century manipulations of the legends of King Arthur and Robin Hood, notes that like 'many other European nations in this period, Britain turned to the past as a potential source of unity in the present, and again as in those other nations – this process required considerable manipulation and at times blatant fabrication'.[14] The findings of these scholars suggest that apart from continuing to be the reservoir of literary tradition, England was subjected to the same pan-European trends as Ireland. A comparative study of English and Irish turn-of-the century authors, such as Hardy and Synge (or perhaps Kipling and Yeats) involves looking beyond the ideology of the Irish revival. But when taken in conjunction with the examination of the similarities and differences in their respective social and historical contexts it may help us to arrive at a better understanding of the literature of that period.

---

[1] Thomas Hardy, *The Life and Death of the Mayor of Casterbridge: a Story of a Man of Character*, New Wessex Edition (London: Macmillan, 1974): 91.

[2] John Millington Synge, *The Collected Works*, ed. Ann Saddlemyer, vol.4 (London: Oxford University Press, 1962-1968): 59.

[3] Rosangela Barone, 'Thomas Hardy e John Millington Synge: Alcune Affinita', *Annali della Facolta di Lingue e Letterture Straniere*, 1. 2 (Universita di Bari, 1970-1971): 6-32. Concentrating mainly on Synge's *The Aran Islands* with reference to passages from various works by Hardy, Barone shows the similarity in writers' conceptions of nature, mortality, peasantry, and women.

[4] W.J. McCormack, *The Fool of the Family: A Life of J.M. Synge* (London: Weidenfeld & Nicolson, 2000). McCormack notes that Synge's Deirdre is 'closer to Hardy's tragic women than any other dramatic character in the Anglo-Irish repertoire'(368) and compares the tragic tension in Synge's plays to the 'mood of enchanted frustration to initial chapters by Thomas Hardy', (23).

[5] Ibid. 24.

[6] Cited after George Wotton, *Thomas Hardy: Towards a Materialist Criticism* (Totowa: Barnes and Noble, 1985): 190.

[7] Thomas Hardy, *The Well-Beloved A Sketch of A Temperament* (London: McMillan, 1927): v.
[2] This connection was also noted by Mary C. King in a lecture on Synge given in Galway in Spring, 2004, as part of the *DruidSynge* series of public talks. She examines the Jimmy and Philly interchange in *The Drama of JM Synge*, noting the function of the 'appropriate comic combination of history and biblical myth' in the play's overall blending of fact and fiction, heroic and mock-heroic. See Mary C. King, *The Drama of JM Synge* (Syracuse: Syracuse University Press, 1985): 149-50.
[8] Gregory Castle, *Modernism and the Celtic Revival* (Cambridge and New York: Cambridge University Press, 2001): 9.
[9] McCormack, *Fool of the Family*: 26.
[10] Declan Kiberd, *Inventing Ireland: the Literature of the Modern Nation* (London: Vintage, 1996): 29.
[11] George Laurence Gomme, *The Village Community, with Special Reference to the Origin and Form of its Survivals in Britain* (London: Walter Scott, 1890).
[12] Deborah Fleming, *A Man Who Does not Exist: the Irish Peasant in the Work of W.B. Yeats and J.M. Synge* (Ann Arbor: University of Michigan Press, 1995): 54.
[13] Stefan Collini, 'Genealogies of Englishness: Literary History and Cultural Criticism in Modern Britain', *Ideology and the Historians,* ed. Ciaran Brady (Dublin: Lilliput Press, 1991): 132-3.
[14] Stephanie L Barczewski, 'Myth and National Identity', *Nineteenth-Century Britain: The Legends of King Arthur and Robin Hood* (Oxford and New York: Oxford University Press, 2000): 7.

6 | Sean O'Casey and The Abbey Theatre: A Conflicted Relationship

Paul O'Brien

There are many parallels between the Irish Literary Theatre and the Moscow Arts Theatre, quite apart from the fact that both were launched in 1898. Konstantin Stanislavsky defined the policy of the Moscow Arts Theatre as follows:

> Our programme was revolutionary, we rebelled against the old way of acting, against affectation and false pathos, against declamation and bohemian exaggeration, against bad conventionality of production and sets, against the star system which ruined the ensemble and against the whole spirit of performance and insignificance of repertory.[1]

Yeats's manifesto for the Abbey Theatre in Dublin can stand alongside that of the Moscow Arts Theatre or the Independent Theatre in London as one of the founding documents of the modern theatre because it 'fulfilled, more than any other theatre he knew, the possible definition of a people's theatre, where the actors were chosen from the general mass of people, the plays written by people chosen from the general mass. In the same way they drew their plays from all classes.'[2] But there is also an elitist strand in Yeats's manifesto that was the starting point for the artistic rupture that took place between Yeats and O'Casey in 1928: 'I want to create for myself an unpopular theatre and an audience like a secret society where admission is by favour and never to many.'[3] Paradoxically, by rejecting *The Silver Tassie* in 1928, Yeats was rejecting the very arguments for a new kind of drama that he had advanced in 'A People's Theatre' in 1919.

Yeats's statement of his democratic artistic principles was to be tested by the gaunt ill-fed working-class man in cloth cap and hobnail boots who from 1919 onwards bombarded the Abbey directors with manuscripts before they finally accepted *The Shadow of a Gunman* in November 1922. We can see why Yeats was so excited by those early manuscripts:

> When the Abbey Manager sends us a play for our opinion ... if the handwriting of the MSS, or of the authors accompanying letter suggests a leisured life I start prejudiced. There will be no fresh observation of character I think, no sense of dialogue ... On the other hand ... a handwriting learned in a national school always made me expect dialogue, written out by some man who had admired good dialogue before he had seen it upon paper.[4]

For too long we have lived with the simplistic view that O'Casey arrived at the Abbey 'a rough-hewn, almost forty-year-old candidate for discovery by William Butler Yeats and Lady Gregory'.[5] O'Casey learned his craft the hard way, first as a contributor to Larkin's paper, the *Irish Worker*. After its demise in 1914, O'Casey was unemployed and unlikely to obtain work because of his public support for the Irish Transport and General Workers Union. Writing became a necessity if he was to earn a living. Between 1917 and 1920 he published a series of pamphlets, verses and songs for the publishers Fergus O'Connor and Maunsel & Co.

As a young man he had absorbed vast quantities of Shakespeare, Shelley, Dickens, and Boucicault. If the Abbey Theatre was financially beyond him, amateur drama, which was all the rage in Dublin at the turn of the century, fired his enthusiasm for the stage. His brother Isaac, a keen amateur actor had helped organize the Irish Transport and General Workers Union drama society, the Liberty Hall Players. A stage was constructed in the living room of Hawthorn Terrace and extracts from Shakespeare and Boucicault were performed with the help of the neighbours. This was put on a more formal basis when an unused stable in Hill Street was converted into a theatre. O'Casey learned the tools of his trade in the numerous fund-raisers and concerts that he organized and in which he performed. He acted in Thomas Moylan's *Naboclish* at the Empire Theatre in 1917 and played a minor part in Bernard Duffy's *Special Pleading* in 1921 at the Foresters' Hall in Mountjoy Square. A drama club developed within the St Laurence O'Toole Club and O'Casey used his talent for singing and storytelling in an effort to sustain the club during the difficult months after the 1916 rising. O'Casey submitted his first dramatic attempt, *The Frost in the Flower*, to the St Laurence O'Toole Drama Club in 1918, but it was rejected because the central figure was an obvious caricature of Frank Cahill, a leading member of the club. He spent the summer of 1918 working on *The Harvest Festival*, which he submitted along with a revised version of *The Frost in the Flower* to the Abbey in late 1919 and thus began a literary relationship that was to transform the fortunes of both O'Casey and the theatre itself.

When the Abbey rejected O'Casey's experimental anti-war play *The Silver Tassie* in 1928 they administered a serious blow to the future of the theatre as well as to the future of O'Casey. That controversy has been well rehearsed, but little attention has been paid to the first five plays that

O'Casey submitted to the Abbey Theatre between 1919 and 1922 and the impact they had on the relationship between O'Casey and the Abbey Theatre.

After the success of his first play, *The Shadow of a Gunman,* O'Casey became extremely proprietorial, refusing to allow anyone to revise his work. Whatever cuts were to be made were restricted to the discretion of Yeats and Lady Gregory. After the breach with the Abbey even this possibility was lost, to the extent that in 1961 he refused Alan Simpson and the Joan Littlewood Theatre Workshop permission to produce one of his later plays, because of her reputation for changing or even rewriting some of the plays she directed:

> I have never liked the ways of Miss Littlewood ... I am of the opinion that she took too much upon herself in the ways of handling the work of playwrights; and certainly wouldn't allow it with mine ... It is well known, too, that Miss L. tempered the method, or tampered with them, of the plays by Behan and Delaney. She may have improved them, but the point with me is that, even so, they ceased to be the work of the playwrights and became the work of J. Littlewood. This, to me, is bad for playwrighting.[6]

Alan Simpson makes the point that while 'it is accepted that O'Casey was ahead of his time, notably in his conception of dramatic technique' it is only recently that 'a number of talented directors acquiring the basic crafts required to handle well plays of a type that O'Casey was turning out in the Thirties, Forties and Fifties'[7] have emerged. O'Casey's 1934 play, *Within the Gates,* which was first envisaged as a film and retains all the hallmarks of that endeavour, made heavy demands on the director and musical arranger that were beyond the capabilities of the first London and New York productions. The traditional theatre was incapable of responding to O'Casey's vision, a fact that he recognized: 'Apart from the Irish players in their heyday, and the production of *The Silver Tassie,* all were bad, a few worse than others, and one worst of all.'[8]

His insistence on the artistic integrity of the writer has to be accepted, although his later work suffers in many cases from overwriting and the near impossibility of presenting them on the stage in the way that O'Casey intended. Living in Devon, he was isolated from modern theatre and the transformations that the workshop methods of Brecht and Littlewood were having on theatre production. This approach was to hinder the development of O'Casey as a living writer. He had, in the past, always been willing to incorporate changes that were obviously suggested in rehearsal and production, and Mary Todd notes the way in which the living stage served as a workshop for O'Casey that allowed him to reach his final form as published in the later editions of his plays.[9] Heinz Kosok draws attention to the fact that 'there are no less than four published versions of

Purple Dust, three of *Red Roses for Me* and two of *The Star Turns Red* and *The Silver Tassie*.'[10]

Ronald Ayling suggests that 'no other person helped write, revise, or shape O'Casey's work',[11] a point on which O'Casey in his later years was quite emphatic. Ayling, correctly, was defending O'Casey's integrity as a writer from those whom Christopher Murray calls 'the begrudgers', but he goes too far in O'Casey's defence. O'Casey's development as a writer arose from the collaboration and support for his work by the directors and actors of the Abbey Theatre. If we examine the evidence surrounding the writing and development of the five plays rejected by the Abbey prior to 1922, a different story emerges. With the help and encouragement of Lennox Robinson and especially Lady Gregory, O'Casey worked to develop his style and technique. Robinson thought his early plays were too didactic, though well conceived, and encouraged him to move away from stereotypical characters and 'replace them with characters drawn from his own experience'. Lady Gregory convinced him to 'throw over my theories and work on my characters' and it was this character-based technique that brought him success. The Reader's Opinion, which accompanied the rejection of the first two plays, was encouraging and constructive in its criticism. Lady Gregory found *The Crimson in the Tricolour* 'extremely interesting' and contained 'some good ideas about Labour and Sinn Fein which however were too provocative to be staged during the rebellion'.[12] She 'wanted to pull that play together and put it on to give him experience';[13] Yeats, on the other hand, felt that it pandered to an Irish audience's prejudice – that it was 'Queen's melodrama brought up to date'.

Yeats's support and encouragement for young writers has been well documented, as evidenced by the Reader's Opinions in his papers in the National Library: 'Yeats and Lady Gregory read, criticized and rewrote parts of almost every script submitted to the Abbey Theatre.'[14] Christopher Murray makes the point that 'the reader's report offered some consolation'[15] to O'Casey and that he took Yeats's advice seriously is evident from the inscription in the presentation copy of *Juno and the Paycock*: 'The man who by the criticism of a bad play of mine made me write a good one.'[16] *The Frost in the Flower* was returned to O'Casey with the statement 'that they thought well of it, but the central character stood out too dominantly, dwarfing the others'. He amended the play on the lines suggested but it was returned again, now with the comment that they 'liked the first version better'.[17] Peter Harris makes the point that 'whether simply forgetful or wilfully inaccurate, O'Casey's faulty recollection of the detail of the Reader's Opinion, provides him with an opportunity in his autobiography to deny the possibility of the Abbey Theatre having influenced him, the establishment of which point, as we have seen before, was of great importance to him.'[18] On the other hand, in an interview in 1925, O'Casey seemed anxious to stress his connections with the Abbey:

'His last job, oddly enough, was on a building near the Abbey Theatre, which he has visited for the past ten years and into which he drops nearly every evening.'[19]

O'Casey always believed in his own ability, and was never afraid to stand over his work, sometimes with an overconfidence that may have hindered his development. He resubmitted *The Crimson in the Tricolour* to Michael Dolan, the Abbey Director, with Lady Gregory's more favourable critique, and suggested that Dolan direct the play on a Sunday in the off-season when the Abbey actors gave special performances to supplement their earnings. O'Casey accepted that on foot of Lady Gregory's criticism, Dolan could make 'any alteration thought necessary'. After taking the advice of the actors Arthur Shields and F.J. McCormack who did a read through, Dolan reluctantly came to the conclusion that he could not stage it. He felt that a poor production would undermine the reception for *The Shadow of a Gunman*, which had already been accepted by the Abbey.

Two of his earliest plays survive, though only *The Harvest Festival* from 1919 has so far been published. The limitations of the apprentice writer are evident but, as O'Casey has reminded us; he never thought of his rejected plays as poor stuff and felt that they were 'a lot better than many of the atrocities welcomed and staged by the Abbey at the time'.[20] O'Casey never gave up on *The Harvest Festival* and in 1942 used the text as the basis for *Red Roses for Me*. O'Casey returned to much of his earlier work for material in his later plays. *The Cooing of the Doves* formed the second act of *The Plough and the Stars* and two characters from *The Crimson in the Tricolour* were also incorporated into the play.

After the success of *The Shadow of a Gunman* 'he was a frequent visitor to the theatre where his friendship with some of the players gained him access to the Green Room, which in a sense was a kind of theatre workshop, where he could air his views on playwriting and staging.'[21] This was a vital and lively period in the life of the Abbey Theatre: the Green room had the atmosphere of a club and the company had achieved a level of teamwork that has probably never been surpassed. Nevertheless, criticism was by no means a one-way street. O'Casey was always willing to express his opinion on the shortcomings of the Abbey. In 1925 in a letter to Michael Dolan, he set down his impressions of the Abbey's production of Shaw's *Man and Superman*:

> The acting, the settings and the general balance and interpretation of the play were painfully imperfect ... I have written this primarily to show that no savage attack upon me by you or by Mr. F.J. McCormack will prevent me from venturing to give an answer for the hope that is in me, and to point out that while the Abbey Players have often turned water into wine, they may occasionally, turn wine back into water.[22]

This led to a cooling of relations between Dolan and O'Casey and eventually a ban on O'Casey's access to the Green Room – a disagreement that not only deprived him of this privilege but also did considerable damage, in the view of Gabriel Fallon, to the production of *The Plough and the Stars*.

O'Casey's visit to Coole Park in August 1925 for a read through of *The Plough and the Stars* was an ideal setting to fine tune the play before it was sent to George O'Brien for a final decision. A letter to Gabriel Fallon[23] shows how clearly O'Casey identified his work with the Abbey Theatre. He regretted that he had not read the play to the Abbey actors Gabriel Fallon and Barry Fitzgerald to test their reactions and any suggestions they may have had before it went into production. This letter also makes clear that by this time O'Casey's characters were written with particular Abbey actors in mind. He attended all the rehearsals and sometimes acted the characters for them. Cyril Cusack, the actor most associated with O'Casey in the post-war years, believed that creative theatre is best built from collaborative interchange between playwright and player and that 'O'Casey's work has not been without the stimulus of collaborating native genius.'[24]

The directors feared that *The Plough* was too sexually outspoken and Michael Dolan refused to direct it. O'Casey wrote to Lady Gregory in September 1925: 'I am going up on Sunday to Mr. Yeats to speak about some cuts in my play ... I've no objection to cuts made by him, or you or Mr. Robinson.'[25] Robert Hogan seems to support O'Casey's view that some of the changes were to the detriment of the play and that the Yeats/Gregory revisions were not made for artistic reasons but to make it acceptable to the potential audience.[26]

In Christopher Murray's opinion *Juno And the Paycock* 'is the best constructed of all of O'Casey's plays' and 'some of the credit must go to Robinson, a master craftsman who tried to get him trained in the writing of the so-called well made play.'[27] O'Casey had written an extra scene for the third act in which he described the shooting of Johnny, which was cut during rehearsals, no doubt influenced by the opinion of Yeats and Robinson. He wrote the part of Captain Boyle for Barry Fitzgerald, Juno for Sarah Allgood, and Joxer for F.J. McCormack. According to Ronald Ayling this perhaps accounted for 'even its shape and dramatic proportions to some extent'.[28] Details of these changes are recorded by Ayling in 'Juno and the Paycock: A Textual Study', which appear to contradict his assertion that no one helped O'Casey with his plays. By the time he had started writing *The Plough and the Stars* in 1925, a truly collaborative relationship, in the sense that Brecht or any of the innovators of continental theatre would understand it, was in the making.

O'Casey, in later life came to believe (with little justification) that the revisions and advice he had received from the Abbey directors had been harmful to his work. O'Casey records his own reactions to the demands for changes: 'Like other writers before him, O'Casey felt the pressure to amend his work to conform to social standards, or to actors and producers' preferences stifling, and so he left Dublin permanently for the comparatively greater freedom of London.'[29] There he felt free to develop his skills without, what appeared to him, the petty restrictions that the Abbey imposed.

By 1928 O'Casey had taken his work to the limits of its form; he needed to broaden his horizons and experience the innovations taking place in the international theatre movement. The tragedy of *The Silver Tassie* episode was not that O'Casey left Ireland but that he left in anger at a time when developments in that country could have provided him with the stage and workshop that he required. O'Casey needed freedom but he also needed to understand that:

> All plays require rewriting after their first presentation for the obvious reason that they do not really exist until they have had to face up to the reactions of a sensible objective audience ... All these [changes] indicate a healthy state of affairs that the play is a living thing, undergoing modifications that all serious drama must undergo in the course of production.[30]

The Gate Theatre in Dublin, which opened in October 1928, might have provided the environment for O'Casey's work to develop, in the way that the Abbey was, by that time, incapable of doing.

Because of O'Casey's reluctance to acknowledge any influence on his work we have to piece together the evidence for this from other sources. The crude division of the Dublin plays representing his realist period, and the later plays his expressionist or modernist phase, has long been rejected – both *Juno and the Paycock* and *The Plough and the Stars* combine elements of realism and expressionism. Gabriel Fallon has described his 1923 one-act play *Cathleen Listens In* as 'Brecht before Brecht of whose existence neither the author nor the Abbey Theatre had then the slightest idea'[31]. In *Nannie's Night Out* (1924) he incorporated expressionist methods into the development of his characters.

Though Yeats had always intended to produce foreign plays, his distaste for Ibsen, the dominant playwright in European theatre at the turn of the century, allied to the emergence of Irish writers, meant that the Abbey was able to subsist on a diet of native plays, and the plan was quietly forgotten. Both James Joyce in *The Day of the Rabblement* and George Russell had pleaded for an internationalist outlook: 'We cannot be intellectually self-sustaining any more than England, France, Italy or Germany could ... We must penetrate Irish culture with world wisdom, or it will cease to be a culture, and our literature will lose its vitality and become a literature of conventions.'[32]

In 1918, Lennox Robinson and Arthur Shields formed the Dublin Drama League. Their intention was to produce on Sunday and Monday nights at the Abbey plays from the international repertoire by such writers as Chekhov, Pirandello, Strindberg, O'Neill, and others. The Abbey patent at the time disallowed what were called foreign plays and Robinson and Shields had to find some way round this. The Dublin Drama League was the answer, as Shields explained: 'It was not the Abbey, but we used the Abbey stage. The intention was to prevent the players, playwrights, and audiences of Dublin from becoming too narrow, too provincial and too exclusively interested in their Irish selves.'[33] For the first time Irish audiences were able to see avant-garde work that was transforming continental theatre and according to Harold Ferrar this 'was to have a persuasive influence on the work of O'Casey, Lennox Robinson and Denis Johnston'.[34] Lady Gregory and Yeats both encouraged the project and while it may have been beyond their experience or indeed their taste, they understood that this development provided a healthy training ground for young theatre practitioners.

From 1925 onwards, when he returned to Dublin, Denis Johnston's involvement as actor and director with the Drama League and The New Players helped in large measure to make the expressionist method available in Ireland. Two of his productions for the Drama League between 1927 and 1929 were of plays by the German expressionists Kaiser and Toller. In London, he regularly attended the performances at Peter Godfrey's Gate Theatre Studio, often in O'Casey's company. The Gate was the one London playhouse that offered an expressionist repertoire, since being a club theatre they could ignore the ban imposed by the Lord Chamberlain on public performances of German political theatre. Gabriel Fallon estimates that O'Casey attended about sixty per cent of the Dublin Drama League's productions and this was a key factor in his turning to the experimental methods of *The Silver Tassie* in 1928.[35]

The London premiere of *The Silver Tassie* in 1929 with sets by Augustus John and direction by Raymond Massey (who went further in his non-realistic presentation of act two than O'Casey himself had dared) critically exposed O'Casey to the potential of theatrical modernism. His work was transformed and he began to move towards a form of theatre developed by such practitioners as Lee Simonson, who worked with the Theatre Guild in New York, and the radical productions of the French playwright Antonin Artaud. But having taken the first steps in that direction, O'Casey then drew back, as if he feared losing control. Artaud's emphasis on music, dance, texture, mime, lighting and décor all find an echo in his work. But the view that it was possible to stage a work 'without regard for the text' or Gordon Craig's proposition that the extreme achievement of theatre is when we will 'no longer need the assistance of a playwright'[36] was a step that O'Casey could never contemplate. While Gordon Craig's view of theatrical developments may have been anathema to O'Casey, his view that directors should discard writers' stage directions makes sense. O'Casey, following Shaw, always left little to the imagination of the director. In the early plays his stage directions are precise, a tendency he takes to extremes in the later plays, which were written mainly for publication. What is missing is a living contact with a working theatre, engaging the attention of the audience at the instance of performance. Incredibly, O'Casey did not see a play of his produced between 1934 and 1946. Without the discipline of constant production all the flaws of the later work are steps, in the words of Brooks Atkinson, 'that lead into the library'. In contrast, Frank O'Connor, writing on the art of the theatre in 1947, takes up the Brechtian idea of a theatre as 'a workshop where plays are manufactured and a writer's job is to help manufacturing them' and makes the point that could be taken as a direct criticism of O'Casey that a writer's 'place is not at home but in the theatre'.[37]

O'Casey, for his own reasons, constantly downplayed his knowledge of modern dramatic developments, but he was well-read and his letters indicate more than a passing knowledge of theatre outside the English-speaking world. The second act of *The Silver Tassie* owes much to Ernst Toller, the German expressionist playwright who had a lasting influence on O'Casey. In a letter to Jack Lindsay he writes of Gorky's battles with the Russian Futurists' attempts to develop a new kind of drama, which were reported in *International Theatre* in Moscow in 1924: 'Don't let them try to break away from the great and gracious things of the past. The Soviet writers and play producers tried to do this; but it didn't work.'[38] However much he was aware of theorists such as Eric Bentley or Konstantin Stanislavsky, they appear, with the exception of Toller, to have made little impact on him. He felt Stanislavsky's book *An Actor Prepares* was 'too learned' and it left him bewildered. Reading Bentley's book *Playwright as Thinker*, he confesses that he 'can't catch hold of a thing in it'. He disagreed with the theories of Bertolt Brecht, who he felt had banished emotion from the stage, that he was 'a bit disorderly in his dramatic conceptions, too much diffusion, too hasty in his conception of incident and act'.[39]

Nevertheless, the production values of Brecht, Helene Weigel, and the Berliner Ensemble, in which all the elements of theatre including those pertaining to production were brought together, could have provided the template for O'Casey's later plays to be realized. Brecht's lesson is clear: 'a playwright cannot be merely literary; that he must know what he wants of actors and producer and composer and designer; and that he has to plan his work with all the elements of the combined operation in view'.[40] The Russian director Boris Zakhava described this process as a 'creative reciprocity' and towards the end of his life O'Casey expressed regret that he 'hasn't had a theatre or group in which to try out his plays before they were presented to the public'.[41] This was the nearest he ever came to acknowledging that his breach with the Abbey in 1928 had damaged his ability to develop his work.

In February 1966, The Berlin Theatre produced *Purple Dust*, which ran in repertory for twelve years and became a legend in the history of the German theatre. *The World Stage* reported that:

> The Berlin Ensemble performed *Purple Dust,* as it were, like a posthumous meeting between O'Casey and Brecht. Both have a lot in common: they were social realists as well as real socialists; both left behind a lifetime's work, full of intellectual energy and lyric beauty, which places them at the top of the dramatic world literature of our century ... Here in this production O'Casey and Brecht met – and it turned out to be a meeting worth viewing. O'Casey was divided by Brecht – and O'Casey was multiplied.[42]

Unfortunately, O'Casey had died two years earlier and he was never to see his vision 'glowing on a stage'[43] in the way that he often imagined. The disparate styles, the demands made on set designers, the need for ensemble acting with the ability to incorporate sound, dance and mime have all placed restrictions on successful productions of O'Casey's later work.

O'Casey struggled from the beginning of his career to break free from naturalistic dramatic forms but he was unable or unwilling to accept the theatrical methods that could have enabled him to do so. His plays as social documents, with some exceptions, are still relevant, but 'as poetical creations they have not even begun to be realized'.[44] Contemporary directors need to mould and adapt his work 'so as to highlight for contemporary audiences the universal truths contained in the plays'.[45] Garry Hynes's production of *The Plough and the Stars* at the Abbey in 1991, on the seventy-fifth anniversary of the 1916 Rising, showed what modern interpretations could do for O'Casey's work, though it was not to everyone's liking. Hugh Leonard in *The Irish Times* criticized the production, amongst other things, for its Brechtian techniques.

Gordon Rogoff, in his obituary of Sean O'Casey, lamenting the absence of any productions of the later plays, wrote: 'what may well be missing is some gloriously dotty Irish Berlin Ensemble.'[46] We need to open our minds to the potential of O'Casey's drama. This need not entail changes to the text. The German director Peter Stein, a founder-member of the Berlin Schaubühne, trained in the Brechtian tradition, and directed Sean O'Casey's *Cock-a-Doodle Dandy* at the Schauspielhaus in Zurich, is obsessed with the ultimate sanctity of the text. Brian McMaster, who has brought much of Stein's work to Britain, writes of Stein's policy regarding the text: 'We've got all these multimedia directors at the moment, which is fine. But that is exactly why the simple act of going back to the text is the most radical thing that you could do now.'[47] This must be the way forward; theatre groups and directors transforming work with an imaginative collective approach that brings to life the magic and excitement that is at the heart of O'Casey's drama.

1 M. Knebel, 'The Abbey and the Moscow Arts Theatre', *The Abbey – Then and Now*, ed. Micheál Ó hAodha (Dublin: The Abbey Theatre, 1969): 63.
2 Robert Hogan and Richard Burnham, *The Years of Sean O'Casey, 1921-1926*, (Gerrards Cross: Colin Smythe, 1992): 26.
3 W.B. Yeats, 'A People's Theatre', *The Irish Statesman* 23-4 (1919): 572.
4 Yeats, *The Irish Statesman*, 548.
5 Sean O'Casey, *Selected Plays Of Sean O'Casey*, introduction, John Gassner (New York: George Braziller, 1954): viii.
6 Sean O'Casey, *The Letters of Sean O'Casey 1959-1964*, 4 vols (Washington: The Catholic University of America Press, 1992): Vol. IV, 231.
7 Alan Simpson, 'The Staging of O'Casey's Plays', *The Sean O'Casey Review* 5.2 (1979): 134.
8 Sean O'Casey, *Autobiographies*, 2 vols (London: Macmillan, 1963): Vol. II, 655.
9 Mary Todd, 'Two versions of within the Gates', *Modern Drama* 10. 4 (1968): 346.
10 Heinz Kosok, 'The Three Versions of Red Roses for Me', *O'Casey Annual*, 1 (1982): 141.
11 Ronald Ayling, 'Sean O'Casey and the Abbey Theatre Company', *Irish University Review* 3.1 (1973): 5.
12 Sean O'Casey, *Letters* (New York: Macmillan, 1975): Vol. I, 90.
13 Mary Fitzgerald, 'Sean O'Casey and Lady Gregory', *Sean O'Casey Centenary Essays*, eds David Krause & Robert Lowery (Gerrards Cross: Colin Smythe, 1980): 71.
14 James Flannery, *W.B. Yeats and the Idea of a Theatre* (New Haven: Yale University Press, 1976): 350.
15 Christopher Murray, *Sean O'Casey: Writer at Work* (Dublin: Gill & Macmillan, 2004): 127.
16 Peter Harris, *Sean O'Casey's Letters and Autobiographies* (Trier: WVT, 2004): 94.
17 O'Casey, *Letters* (1975): Vol. I, 92.
18 Harris, 71.
19 *The Observer* 22 November 1925.
20 Bernard Benstock, 'The Harvest Festival', *O'Casey Annual* 1 (1982): 225.
21 Gabriel Fallon, 'Afterword', *Irish University Review* 10.1 (1980): 159.
22 O'Casey, *Letters*: 139.
23 O'Casey, *Letters*: 141.
24 Cyril Cusack, 'In the beginning was O'Casey', *Irish University Review* 10. 1 (1980): 21.
25 O'Casey, *Letters*: 147.
26 Robert Hogan, *The Experiments of Sean O'Casey* (New York: St Martin's Press, 1960): 42.
27 Murray, *Sean O'Casey*, 149.
28 Ayling, 'O'Casey and the Abbey', 9.
29 Fitzgerald, 'O'Casey and Lady Gregory', 98.
30 Denis Johnston, 'Waiting with Beckett' 34, *Irish Writing* (Spring 1956) :25.

[31] Gabriel Fallon, *Sean O'Casey: The Man I Knew* (London: Routledge & Kegan Paul, 1965): 14.
[32] Michael J. O'Neill, *Lennox Robinson* (New York: Twayne, 1964): 113.
[33] Homer Swander, 'Shields at the Abbey', *Eire/Ireland* 5.2 (1970): 30.
[34] Harold Ferrar, *Denis Johnston's Irish Theatre* (Dublin: The Dolmen Press 1973): 9.
[35] Brenna Katz Clarke and Harold Ferrer, *The Dublin Drama League 1919-1941* (Dublin: The Dolmen Press, 1979): 16.
[36] Gordon Craig, 'The Art of the Theatre', *The Theory of the Modern Stage*, ed. Eric Bentley (London: Penguin, 1990): 119.
[37] Frank O'Connor, *The Art of the Theatre* (Dublin: Maurice Fridberg, 1947): 30.
[38] Robert Lowery, 'O'Casey Letters', *The Sean O'Casey Review* 1.2 (1975): 22.
[39] O'Casey, *Letters* (1992): Vol. IV, 230.
[40] John Willett, *The Theatre of Bertold Brecht* (Connecticut: New Directions, 1959): 224.
[41] Victoria Stewart, *About O'Casey* (London: Faber & Faber, 2003): 75.
[42] Hans-Georg Simmgen, 'O'Casey Stage Productions in the German Democratic Republic', *The O'Casey Enigma*, ed. Micheál Ó hAodha (Cork: Mercier Press, 1980): 7-8.
[43] David Krause, 'Sean O'Casey', *The Massachusetts Review* 6.2 (1965): 249.
[44] John Arden, 'Ecce Hobo Sapiens: O'Casey's Theatre', *Sean O'Casey*, ed. Thomas Kilroy (New Jersey: Prentice-Hall, 1975): 76.
[45] Simpson, 'Staging O'Casey's Plays', 134.
[46] Gordon Rogoff, *Commonweal* 23 October 1964.
[47] John O'Mahony, *The Guardian* 9 August 2004.

7 | *Observe the Sons of Ulster*: Historical Stages

Helen Lojek

When Frank McGuinness's *Observe the Sons of Ulster Marching Towards the Somme* premiered on the Abbey's Peacock Stage in 1985, the play received widespread praise and notoriety as a powerful dramatic consideration of Ulster Protestant soldiers fighting in World War I. The fact that the drama was written by a Catholic from the Republic of Ireland, at a time when unionist/nationalist tensions in Northern Ireland dominated the headlines, cried out for commentary, garnering the play social and political as well as artistic responses. Since then, productions have become a bell-wether for cultural discussions both in the English speaking world and in Europe. Such discussions go beyond nationalist-unionist relations: the Battle of the Somme, gay rights, European politics, and the War in Iraq have also been major contexts. The play has inevitably been seen through the multi-faceted lens created when text, productions, and audiences come together at particular cultural/historical moments. The ease with which different observers have located different themes is one sign of the play's value and complexity.

Lionel Pilkington notes that *Sons of Ulster* was written 'in the wake of a hostile unionist reaction to the New Ireland Forum', and 'elevated to the main Abbey Theatre stage just one month after the signing of the Anglo-Irish Agreement'. Pilkington's point is that the Irish national theatre leaned toward 'ideological conformity to the political interests of the state', and he argues his perspective persuasively in relation to various productions.[1] However, although McGuinness has been remarkably willing to discuss the play's origins and import, he does not connect it with either the Forum or the Agreement. The play endorses no particular step toward resolving tensions. It does raise issues that were (and are) 'political interests' not just of the state but also of numerous citizens on both sides of the border. That fact, rather than manipulations by the Abbey or the state, seems the likely explanation for the play's political impact.

Nevertheless, its first production established *Sons of Ulster* as a model for cross-cultural understanding, and subsequent Irish productions emphasized this aspect. The programme for the premiere included the Roll of Honour of the 'Invincible True Blues' of Coleraine,[2] World War I photographs, Psalms 82 and 88, Wilfred Owen's 'Strange Meeting', and Emily Dickinson's 'The Soul unto itself'. The programme, then, emphasized World War I and the play's religious dimension, though only Keith Jeffery seems to have noted implications that the play has a religious dimension beyond the simplistic political/religious split between Catholics and Protestants. Despite the programme's silence about the contemporaneous movement toward peace in Northern Ireland, most commentators made that connection. The Hampstead (London) production in 1986 included the Psalms, information about the Boa Island statues, quotes from World War I writings – and a timeline that, jumping from 1920 to 1985, mentioned both the Anglo-Irish Agreement and the 70th anniversary of the Battle of the Somme. Such direct references to cross-cultural understanding have continued to increase.

In order to perceive the play as an emblem of cross-cultural understanding, audiences need to know something about the fierceness of tensions between Irish factions, and about the extent to which McGuinness's life illustrates those tensions. A Catholic from the Republic, he wrote about Ulstermen. A native of Donegal, which was separated by partition from the rest of Ulster, he is himself a Son of Ulster – 'from that part of Ulster which is within the Irish Republic', as Keith Jeffery put it in a 1985 review. Early press reports mentioned these facts regularly, even if the programmes did not. The extent to which the play is a view across cultures is also emphasized by McGuinness's oft-quoted comment that he had begun it knowing the last line would be 'I love my Ulster', and that he wanted to create a character who would find it as difficult to say that as McGuinness himself would have.[3] In an Abbey production, there is the added layer of watching actors from the Republic's national theatre cross cultural barriers in order to portray Ulster soldiers. Occasionally Northern Irish reviewers complained about the Abbey players' accents,[4] but that is part of the point: the Republic's national theatre actors were stretching to embody Ulstermen who would have heard in their accents the tones of the enemy. Most programmes have provided information about the Battle of the Somme, but audiences must bring with them the late twentieth century awareness that provides such ironic layers for the play, and the cross-cultural elements clearly work best when audiences feel them deeply, without the need for critical preparation.

If audiences in the Republic were captured by the play's importance as a demonstration of cross-cultural understanding, Northern Irish unionists were more likely to respond to it as a rare and respectful view of their culture – a culture not often presented on stage and often stereotypically regarded as uninteresting, lacking artistic imagination, and scarred by negative emotions. Charles Fitzgerald, writing about the Abbey's first production, suggested to Belfast readers that the play

> does for Ulster what O'Casey and Yeats did for Ireland, what Shakespeare did for England, Longfellow for North America – it puts the whole Protestant ethos into perspective .... It is a play that does for Ulster what Ulster's Sons did in Flanders and it is the final, superb tribute to their sacrifice. It must be seen here.[5]

The 1985 production to which Fitzgerald was reacting played to enthusiastic reviews in both Belfast and Coleraine, but the Lyric Theatre's 1990 production was the first professional staging by a Northern Irish company.[6] It too was warmly received by reviewers. Though he did not particularly like the Lyric production, Fitzgerald again concluded that *Sons of Ulster* was 'the play of our time, about our place and about us and should not be missed'.[7]

Reviewing the 1986 Hampstead Theatre production, Christopher Edwards noted that *Sons of Ulster* (which he contrasted with the 'anti-English propaganda' of Brian Friel's *Translations* and Ron Hutchinson's *Rat in the Skull*) 'subtly and successfully' dramatized Protestant experience 'without grinding any axes'[8]. Several years later Joe McMinn pointed out that the play 'was greeted with delight and relief – as if, finally, a tradition not associated with imagination or poetry was getting a chance to be heard with respect'.[9]

The Northern Irish Troubles and Protestant unionist concern that their culture be favourably portrayed were not the only contexts in which *Sons of Ulster* appeared. The play premiered just before the seventieth anniversary of the Battle of the Somme, when commemorative journeys were taking World War I soldiers (most of them from Ulster) back to the French battlefield, and when the Irish Republic was seeking ways to commemorate the World War I contributions of its soldiers. The anniversary of the Easter Rebellion, which coincided with the Battle of the Somme, was also coming up. Particularly among unionist commentators, connections with Ulster's role in World War I were tremendously important. David Nowlan's *Irish Times* review of the Abbey's original production described *Sons of Ulster* as 'one of the most comprehensive attacks ever made in the theatre on Ulster Protestantism' – a judgment that touched off a storm of controversy. Kevin Barry (then an editor of the *Irish Literary Supplement*) and Jennifer Johnston (whose 1974 *How Many Miles to Babylon?* is based partly on a relative's World War I diaries) wrote to praise the play's view of Ulster Protestantism. Nowlan defended (explained?) himself, and Northern Irish poet Michael Longley lauded the play:

> My own father survived the Trenches, and over the years I tried to come to terms imaginatively with his memories and with accounts I have picked up elsewhere of the Ulster Division at the Somme. In light of this

preoccupation I feel honour-bound to praise Frank McGuinness's abundant, profound and humane study of cultural confusions and military heroism. This play moved me to tears.[10]

Subsequent reviews in other publications, although they do not mention Nowlan, were in part responses to his critique.

Northern Irish productions and reviews continued to emphasize the play's use of the Battle of the Somme, generally regarded as a key event in the history of Ulster Protestantism. For its 1990 production, the Lyric displayed World War I photographs and memorabilia from Belfast's Farset Community Centre (which had earlier organized a commemoration trip to the Somme), and the director pointed to the play's importance as an examination of the past as well as a message for the present.[11] Ian Hill, in the *Guardian*, compared the play's events to Vietnam, but Irish reviews were more likely to note its connection to the Somme and its importance as an expression of cross-cultural understanding.[12]

The play's presentation of gay lovers has also resonated in Irish culture. The 1980s witnessed the explosion of AIDS, and a mounting campaign to decriminalize homosexual behaviour in both Irelands.[13] Discussion of McGuinness as a gay playwright and of the play's presentation of gay love became increasingly open. A 1990 Red Kettle production in Waterford coincided with the Lyric's production in Belfast. Few Northern Irish reviews mentioned the characters' sexuality, though Ian Hill in the *Guardian* noted the 'sweat of incipient homosexuality', and Sheila Hamilton in the *Communist Party Weekly* noted that Craig is Pyper's 'lover'. Mary O'Donnell confronted the issue directly in Dublin's *Sunday Tribune*, describing Red Kettle's production as weakened because the '*homosexuality* seems fudged at the very moment when it should provide radiance and dimension to the bonding which takes place between [Pyper and Craig]' (italics in original)[14]. O'Donnell does not mention the Lyric's portrayal of gay characters, which may mean that she found it more successful, though in general she preferred the Red Kettle production. In 1991 McGuinness protested that 'recent productions of *Sons of Ulster* censored Pyper's relationship with Craig'.[15] It seems likely the reference is to Red Kettle, but he used the plural, so there may have been other portrayals he found problematic. In 1985 only Charles Fitzgerald had mentioned sexuality in *Sons of Ulster*, but the 1990 productions coincided with increased discussion of gay rights in both Irelands, and the attention of some reviewers was drawn to the issues.

The Abbey's 1994 production premiered by coincidence at a time when a lasting peace in Northern Ireland seemed possible.[16] Treatment of the play as an icon of cross-cultural understanding, however, was no coincidence. The gala opening night included special guests from both sides of the border and both sides of the conflict—politicians, well-known entertainers, and twenty-four community workers from Belfast's generally unionist-Protestant Shankill Road. Recalling that occasion four years later, David Ervine, who was at the time political spokesperson for Northern Ireland's Progressive Unionist Party, showed his awareness of various contexts:

> Even in the homosexuality that [McGuinness] introduced he was saying we weren't all the same; we were all different – naïve, uncomplicated people having to deal with complicated circumstances. But he was also saying to the nationalist community: this did happen, and it happened to our people, and it didn't happen quite the way you think it happened. Explore. Understand ... We were in a new era.[17]

In conjunction with the 1994 production, *The Irish Times* published a full page of commentary (including assessments from eight well-known commentators) that emphasized cross-cultural understanding.[18] Dorothea Melvin's programme notes suggested the play's importance 'to us here and now, in a time of hope and uncertainty, fraught with all kinds of expectations and challenged by so many other legacies from the past'[19]. The programme also included World War I photographs and a discussion by Kevin Myers in which he pointed to what he felt were historical inaccuracies. Myers also devoted an *Irish Times* column and his comments on RTE Radio's *The Arts Show* to anachronisms he believed falsified the play's view of Ulster Protestantism[20]. Such discussion indicates the emphasis on getting things 'right' about the past, so that Irish people could move forward into cross-cultural understanding and a more peaceful future.

When the Abbey remounted the play in 1995, Director Patrick Mason noted that it was in deliberate conjunction with the IRA ceasefire in Northern Ireland.

> I decided to revive the play when news of the IRA ceasefire came in and I rang Frank and I said, look, I know we were going to do this play in twelve months time but I think we should do it now[,] and on ... the night of our first preview, the Loyalist ceasefire was called and in a strange way ever since this production has gone with all the ups and downs of the ceasefire.[21]

This production also toured. At the Edinburgh Festival, almost every review mentioned its relationship to the ceasefire. Most found hope in the play's effort to create cross-cultural understanding, but Charles Spencer found the characters' adherence to ancient loyalties cause for 'despair that a lasting peace will ... be achieved'.[22] Almost every review also mentioned the production's portrayal of gay lovers, which Benedict Nightingale found 'over-explicit' and Nicholas de Jongh described as 'rather camp and outrageous'[23]. The play arrived in London on the eve of the eightieth anniversary of the Battle of the Somme and (ironically) just as IRA bombs were once more exploding there. It toured to Blackpool, Liverpool, Malvern, Plymouth, and Belfast. Months later McGuinness responded 'to recent English newspaper descriptions of the play, claiming it was all about homosexuality, with a dismissive "grow up".[24] Ten years after its premiere, *Sons of Ulster* had achieved notoriety in Ireland and the UK both for its push toward cross-cultural understanding, and for its portrayal of gay love. French reactions, however, focused elsewhere.

In Paris at the 1996 *Imaginaire Irlandais* celebration, the Abbey production was performed in English, with French subtitles, and the text of McGuinness's play appeared in a French translation by Joseph Long and Alexandra Poulain.[25] French President Jacques Chirac and Irish President Mary Robinson attended the tremendously successful opening performance, which coincided with Robinson's birthday and which Jocelyn Clarke reported ended with demands for 'auteur, auteur!'[26]

The play was featured on the front pages of *Le Monde* and *Le Figaro*, but French press coverage was quite different than Irish and English coverage. Certainly the French knew of the start of the peace talks, but the French press focused not on Irish politics but on European politics. The 1992 Maastricht Treaty had strengthened European unity, and debate about its ratification had revealed the Irish as increasingly willing to challenge the authority of the Catholic church. Ireland's economic boom had begun in 1995. Now, in 1996, Ireland was about to assume the presidency of the European Union. *Sons of Ulster* had premiered in the 1980s, in an economically depressed and socially conservative Republic which had just reaffirmed its opposition to divorce and abortion. By the 1990s, when the play arrived in France, Ireland was prosperous, and legal restrictions on divorce and abortion had eased. Heavily Catholic France was interested in the role of religion – in the play and in Ireland – and there were reminders that Ulster's soldiers had come to the Somme to resist the German invasion of France. Under a headline pointing to the need for liberation from malignant (*haine*) nationalism and conservative religion, Catherine Bédarida noted in *Le Monde* that McGuinness's emergence as a playwright had coincided with Ireland's entry into the European Union, and with the country's exit from post-colonial isolation and poverty.[27] Olivier Schmitt described the play as 'the best work of an author representative of the rebirth of Irish theatre' and quoted McGuinness about changes in Ireland: people no longer allowed the church to dictate their lives and the climate was freer, so that he had no need to go into exile as had earlier Irish writers: 'I can write without fear of censure and lead my private life as I choose,' he stated.[28] McGuinness also noted the prevalence of racism in Ireland, paralleling Irish prejudice against the English with prejudice against Blacks and Asians elsewhere. Schmitt suggested that racism was one traditional Irish value that the play attacked, implying that a mark of McGuinness's modernity was his move beyond that traditional value. French struggles with an increasing Arab population were an unstated context, but the need to escape inherited loyalties and move toward a federalized Europe were more immediate concerns. The French press seems not to have mentioned the play's presentation of gay characters, focusing instead primarily on ways *Sons of Ulster* showcased new European values, and Ireland's emergence into the modern world. Hope for a breakthrough in Northern Ireland's peace talks was simply another indication of Ireland's modernization. French perception of the play as innovative in form and progressive in theme was no doubt one factor that led a year later to the awarding of the French Order of Arts and Letters to McGuinness.

The French interest in McGuinness as a herald of new directions in Irish theatre parallels the assessment of Christopher Morash, who characterizes Irish theatre in the 1970s as 'strangely out of date' and cites McGuinness as one of the 'new Irish Theatre' playwrights whose university backgrounds enabled them to 'generate a different sense of tradition'.[29] By 1996, when *Sons of Ulster* appeared in Paris, this 'new Irish Theatre' was at its height. Five years earlier, Maeliosa Stafford, having left Galway's Druid Theatre to work in Australia, used similar terms to describe his decision to stage *Sons of Ulster* there: 'I want to get away from the stereotype of people's associations with Irish theatre.... modern Irish writers explore a wealth of subjects and issues.'[30]

The Abbey's production went from Paris to Brussels, where it was sponsored in part by the Northern Ireland Group, an organization of ex-patriots living in Belgium. Connections with the peace process were prominent, but Belgians also noted the play's universality, citing parallels between varying dialects of Irish English and varying dialects in Belgium.[31] From Brussels the production went to Bonn, opening the same week as the Northern Ireland peace talks. The only press report I've located focused on the play as a play, praising its 'classical stringency' and daring interjection of humour into events focused on the 'deadening awareness of death'. There was no mention of contemporary events.[32]

In July 1998 the play again appeared in the context of Irish efforts to enhance cross-cultural understanding. Irish President Mary McAleese organized a reception for Orangemen from the Republic, a group whose presence had not before been generally noted or appreciated by the state. McAleese was reaching out to under-recognized communities and seeking to heighten awareness of the Republic's diversity. A cross-community drum group from Derry, Northern Ireland, performed, and McGuinness read from *Sons of Ulster*.[33]

When McGuinness's play finally arrived in the US (Williamstown Theatre, spring 2001), September 11 and the War in Iraq were still in the future. When director Nicholas Martin remounted that production in Boston (Wilbur Theatre, spring 2002), though, reviewers regularly mentioned its anti-war content and one drew analogies with Palestinians and refugee camps.[34] By the time Martin brought the production to New York (Lincoln Center, February 2003) its relevance to US history seemed so compelling that one reviewer suggested the play be re-titled *Observe the Sons and Daughters of America Marching Towards Iraq*. Despite the programme's extensive presentation of historical background, reviewers routinely focused on more general issues, describing the play as anti-war and noting its timely relation to 'American drums of war' and the 'war obsessed environment' of the United States. 'Anyone urging the rush to war', concluded Jeanne Lieberman, 'should be compelled to see Frank McGuinness's poignant, touching and intimate portrait of the effects of combat....'[35] The emphasis on the play as 'anti-war' contrasts with frequent Northern Irish descriptions of it as a celebration of the noble sacrifice of Ulster soldiers. The play emphasizes both individual nobility and the collective futility of war, but reviewers in different times and places have been struck more forcefully by one element than the other. McGuinness himself pointed from the start to the anti-war themes, declaring in 1985 that 'The Battle of the Somme is strongly a metaphor for the nature of multi-violence in the twentieth century. And I wanted to say that something as banal, but I hope as deep, as the human male and the human species of which he is part, is worth preserving, and that we're now all standing on the verge of going over the top at the Somme....'[36] Now, almost twenty years later, the playwright again noted the play's anti-war sentiment and its presentation of a 'different type of Irishness' than the Catholic nationalism familiar to US audiences.[37] Mentions of the 'unfamiliar' Irishness and of the actors' difficult, often inconsistent accents were also common. Reviews in mainstream publications often mentioned gay issues, and a number of publications aimed at gay readers reviewed the play.[38]

The minimal familiarity of US reviewers with Irish (or, at least, Northern Irish) culture was evident when one saw in the soldiers' raised red hands only a reference to the blood and violence of war, despite the programme's explanation of the Red Hand of Ulster. McGuinness's roots in the Catholic Irish Republic were ignored. A focus on cross-cultural understanding is notably missing. Only *The Wild Geese Today*, an Irish heritage internet site, noted the cross-cultural issues that are typically prominent in Irish reviews. Nor do any of the US reviews echo the French discussion of a 'new' Irish drama, coming from a more modern, more European, less post-colonial society. Clearly preoccupation with the progression toward a pre-emptive strike in Iraq shaped United States response to the play, but more than that seems to be involved. United States audiences were simply less interested in European developments and less familiar with Ireland's deep cultural divisions. New York reviewers, in fact, often voiced puzzlement about the cultural and historical references, despite the help offered by the programme. Belfast celebrated the triumph of a Son of Ulster on Broadway.[39]

A second Lyric production coincided with the New York production. Like the Lyric's 1990 production, it featured a lobby display of World War I memorabilia, this time from the Somme Heritage Centre collection. The programme included war photos, battlefield maps, and an essay by Philip Orr outlining the emblematic importance of the Battle of the Somme. Members of the Ulster Division at the Somme had largely come from 'the old Ulster Volunteer Force, set up to oppose Irish Home Rule and to maintain Ulster's place at the heart of the British Empire'. Fiercely loyal to Britain, suspicious that Britain did not really want them, suffering horrific casualties, these Ulster soldiers occupied a position parallel to that of contemporary Ulster loyalists. Understanding what the Somme represents, Orr argued, is 'key to a true understanding of Northern Ireland's place on these islands'.[40]

Pre-opening press reports focused less on Ulster history and more on connections between the play's anti-war stance and the contemporaneous American/British movement toward war in Iraq. The cast and crew of the Lyric production were almost all from Ulster, and numerous regional papers (from Anderstown, Antrim, Lurgan, Portadown, Newry, and Armagh, for example) celebrated the appearance of favourite sons, in a play about their own province. Most of those pieces also connected the play to the looming war in Iraq, in language that is so similar (often identical) that it seems possible the papers were relying on a common source. Director Michael Duke also connected *Sons of Ulster* to the 'relentless' pursuit of war by Blair and Bush, concluding

> If I was to write about producing this play at any other time, I'm sure I would be consumed by the artistic brilliance of the drama. For what it dares, and how it dares, the play is a must see at any time. But now, on the threshold of another major conflict, it is clear that how it deals with men and war transcends the men and the war in question, and gives us a unique perspective on our own dangerous present.[41]

Several reviews mention the presentation of gay love, sometimes in coded language: the men 'question' their sexuality or 'illustrate their feelings'.[42] Gay love was mentioned directly by Ian Hill, Karen Fricker, and Director Michael Duke, who neither lingered on nor avoided the play's 'hymn to the love which did not then dare to speak its name'.[43]

The remarkable coverage in local papers indicates the close connections felt between the play and Ulster, as well as the pride individual communities took in the success of local performers. Almost all of this press coverage also focused on history and Iraq. There was no significant mention of the play as a play. For reviewers, as for the director, contemporary realities trumped artistry as a primary concern.

Sons of Ulster has won a remarkable string of awards and has attracted talented professionals, particularly in Ireland and England, where productions have reached large audiences. It is now a text on the Advanced Subsidiary Exam set by the Northern Irish Council for the Curriculum. Among a wide variety of options on the exam are questions that focus on the portrayal of Protestant Ulster culture. The 2001 exam noted that 'McGuinness suggests ... that blood sacrifice plays a significant part in the culture of Protestant Ulster' and suggested discussion of 'distinctive features of Ulster Protestantism as presented in the play' or 'the importance of the characters' Protestant culture to their bonding'. A 2002 exam pointed to the characters' 'involvement in a common cause' and to the 'relationship between past and present' in the play, suggesting discussion of 'shared values, traditions, attachments' or the 'place of the Somme in Protestant tradition'. In 2003 and 2004, when cultural tensions had eased and awareness of cultural diversity had increased, exam questions were phrased more generally and less prescriptively: the 'hardening effects of war' and the 'importance of religious belief to characters', for example.[44]

Sons of Ulster opened once more on the Abbey stage as part of the celebration of the Abbey's first hundred years. Its selection as part of that celebration is another indication of the extent to which the play has become an icon in Irish theatre. The programme for abbeyonehundred describes the play as

> magnificent and elegiac....A compelling portrait of a group of men divided by religion, politics and class but united in their common belief in God and country. McGuinness' play at once celebrates their willingness to fight and die to preserve a way of life while offering a timely critique of the futility of war.[45]

I'm uncertain what to make of this description: if the production indeed reveals divisions of religion and politics among these soldiers (or even shows how to separate religion from politics in Northern Ireland) it will be a more nuanced interpretation than past productions have offered. Pyper (hardly an orthodox Protestant), Crawford (product of a mixed marriage), and Roulston (a failed minister) are divided in some ways from their unreflective Protestant companions. Not, however, divided enough to separate them from the general community of Ulster Protestants. But perhaps the abbeyonehundred programme merely means that these soldiers are divided from the Irish Republic, whose national theatre will again be placing them on stage – revealing once more the complexity of the play's presentation of social and cultural issues, and the extent to which particular audiences have been able to find in it powerful messages about their times.

---

[1] Lionel Pilkington, *Theatre and the State in Twentieth Century Ireland: Cultivating the People* (London: Routledge, 2001): 221-23.

[2] McGuinness was teaching at what was then the New University of Ulster in Coleraine when he began to think about the play; he returned to Coleraine later to do research for it and has repeatedly cited the play's connection to Coleraine.

³ John Waters, 'Alone again, naturally,' *In Dublin* (14 May 1987): 18.
⁴ Grania McFadden, 'Southern discomfort on the road to the Somme,' *The Telegraph* (Belfast) 5 August 1996, 16.
⁵ Charles Fitzgerald, 'Face to face with Ulster', *Belfast Newsletter* (March 1985).
⁶ Amateur theatre groups in Bangor and Newry staged the play in 1989.
⁷ Charles Fitzgerald, *Belfast Newsletter* 4 April 1990.
⁸ Christopher Edwards,'*Protestant passion', Spectator* 2 August 1986.
⁹ 'Language, literature and cultural identity: Irish and Anglo-Irish', *Styles of belonging: the cultural identities of Ulster*, eds Jean Lundy and Aodán MacPóilin (Belfast: Lagan Press, 1996): 48.
¹⁰ Nowlan's *The Irish Times* review appeared 19 February 1985: 10. Letters from Barry and Johnston: 23 February 1985: 19; Nowlan's letter: 28 February 1985; Longley's letter: 2 March 1985: 23.
¹¹ Una Brankin, 'Marching towards a full house'. Lyric Theatre Archives, March 1990
¹² Ian Hill, 'Great Portrayal of the "Shallowness of Governments and the Horrors of War"', *Newsletter* 13 February 2003.
¹³ Parallel cases about gay rights in Northern Ireland and the Republic succeeded before the European Court of Human Rights in 1981 and 1988; in 1993, Ireland's Sexual Offences Act effectively equalized the code for heterosexuals and homosexuals.
¹⁴ Mary O'Donnell, 'Blood Sacrifice and Faith Under Duress', *Sunday Tribune* 22 April 1990: B4.
¹⁵ 'An Irishman's theatre', *Studies on the Contemporary Irish Theatre*, eds Jacqueline Genet and Elisabeth Hellegourac'h (Caen, France: GDR D'Études Anglo-Irlandaises du CNRA, 1991): 62.
¹⁶ Joe Dowling was ill, so the Abbey cancelled the production he was scheduled to direct and re-mounted *Sons of Ulster* to fill the vacancy.
¹⁷ David Ervine, *Clear the Stage*. BBC Northern Ireland, 1998.
¹⁸ Dorothy Melvin, 'Mining a rich heritage, or digging trenches?' (19 October 1994): Arts, 12.
¹⁹ Dorothea Melvin, Programme Note, *Observe the Sons of Ulster Marching Towards the Somme* (Dublin: Abbey Theatre, 1994).
²⁰ Kevin Myers, 'An Irishman's Diary', *The Irish Times*, 22 October 1994: 15.
²¹ *Morning Ireland*, RTE Radio 1, 10 June 1996.
²² Charles Spenser, 'Pack up the troubles in an old kitbag', *Daily Telegraph* 22 August 1995.
²³ Benedict Nightingale, 'Recognising the Somme Total', *The Times*, 22 August 1995. Nicholas de Jongh, 'Powerful Topicality...' (Source: Abbey Theatre Archive).
²⁴ Dermott Hayes, 'Tony hero of late night metro drama', *Evening Herald* 23 May 1996.
²⁵ Long directed a 1976 University College Dublin production of *Richard II* that gave McGuinness his first stage experience.

[26] Jocelyn Clarke, 'Irish Eyes are Smiling After a Tour de Force', *The Tribune Magazine*, 26 May 1996.
[27] Catherine Bédarida, 'Les plaies de la guerre au Coeur de theater de Frank McGuinness', *Le Monde* 24 Mai 1996: Culture 27.
[28] Olivier Schmitt, 'A la recherche de la paix sur les rives de la Somme, résister à l'envahisseur allemand', *Le Monde* 24 Mai 1996: Culture 27.
[29] Chris Morash, *A History of Irish Theatre, 1601-2000* (Cambridge: Cambridge University Press, 2002): 242ff.
[30] Aine dePaor, 'Druid in Oz', *Theatre Ireland* (Winter 1990-1991): 47.
[31] See Patrick Smyth, 'Stage drama provides relief from beef war', *The Irish Times* 14 June 1996, 10. And *'Observe the Sons of Ulster* European tour,' *Morning Ireland*, RTE Radio 1, 10 June 1996.
[32] Kölnische Rundschau 'Von Clownerie zum Totentanz', *Kölnische Rundschau* (Cologne, 15 June 1996).
[33] Frank McNally, 'Orangemen are invited down an untraditional route to the Aras', *The Irish Times* 11 July 1998, 1.
[34] See Suzanne Bixby, 'Boston' (2002) http://www.talkinbroadway.com; Robert Nesti, 'Waiting for God-knows-what', 2002, http://www.baywindows.com; and Will Stackman, *'Observe the Sons of Ulster Advancing on the Somme* [sic]', 2002, http://www.aislesay.com .
[35] 'Observe the Sons of Ulster Marching Towards the Somme' (2002) http://www.theatrescene.net.
[36] Frank McGuinness in *Kaleidoscope*, with Paul Allen, BBC Radio, 12 November 1985.
[37] Maureen Dezell, 'Fighting Irish (on the side of the king)', *New York Times* 23 February 2003: 28.
[38] See Lawrence Pfeil, Jr., 'A kiss before dying', *New York Blade* 7 March 2002: 49 and Gerard Raymond, 'Gays and the military', *The Advocate*, March 2003. http://www.advocate.com.
[39] Eamonn O'Hanlon, 'Observe as a son of Ulster marches on Broadway', *Sunday People* 9 March 2003.
[40] Philip Orr, Programme Notes *Observe the Sons of Ulster Marching Towards the Somme*, Lyric Theatre Programme (2003): 11.
[41] Michael Duke, 'Opening your eyes to war', *Fortnight* (March 2003).
[42] Keith Gilmore, 'Observe the Sons of Ulster at the Lyric', *Down Spectator* 13 February 2003 and Stephen Gray, 'Review corner,' *South Belfast News* 22 February 2003.
[43] Ian Hill, 'Great portrayal of the shallowness of governments and horrors of war', *Newsletter* 13 February 2003.
[44] The exam is given to students in the lower sixth (seventeen year olds), who would typically complete their A Level studies the following year. I am grateful to Amanda Simpson for providing copies of the Advanced Subsidiary exams. McGuinness's *Someone Who'll Watch Over Me* is on the Irish Republic's Leaving Certificate Exam.

45 Abbey Theatre, *abbeyonehundred* commemorative programme (Dublin: Abbey Theatre, 2003): 23.

8 | 'Am I a con man?': Brian Friel's idea of the self-reflective artist, viewed in the light of Adorno's aesthetic theory

Christa Velten-Mrowka

'On the stage one must have reality and one must have joy': John Millington Synge thus sums up his aesthetic in his Preface to *The Playboy of the Western World*.[1] Ironically, it is a play that shows reality to be utterly deceptive. It suggests that only someone who has learned that fixed, volitional truths are falsities, and that human reality is marked by delusion can, like Christy Mahon, be 'the master of all fights' (163) and even that assertion may be fictitious. Synge's *Playboy* reveals a harsh world, full of folly and atrocities, and yet the spectator, being magically transformed by the artistic representation of human absurdities, experiences deepest aesthetic satisfaction. Joy comes through the unconscious, and if it is 'the rich joy', which Synge opposes to the 'false' one of shallow entertainment, it blends with the conscious experience of 'what is superb and wild in reality' (103), of what is indomitable and awesome, because it exceeds rational thought. Human fragmentation is thereby transcended, heightened to a wider context of being, in which the isolated and destitute are illuminated by the reflection of wholeness. Within, and in spite of the limitations and inevitabilities of a broken world, these moments of aesthetic experience convey a sense of escape and restoration – a sense of happiness.

Such an experience of what might be described as metaphysical truth naturally resists definition and reification; it remains ambiguous like the work of art, through which truth becomes transparent. For, as Theodor W. Adorno (1903-1969) *spiritus rector* of the Frankfurt School, put it in his *Aesthetic Theory*, 'art completes knowledge with what is excluded from knowledge and thereby once again impairs its character as knowledge, its univocity.'[2] In *Twilight of the Idols*, Friedrich Nietzsche formulates an aesthetic that is dialectically integrated, included and transmuted in

Adorno's own theories and that holds true in all great art. It has proved to be of specific significance in Irish writing from Wilde, from Yeats and Synge, to Friel:

> To divide the world into a 'real' and an 'apparent' world ... is [a] symptom of declining life ... That the artist places a higher value on appearance than on reality constitutes no objection to this proposition. For 'appearance' here signifies reality once more, only selected, strengthened, corrected ... The tragic artist is not a pessimist – it is precisely he who affirms all that is questionable and terrible in existence, he is Dionysian.[3]

In other words, tragic artists, whether or not they are writers of tragedies, do not seek to negate the negativities of life but try to transmute them in a ceaseless process of re-creation. Almost a century after Nietzsche, Brian Friel pithily expresses the aim of the creative artist with the words: 'To see the thing exactly as it is, and then to create it anew'.[4] This reveals a dialectic also in the Adornian sense: one in which the logic of critical analysis and the irrational 'Dionysian' element, 'the driving impulse of the artist, of all great men, of nature itself',[5] as James Flannery has put it with regard to W.B. Yeats, are the complementary constituents of creative and artistic work.

Synge's 'reality' on the stage, as well as Brian Friel's artistic re-creation of reality, may be equated with Nietzsche's aesthetic 'reality once more'. All three versions of the same idea point to the mimetic character of art. As Adorno explains, 'mimesis implies knowledge of the innermost nature of an object expressed by art, not in the narrow context of what is, but in the large context of its possibilities' (112). Mimesis means assimilation to the object, not its imitation; it means production, not reproduction. Mimetic recreation takes place on three interrelated levels. It concerns the artist's approach to the nature of his object – his 'divining', and his capability of expressing his object 'in the large context of its possibilities'. The artist must attempt to approximate the essence of his object and its expression so closely to one another that the difference fades.[6] The artwork in turn is mimetic re-creation in that, like the artist, it represents what is not. It mimes truth, unable to make it immediately comprehensible, which accounts for the artwork's dialectic: it is at once spiritualized object and objectified spirit, reality and imagination. Also, it is both subject and object in that through the artist's subjective form of expression, something objective speaks. Finally, mimetic re-creation is demanded of the recipient of art in that he or she has to re-translate the cryptic language of the artwork into significative human terms. They reflect the work without being identical with it, but at the same time they signal an understanding, which exceeds verbal expression. It derives from emotion, from the ecstatic experience of the unspeakable truth that the magic of art's mimetic language transmits. It causes the recipient to reflect on what the work of art reflects, or, putting it with Adorno, 'art's linguistic quality gives rise to reflection over what speaks in art; this is its veritable subject, not the individual who makes it, or the one who receives it.' (*Aesthetic:* 166-67)

The moments, when, in the perceptive mind, intellect and emotion are dialectically balanced, are the rare and elusive moments of joy and reality, the joy of transcended reality. They are tantamount to a sense of liberation that may be characterized as the felt simultaneity of enchantment and enlightenment: aesthetic experience as visionary moments, and 'not a morsel of that from which' the mind has 'escaped' (*Aesthetic:* 21). Although the man-made catastrophes of the twentieth century have made it impossible to create and enjoy art in a naive way, they have not been able to annihilate the longing for peace and, along with it, the magic of art, despite art's modern affinity to the sinister. 'The transcendent is, and it is not. We despair of what is, and our despair spreads to the transcendental ideas that used to call a halt to despair' (*Dialectics:* 375). The firm belief in human reason has generally been upturned and revealed in its self-delusive and violating tendencies. Converging with Nietzsche's visionary judgment of modern civilization, and Adorno's philosophical and aesthetic conclusions after the Holocaust, Friel, in the context of the Northern Ireland Troubles states that 'everything has failed – politics, art, science, philosophy', and, in Beckettian fashion, he adds: 'man wastes and pines, wastes and pines' (*Essays* 21). Yet, like the philosophy and art of Nietzsche, of Adorno, and of any other 'tragic artist', Friel's work continues unabashed. It is marked, however, by the characteristic dilemma of the artist, the same dilemma that Nietzsche attributed to the philosopher: 'To be crushed by a burden one can neither bear nor throw off'.[7] What indeed appears to be a tragic situation is interlinked with the happiness of stoically 'standing firm' in the face of despair, and of mimetically correcting and restoring a damaged world by giving it aesthetic expression (*Aesthetic:* 15). When dramatists 'depict in mean and gruesome detail only one portion of our existence, perhaps in our generation the dominant portion', Friel writes in 'The Theatre of Hope and Despair', 'they are crying out for recognition of the existence of something less ignoble, something more worthy' (*Essays* 24). Similarly, to Adorno despair does not mean absolute negativity but is inseparable from the idea of redemption: 'Greyness could not fill us with despair if our minds did not harbour the concept of different colours' (*Dialectics:* 377-78).

Even the experienced horrors of the past and, so far, the global ones of the present century have not been able to extinguish faith: faith that remembers wholeness without fixing itself to totalizations by which it would annihilate its very nature. The premise of faith is unfathomable uncertainty. This is the driving impulse of creativity, the ever-changing constellations of the elements of being, in the process of becoming. Faith is dialectically related to liberation in that it presupposes the intellectual freedom to assess what is and to imagine what ought to be, combined with the heroic readiness to face the foreign and unknown. Such faith is the source and fundament of both philosophical reflection and creative work, in which steadfastness and the passionate will to change, certainty and uncertainty, form a dialectical balance. Faith relates itself to something entirely intermediatory, to the doubleness of possibility and impossibility, which is utopia. Given the ambiguity of their objective, artist and art alike must persistently question themselves so as to avoid their self-annihilation by falling prey to a delusive status quo, or illusive sentiment. While Brian Friel's entire work centres around this idea, he has made it the explicit subject of his 1997 play, *Give Me Your Answer, Do!*

Art, with the artist as its executer, is a medium of both faith and truth. Yet truth only becomes apparent as reflection, and while it persistently necessitates expression and interpretation – just as the individual work of art demands interpretation and reinterpretation – truth affirms itself as continuous presence. At the same time, it negates itself as conceivable objectivity. Its ambiguity places the truth-oriented artist in a difficult position. The question of whether or not he or she is able to express truth is the central aspect of the artist's dialectics of hope and despair. The term 'dialectic' originally denotes 'the investigation of truth by discussion'.[8] Adorno points out its derivation from sophism, initially the wise and skilful rhetoric aimed at shaking myths and dogmatic assumptions. Later, lawyers and comedians applied it as the method 'to turn the lesser word into the major one' (*Aesthetic:* 330). In addition, it may be observed that, with the Greek preposition 'dia' meaning 'through / beyond', sophists and ironists are among those who are able to look through, or beyond, the outer appearance of things, discerning in them their inherent mirror image. As adverb, 'dia' means 'through' in the sense of 'apart' or 'in two', thus indicating dichotomy. Stressing the verbal constituent of the term, Adorno, however, emphasizes that 'in the most literal sense of the word, dialectics postulates language' (*Dialectics:* 163). It is, in fact, 'double talk' by virtue of its ability to speak in a dual way of things that have been perceived in their double nature. A generation after Adorno, George Steiner made the dialectics of verbal language the major theme of his language theory, showing language to be both bridge and barrier to cognition and above all, to inter-human communication. It is well known that on the basis of Steiner's language theories, Friel dedicated his *Translations* (1980) to this subject. Moreover, the fact that communicative human language is essentially different from and yet (by its ambiguity) related to the mimetic language of art, makes the dialectics of language a key element of aesthetic theory.

The investigation and artistic expression of truth, the objectification of the unobjectifiable, constitute the artist's dilemma: the source of what Friel calls 'the terrible and taunting questionings' (*Essays* 23). 'Whether the promise (of truth, the author) is a deception – that is the enigma', as Adorno defines the problem (*Aesthetic:* 127). Its solution can only be an aporetic one. For 'the chasm between the mind that suffers and the man who creates', as Friel puts it with silent reference to T.S. Eliot (*Essays* 59), is overcome by art itself: the answer is given by the question. Therefore, the artist must persistently put himself and his art into question, as does Brian Friel through his notorious self-scepticism and self-irony. He is conscious that what his art promises is not a copy of reality, but 'the cipher of its potential' (*Aesthetic:* 33). The artist keeps promising, uncertain whether he can keep the promise. In contrast to the immediate, false happiness that the culture industry promises, the artist breaks his promise 'in order to stay true to it' (311). This fundamental equivocation is accompanied by yet another uncertainty to which the artistic mind delivers itself to the point of self-denial. Friel's statement that 'in writing you put all you've got into it, although it may be a complete failure' (*Essays* 30) coincides with Adorno's characterization: 'That no artist knows with certainty whether anything will come of what he does, his happiness and anxiety ... subjectively registers something objective: the vulnerability of all art' (353-4). In a personal way, the artist is equally vulnerable. But his dilemma is as much a burden as it is a blessing: through his re-creative acts, 'the artwork is not only the echo of suffering, it diminishes it; form, the organon of its consciousness, is at the same time the organon of the neutralization of suffering' (39).

In his 'Seven Notes for a Festival Programme' of 1999, Friel recalls the ancient story of Kitezh. In the midst of confusion, on the brink of extinction, that legendary Russian town is saved by vanishing into a mist, while its church bell goes on ringing. Friel takes this story as a parable to illuminate the nature of art, and he concludes: 'The real benediction of all art is the ringing of the bell reverberating in the head long after the curtain has come down ... Because until the marauders withdraw and the fog lifts, that sacred song is the only momentary stay we have against confusion' (*Essays* 180).

Conjuring up our own imaginative powers, Friel evokes in us a most vivid idea of the double character of art that is part of contingent reality and yet without it, sounding both perdition and salvation. Paradoxically, art participates in both a beleaguered world and the spiritual realm of freedom. In this innate tension lies its simultaneous redemptiveness. By its duality, the 'sacred song' of art can only be the reflection of redemption, never redemption itself. Moreover, besides its own mediation between opposites, art needs a mediator, a performer, to connect it to an audience. The artist as performer, receiving the elusive sound, seeks to give it expression, that is, to translate the inconceivable into human terms. Bearing 'the burden of the incommunicable', as Friel puts it (*Essays* 68), the artist labours to give it form. By the perfection of artistic form, he or she creates the semblance of wholeness with all its immanent tensions. The artist creates a mimetic correspondence to the metaphysical whole that cannot be immediately realized and expressed. Calling artistic expression a 'second-hand' version of truth would still imply that it *is* truth in all its enigmatic being. As has been discussed in some detail already, using physical form to mediate the intangible, whose language is supra rational, places the artist in an aporetic situation. The power to endure it comes from his faith in the utopia of wholeness, while his dilemma fills him, at the same time, with hope and desperation. This same aporia distinguishes Brian Friel's art, his theatre of hope and despair.

In his work and personal utterance, Friel shows his keen awareness of the discrepancy, but also of the reciprocity between the healing power of art and the artist's dubious power of healing. The previously quoted passage from Friel seems to betray nothing of the uncertainties, the 'maddening questions' and 'atrophying terror' that befall the conscientious artist, as is so breathtakingly portrayed in *Faith Healer*. It is the first of four plays that acutely reveal Friel's preoccupation with the inner reality of the artist and his role and achievement in society.[9] Each play, self-contained as work of art, nevertheless complements the others. But it is *Faith Healer*, in which the tension between artist and art is most dramatically expressed and most poetically resolved. Ulf Dantanus calls it 'a play where form is perfectly wedded to content, held together by a strong vision of thematic unity';[10] Anthony Roche observes that it is 'a rehearsal of the very process it describes'[11]; and Nicholas Grene, in *The Politics of Irish Drama* concerned with other Frielian plays, remarks that he still regards *Faith Healer* as 'Brian Friel's greatest play'.[12] Declan Kiberd, too, points to the play's apparent self-reflection, arguing that it 'turns out to be about itself, since it, like the healer, veers between confidence trickery and brilliant innovation.' Kiberd argues that 'the first audience which the artist must con is himself' and reasons that 'if the artist becomes overly self-analytical, he will kill his very gift and it will even sooner desert him.'[13]

From an aesthetic point of view, this statement rouses some critical attention. For though noting the structural unity of *Faith Healer*, Kiberd tends to interpret the play under the sign of ultimate dichotomy, namely, the antagonism of thought and creative impulse, as well as the antinomy between delusion, or illusion, and true innovation. This view of the either-or seems to neglect the aspect of the dialectic correspondence between oppositions, while *Faith Healer* underlines that view. Adorno has made the reciprocity of oppositions the fundamental thesis of his philosophy and aesthetics. In the present text, I argue from the stance of Adornian theory which claims the dialectic unity of truth and delusion. This insight both presupposes and reinforces critical self-reflection as an attitude, a necessary constituent in the inner and outer process of self-renewal. Brian Friel's dictum that 'impermanence is the only constant' (*Essays* 16) points to such a process in art and artist alike. With *Faith Healer*, however, Friel presents the inner liberation from constant seeking and 'chancing'. His resolution finds its parallel and support in Adorno's dialectic, which negates negation without setting a position. According to one of Adorno's nonetheless stringent definitions, 'dialectic is the self-consciousness of the objective context of delusion; it does not mean to have escaped from that context. Its objective goal is to break out of the context from within' (*Dialectics*: 406).

The faith healer Frank Hardy shows that turning against one's own delusions or illusions without seeking new, equally delusive affirmations, is a mode both of dying and living. He shows that there is no redemption without conscious self-surrender to the non-identical – to that which is outside the self. In the utopia of aesthetic experience that he creates, such liberating self-surrender becomes reality. *Faith Healer*, even more compellingly than the later *Molly Sweeney* (1994), is self-reflection on stage and in stages. The minds of its three characters express various levels of self-identity, of consciousness and self-consciousness. Yet in each, the critical distance which self-reflection demands is both clarifying and deceptive. This critical distance is emphasized through recollection; in fact, the entire play, as staged self-reflection, embodies recollection in all its ambiguity, being as fallacious as it is illuminating. The ambivalence of memory as imaginative transformer of fact into fiction and fiction into fact is a well-known dramatic device not just in *Faith Healer*, but also in Friel's entire work. While he shows the falsity of exclusive, one-sided positivities, it is, ironically, the iridescence and fallibility of memory by which Friel evinces the experience of restoration to wholeness that the concept of recollection implies. The ambiguity of memory upturns the received notions of truth and untruth. It transcends the limitations of common logic and puts the mind in a position to discard the negativities of contingent reality as untruth, and to blissfully remember the possibility of fulfilment as truth.

The idea of memory as being the mutual mirror image of fact and fiction involves the mutual entwinement of consciousness and unconsciousness, of analytical thought and imagination, of empiricism and utopia. The theatrical function of memory in Friel's *Faith Healer*, for example, is thus heightened to philosophical and aesthetic dimensions. Memory becomes a metaphor for the enigma of art, its inherent contrariety and simultaneous conciliation, an ambivalence, by which the mind of the recipient is both deluded and illuminated. Adorno, in his *Aesthetic Theory*, points out that 'the effect of artworks is that of recollection' (*Aesthetic*: 242), recollection being utopia, which knows neither actual adversities, nor separation between past, present and future. It is 'the eruption of the subject's collective essence, ... the anticipation of a condition beyond the diremption of the individual and the collective. The object of art's longing', Adorno continues, 'the reality of what is not, is metamorphosed in art as remembrance.'[14]

The artist healer's desperate restorative efforts are driven by this primordial longing for paradisiacal wholeness. Frank Hardy attains all the redemption that is attainable in an unredeemed world. In the state of transformation in which he appears in the play, his vacillations between hope and despondency, self-assurance and self-doubt are resolved in that they are remembered, and thereby transcended: they are present, though no longer existent as immediate split reality. In aesthetic terms, the subject's contrariness is resolved in the objectivity of artistic expression; in the aesthetic experience, the dialectic unity of subject and object is restored. The artwork's prevalent objectivity is embodied in the thing expressed; but its very objectivity demands the artist's subjectivity. Reciprocally, the artist sacrifices his subjectivity to the object of expression: the what and the how are in need of each other. Art's dialectical balance of opposites finds its analogue in the relationship between artwork and artist. Finally, the mediating character of both art and artist calls for the dialectic relation between artist, artwork and audience. Their unity illuminates the elusive moments of aesthetic experience, an experience, in the faith healer's description, 'of exultation, of consummation'.[15] Each part of the triad, in its own way, realizes the utopia of peace that Adorno defines as 'the state of distinctness without domination, with the distinct participating in each other'.[16] Not without reason does Friel choose a wedding guest as the faith healer's crucial object of healing. But ironically, to preclude any proud, delusive positing, the healing fails. With the paralysis persisting, the faith healer's self-sacrifice, 'that final, impossible chance',[17] leads to his own spiritual restoration. From his very deficiency he draws the ability to become whole, according to the 'ancient topos', quoted by Adorno, of 'healing the wound with the sword that afflicted it' (*Aesthetic:* 134). Self-sacrifice turns out to be the ultimate expression of personal endurance, while persistence in the face of despair indicates true self-identity.

Like the other characters of the play, Frank Hardy is speaking from an 'autonomous space, reflecting nothing beyond itself', as Thomas Kilroy suggests.[18] It is the 'Nowhere Land' of redemption – the intermediately human sphere of aesthetic experience. This space is indefinable, 'neither reality, nor dreams',[19] its intermediate status making it essential to human reality by saving it from utter negativity. In the play, this finds dramatic expression in the fact that by being imparted to an audience, the faith healer's introspection is simultaneously an act of self-revelation. The ultimate, intrepid self-surrender to an unknown and thus threatening other that Frank Hardy – *nomen est omen* – recalls, is reiterated and transformed in that it is performed. Such self-surrender of a different order, no less ruthless and dramatic than the one recollected, includes the author's own self-exposure to uncertainty and possible failure in his endeavour to communicate the incommunicable (*Essays* 68). *Faith Healer* mimetically expresses the philosophical idea of the subject giving itself over to a non-identical object and thereby effecting its own liberation from the bonds of its myths, its false identifications and fatal totalizations.

Finally rejecting all finalities, the faith healer casts himself away, as it were, so as to become whole in himself, to gain true identity, the identity of the nonidentical. Rather than representing a particular, delimitable entity, it denotes the dual attitude of criticism and faith, as the dynamic power within a living process. This potentiality unites past, present and future in that it is the openness to face what is, to comprehend its context of *being* through critical analysis and, through faith in infinite possibility, to 'create it anew' (*Essays* 67).

Adorno has said that 'the idea that consciousness kills, for which art supposedly provides unimpeachable testimony ... [is] a foolish cliché' (*Aesthetic:* 174). Thus the faith healer's performed recollection demonstrates restoration from within, because of, and despite, the refracted human mind. Critics of *Faith Healer* have commented upon the liminality of the minds of its characters. But of the three, the faith healer alone is able to assume, in Adorno's phrase, 'a position at least minimally outside the thrall of existence'.[20] While his wife Grace has taken her life in the utter negativity of despair, Teddy the manager survives by virtue of his natural soundness and unquestioning faith. It makes him a mediator among the outer necessities of life, while the faith healer, from his (literally) critical position, aims to mediate between deficiency and wholeness as between the physical and the metaphysical. However, the majority of the sufferers come to the faith healer to find ease and cheap consolation rather than healing as re-creation that involves the pain and happiness of transformation. They prefer their 'sealed anguish' to the risks of self-deliverance, the dynamics of death and renewal, that truth-seeking implies. 'In their hearts they had come not to be cured but for confirmation that they were incurable.'[21] Their curable disease becomes their myth; their myth-making is their incurable disease.

In the play, the uncertainty and possible failure of faith healing is discreetly opposed to the mock-certainty of the assured message that excludes the possibility of difference. Art as faith healing is not the calculable, tangible result of immediate directing. Since absolute truth, as the object of faith, is incomprehensible, faith, too, becomes indefinable. Nonetheless, to make itself known, faith must be performed, by which means it reveals its duality and its simultaneous mediation of thought and action, of rationality and emotion, ultimately of the finite and the infinite. The consciousness of its inherent split gives faith its identity: fissured and yet whole. It is the paradox of faith's 'necessary uncertainty', which relates it so closely to art.[22] Because inconceivable truth is inexpressible in direct conceptual language, its mediation is only possible through tricky assimilation, through artful mimesis: the mimesis of art. In an interview with Fintan O'Toole about *Faith Healer* in 1982, Friel pointed to 'the element of the charlatan that there is in all creative work' (*Essays* 111) In that sense, Adorno, too, writes of the truth-seeker: 'the unnaive thinker knows how far he remains from the object of his thinking, and yet he must always talk as if he had it entirely. This brings him to the point of clowning. He must not deny his clownish traits, least of all since they alone can give him hope for what is denied him' (*Dialectics:* 14).

Suspecting himself of 'masquerading', of being a 'con man', a 'mountebank', the introspective Frank Hardy, therefore, is both right and wrong. He must keep promising without being able to keep his promise. But as long as he is conscious that there is no other way of telling the truth than by conning, he is a con man in an unorthodox sense: not 'one who robs and swindles by means of confidence', as the Oxford English Dictionary explains, but one in whom to confide, whose 'make-believe' is so accomplished that the semblance of truth reveals truth as semblance: 'the semblance of the illusionless' to use the Adornian term (*Aesthetic:* 132). 'Con man' thus becomes a metaphor for the ambivalence of the artist as a mediator of enigmatic truth. Double-faced as he must be for truth's sake, the con man / artist is simultaneously redeemed by his 'attempt to see and present all things as they would present themselves from the point of view of salvation'.[23] 'Con', according to Roget's *Thesaurus of English words and phrases*, has a multiplicity of connotations: to know, scan, examine, cognize, as well as the negation and negativity of these verbs of cognition: not to know, deceive, defraud; and, astonishingly or not, it also means: putting to memory. Like the artist healer and his medium, 'con' dialectically re-unites knowledge and confidence, thereby implicating the enigmatic quality of the cognition of truth. The artist, with his conning neither-nor, posits the impossible and negates it as impossibility. From a perspective very similar to Friel's, Adorno has paraphrased the sacred song of art as 'the sound of peace testifying that the establishment of peace has failed, with the dream of it unfailing'.[24] In *Give Me Your Answer, Do!* art's liberating enchantment (genially manifested through the incorporation of 'On Wings of Song' as one of the play's central metaphors) has the power to win over what Adorno terms 'the spell' of the status quo. It is, in Adorno's words, the 'promise of reconciliation in the midst of the unreconciled' (*Aesthetic:* 33). As imagined experience of mankind's age-old utopia, it is the driving force of life, mimetically represented in art.

By various metaphors, Friel has called to the stage the virtual Fifth Province of the mind, in which the dialectic experience of realized utopia takes place. In *Faith Healer*, it shows itself with special distinction as almost transcended fragmentation. A process towards further distance, towards lightness, towards a place in which the darkness of existence is included and yet fully transmuted, is discernible in Friel's subsequent plays of artistic self-reflection. Adorno, with regard to Beckett, describes this liminal place as follows: 'The slightest difference between nothingness and coming to rest would be the haven of hope, the no man's land between the border posts of being and nothingness' (*Dialectics:* 381). It is this place of self-identity, of reconciliation with the non-identical, from which the faith healer speaks to us. To himself it may be a dream-like place, while as work of art, *Faith Healer* shows and effects a 'second order' of reality: 'magic, freed from the lie of being truth'.[25]

---

[1] John Millington Synge, *Plays*, ed. Ann Saddlemyer (Oxford: Oxford University Press, 1980): 103. Subsequent references appear parenthetically in the text.

[2] Theodore W. Adorno, *Aesthetic Theory*, trans. Robert Hullot-Kentor (London: Athlone Press, 1999): 54. Subsequent references appear parenthetically in the text as *Aesthetic* followed by a page number.

[3] Friedrich Nietzsche, *Twilight of the Gods* and *The Anti-Christ*, trans. R.J. Hollingdale (London: Penguin, 2003): 49.

[4] Brian Friel, *Brian Friel: Essays, Diaries, Interviews: 1964-1999*. Christopher Murray, ed. (London: Faber and Faber, 1999): 67. Subsequent references appear parenthetically in the text as *Essays*, followed by a page number.

[5] James W. Flannery, *W.B. Yeats and the Idea of a Theatre: The Early Abbey in Theory and Practice* (New Haven, Conn: Yale University Press, 1989): 23-4.

[6] Theodore W. Adorno, *Negative Dialectics*, trans. E. B. Ashton (London: Routledge, 1996): 56. Subsequent references appear in the text as *Dialectics* followed by a page number.

[7] Nietzsche, 33.

[8] T.F. Hoad, ed., *The Concise Dictionary of English Etymology* (Oxford: Oxford University Press, 1987): 123.

[9] *Faith Healer*, 1979; *Molly Sweeney*, 1994; *Give me your Answer, Do!* +1997; *Performances*, 2003.

[10] Ulf Dantanus, *Brian Friel: A Study* (London: Faber and Faber, 1988): 172.

[11] Anthony Roche, *Contemporary Irish Drama: From Beckett to McGuinness* (Dublin: Gill & Macmillan, 1994): 109.

[12] Nicholas Grene, *The Politics of Irish Drama: Plays in Context from Boucicault to Friel* (Cambridge: Cambridge University Press, 1999): 3.

[13] Declan Kiberd, *Inventing Ireland: The Literature of the Modern Nation* (London: Vintage, 1996): 631-2.

[14] Adorno, 1999, 131-2. 'Diremption', according to the *Oxford English Dictionary*, is 'a forcible separation'.

[15] Brian Friel, *Selected Plays* (London: Faber and Faber, 1990): 333.

[16] Brian O'Connor, ed., *The Adorno Reader* (Oxford: Blackwell, 2000): 140.

[17] Friel, 337.

[18] Thomas Kilroy, 'Theatrical Text and Literary Text', *The Achievement of Brian Friel*, ed., Alan Peacock (Gerrards Cross: Colin Smythe, 1993): 101.

[19] Brian Friel, *Selected Stories* (Oldcastle: Gallery Press, 1979): 109.

[20] Quoted in *Languages of the Unsayable: The Play of Negativity in Literature and Literary Theory*, eds Sanford Budick and Wolfgang Iser (Stanford: Stanford University Press, 1996): 152.

[21] Friel, 1990, 337.

[22] Brian Friel, *Give Me Your Answer, Do* (Oldcastle: Gallery Press, 1997): 79.

[23] Adorno, quoted in Budick and Iser, 152.
[24] T. W. Adorno, 'Rede über Lyrik und Gesellschaft', *Noten zur Literatur,* I-IV (Frankfurt: Suhrkamp, 1998): 54. Translated by author.
[25] T.W. Adorno, *Minima Moralia. Reflexionen aus dem beschädigten Leben* (Frankfurt: Suhrkamp, 1969): 298. Translated by author.

9 | 'A voice and little else': talking, writing and singing in *The Gigli Concert*

Alexandra Poulain

Tom Murphy's theatre is eminently word-based, and pays extreme attention to the fluctuating rhythms of dialogue and monologue, and the individual variations in the handling of the spoken word. However, it also manifests a constant distrust of language. Language is the instrument with which social institutions shape individual consciousnesses, performing in each individual what the French legal philosopher Pierre Legendre calls a 'social capture of subjectivity': 'The speaking being is spoken, he is spoken by the discourse of institutions, by dogmatizing discourse. Even before he is born, every individual is spoken, just because institutions exist and work.'[1] Murphy shows how 'dogmatizing discourse' surfaces in individual voices, endowing speech with the fixity of the written text. Institutions *are* texts, and one of the aims of the hero's quest is to break free from such texts and find his own voice. Such a process, however, is complicated by the very limitations of language as logos. Murphy's characters are all in search of meaning, but they sometimes find that what they are seeking to apprehend is beyond the reach of words – the dimension of the sacred, the *mysterium tremendum* which can be experienced intuitively but ultimately remains unknowable.

Murphy's great heroic plays: *The Morning After Optimism* (1971); *The Sanctuary Lamp* (1975); *The Gigli Concert* (1983); *Too Late for Logic* (1989); are all structured according to the pattern of traditional initiation, in which the key experience is the candidate's symbolical death and rebirth to a more complete self. As Mircea Eliade has shown, the experience of death, often metaphorized as a descent into Hell or into an abyss, takes the candidate back to original chaos – the paradoxical, atemporal instant which precedes cosmogony:

the novice's regress to the pre-natal stage is meant to make him contemporary with the creation of the world. He no longer lives in the maternal womb, as he used to before his biological birth, but in cosmic Night, waiting for 'dawn', that is, Creation. In order to become a new man, he must re-experience cosmology.[2]

In the course of this experience, the novice acquires the knowledge of the dead and is initiated into the mysteries of the sacred, of death itself, and of sexuality. In Murphy's drama the motif of the descent into the abyss recurs obsessively, with fresh implications: the abyss marks the barrier between the known world, which can be explored and expressed with words, and that which lies beyond words. To re-emerge from the abyss his hero needs to be delivered (in every sense of the term) from language, a preoccupation which makes his drama vitally contemporary. In *The Gigli Concert*, the play in which these issues are addressed most consistently and daringly, singing — the hybrid articulation of text and music — is envisaged as a possible alternative to logos, and a means of leaving it behind.

The play starts as farce, and playfully rewrites the Faustian myth, freely borrowing from Marlowe's and Goethe's plays. JPW, the protagonist, is a rather pathetic English healer of sorts who has settled in Ireland in order to practice 'dynamatology', an occult science which parodies psychoanalysis, and whose basic principle is that 'anything is possible'. The play starts as JPW receives his first-ever patient, a wealthy Irish property developer whose obsessive dream is 'to sing like Gigli'. Thus an Irish Faust appeals to JPW's English Mephistopheles, who promises total success in exchange for blind submission to the demands of dynamatology. The two embark on a series of 'sessions' which are brutally interrupted when the Irish man, just as he is nearing his goal, suddenly takes fright and withdraws from the whole venture; he then leaves a desperate JPW, who has just learned that his lover is terminally ill, to pick up the challenge and sing with Gigli's voice. Parts are thus redistributed halfway through the play, and in the final scene JPW, recast as Faust, parodies the famous tirade of Marlowe's Dr Faustus: 'This night I'll conjure. If man can bend a spoon with beady steadfast eye, I'll sing like Gigli or I'll die.'[3] Murphy allows the supernatural to appear on stage in the final scene, changing the aesthetic rules of the play at the last minute; before walking off JPW throws open the window of his studio onto a new world, where former laws hold no sway.

The Irish man's first cues, spoken offstage as he stands behind JPW's door, draw a misleading parallelism between speaking and singing:

Irish Man: Mr King?
JPW: ... Who is it? ... Who is that?
Irish Man: Can I come in?
JPW: Pardon?

Irish Man: To talk.
JPW: To what?
Irish Man: (*muffled*) To sing (166).

The following scenes, however, display the radical difference between talking and singing. At first sight dynamatology, a New Age version of psychoanalysis, seems to attach great importance to speech. In his study of *Gigli* and *Bailegangaire*, Nicholas Grene points out that 'at a very early stage of writing the play, Murphy did draft scenes in which the character who was to become the Irish Man consults a perfectly ordinary psychiatrist.'[4] When Murphy created the character of JPW and the concept of dynamatology, however, he set out to question the very foundations of the psychoanalytic paradigm. The notion of psychoanalysis is at first unambiguously rejected by JPW:

Irish Man: I haven't much time for psychiatrists – psychologists.
JPW: Candid opinion? Intellectual philistines. Conflicting approaches, contradictory schools. And Freud! (170)

Dynamatology, then, must be something different altogether — and indeed, in the course of the preliminary interview, JPW promises that his patient will need only six days and six 'sessions' to achieve his goal. When sessions do start, however, the reference to psychoanalytical practices is all too obvious. All sessions take place in JPW's studio, furnished only with a couch and armchair. The dynamatological 'movement' is presented as a kind of sect — a portrait of 'Steve, our founder and leader', is reverently displayed on one wall, perhaps a hint at the cult of personality which Lacan inspired and encouraged — and JPW's jargon is fairly impenetrable for the uninitiated. JPW is in fact a caricature of the incompetent psychoanalyst: during the first interview with his patient, perhaps under the stress of this unprecedented situation, he blathers away in pseudo-clinical vocabulary, and seems more concerned to come up with a diagnosis than to listen to his interlocutor, so that within a few moments the Irish man is first declared psychotic, then alcoholic. He is impatient and inattentive, systematically asks the wrong questions, and imposes arbitrary rules and often interrupts, forcing his patient to listen to his own reminiscences and fantasies.

Just like psychoanalysis, dynamatology is indeed based on verbal exchange: the patient is supposed to talk about himself, and to search his memory for childhood recollections. In the course of the first few sessions, however, the Irish man repeatedly points out how difficult talking has of late become for him: 'I was never a great one for talking. Now I'd prefer to walk a mile in the other direction than say how yeh or fuck yeh to anyone.'(173) In the face of such reluctance, the inexhaustible JPW is only too glad to change parts with his patient and to do most of the talking himself. That the analyst should be infinitely more loquacious than the patient is of course an element of farce and parody – but Murphy goes beyond mere caricature when he stages the Irish man's mechanisms of resistance, and plays subtly with the psychoanalytic paradigm. When the Irish man actually starts talking, he substitutes Gigli's memoirs for his own memory, appropriating the text of Gigli's autobiography and reciting it as if it were his own story. The result is a sort of literary ventriloquism, the character talking not only about someone else, but in someone else's voice (in the sense of 'narrative voice'). Instead of analytic discourse, which is produced spontaneously and feeds on the various accidents of speech (verbal slips, digressions, free associations, etc) he delivers a pre-written, already fixed text which exists independently of the play and suffers no improvisation. At first, the insertion of heterogeneous textual material in the dialogue is a source of comedy:

> **Irish Man:** I was born with a voice and little else.
> **JPW:** Naked we came into the world (176).

To the Irish man's opening, borrowed from Gigli's autobiography, JPW spontaneously responds with another quotation, and the flow of verbal exchange is suddenly frozen into an absurd juxtaposition of 'selected pieces'. At this stage, neither JPW nor the audience has yet realized that the man is quoting from Gigli's autobiography, but his cue smacks of melodrama and literary artifice, and quite naturally calls forth another cliché. The situation is emphatically theatrical: the two characters are like actors speaking 'their' lines – lines, that is, which precisely are not theirs. Beyond comedy, however, the Irish man's usurpation of Gigli's text, which he uses as a screen to avoid speaking in his own name, in fact invalidates the very principle of psychoanalysis. As the Irish man recites someone else's memories instead of probing his own, his speech loses its therapeutic value and becomes a symptom in its own right, signalling his alienation.

In spite of an accumulation of obstacles (the analyst's crass incompetence and the patient's fierce resistance), the treatment somehow works, and it seems at first that the impossible work schedule established by JPW in the first scene will in fact be respected. In the course of the fourth session, the Irish man drops his mask for the first time, and evokes a particularly painful personal memory, after which he collapses in hysterics. This is the character's great dramatic moment, when he eventually 'finds his own voice' – in the first editions of the play a stage direction specified: *'the performance an atonal aria.'* It is also the turning-point of the play, as the Irish man, freed from the weight of the past, is cured of his obsession and returns to his usual life; his wife, who had deserted the family home, returns, and everything is back to normal. The play apparently comes to a sudden resolution, in keeping with the dusty conventions of a century-old psychological theatre – re-emergence of an ancient trauma, verbal catharsis, return to order. What, then, may be the point of the parody of psychoanalysis is unclear, since Murphy eventually seems to validate its principles: by gaining access to speech the patient exorcizes his illness, and the symptom (his desire to sing) disappears.

Access to speech, however, was not what the Irish man had set out to gain, and it is repeatedly suggested in the play that singing expresses precisely that which escapes the grasp of words:

> **Irish Man:** Like, you can talk forever, but singing. Singing, d'yeh know? The only way to tell people.
> **JPW:** What?
> **Irish Man:** (*shrugs, he does not know*) Who you are? (179)

Murphy gets hold of a cliché (singing goes beyond words) and explores its theatrical implications. The strange title recalls that the play, punctuated as it is by operatic arias sung by Gigli, is really a hybrid between theatre and music. At first the songs occur extradiegetically as a musical backdrop; but on his third session the Irish man brings his Gigli record with him and plays it to JPW, and from that moment the music is woven into the fabric of the plot. Finally, in the last scene, the actor who plays JPW sings in play-back to Gigli's recorded voice. Thus the text of the play is constantly interrupted, counterpointed and sometimes contradicted by the songs, and Murphy's strategy in this respect is both extremely subtle and paradoxical. A song is the meeting-point of text and music, but according to the Irish man, the words in Gigli's arias are of little import:

> **JPW:** Do you know what he was singing?
> **Irish Man:** You don't have to! –
> **JPW:** Did you understand the words?
> **Irish Man:** You don't –
> **JPW:** What opera was that piece from?
> **Irish Man:** You don't have to know! (201)

A close reading of the play, however, reveals that the words of the arias, and the contexts in which they are sung in the original operas, match the play's dramatic situations very precisely. Some songs provide ironic comment on the action; thus, in the beginning of the play, while the curtain is rising on JPW's dingy studio, Gigli sings 'O Paradiso', from Meyerbeer's *L'Africana* – Vasco de Gama has been shipwrecked on the African coast and discovers a dazzling land of plenty. On many occasions singing expresses whatever remains unsaid in the dialogue: all the feelings and emotions that the characters are reluctant or simply unable to verbalize. The most poignant example is the moment when JPW learns that Mona has cancer; at first he remains petrified, and only after she has left does he give vent to his raw desperation: 'I love! I love you! Fuck you! I love! Fuck you! I love! – I love! Fuck you – fuck you! I love...' (235). This is as close as JPW ever gets to declaring his love for Mona, and it is more animal roar than articulate speech; yet at the end of the scene, with Gigli's voice, JPW sings the aria 'Tu che a Dio spiegasti l'ali', Edgardo's song at the end of Donizetti's *Lucia de Lamermoor*: Edgardo promises the dead Lucia that he will join her in Heaven, and then kills himself. The aria is at once a song of despair, a sublime declaration of love and a challenge to death – precisely the feelings which JPW experiences but fails to articulate. The songs, then, are crucially important in dramatic terms, but Murphy is obviously playing a dangerous game, as the contrapuntal effect of the arias partly depends on their referential value: the reasonably cultured spectator, who may not be familiar with the entirety of the operatic corpus, will necessarily miss out on at least some of the implications of the songs. Murphy thus deliberately exposes his audience to the disturbing experience of a loss of meaning, and calls in question the aesthetics of psychological theatre, which tends towards the completeness of meaning and the exaltation of speech (every secret is disclosed, everything is revealed, verbalized, theorized about.) This formal questioning of the primacy of speech is pursued in the very fabric of the play by JPW himself, when he sets forth the principles of dynamatology.

Halfway through the play, just as the Irish man is nearing his goal, JPW sets out to warn him against the danger of the 'I-am-who-am syndrome'. His great tirade starts with a very irreverent parody of the Bible where the God of the Old Testament and Christ are dismissed off-handedly in burlesque fashion:

> **JPW:** You see, Benimillo, God created the world in order to create himself. Us. We are God. But that neatly done he started to make those obscure and enigmatic statements. Indeed his son did a lot of rather the same thing. The Last Supper, for instance: the wine, the conversation, *Jewish* wine being passed around. (*He rises unsteadily.*) Christ standing up, 'In a little while you will see me, in a little while you will not see me.' They must have thought the man was drunk. But he had learned the lingo from his father (211).

The first sentences are stated casually as if they were self-evident, but they really question the very foundations of Judeo-Christian theology: in JPW's version of Genesis the subject is not prior to the object He creates, but the Creator and his creature are one and the same. This would not be terribly original in itself, if it were not for the specific role which JPW attributes to language; contrary to what is proclaimed in the Gospel according to John, here the Word only intervenes after the completion of Genesis, as a sort of mystifying, superfluous paraphrase: no word precedes the existence of man and dictates its limitations. The parodic rewriting of the Last Supper also tends to destabilize Christ's Word, presented as an alcoholic jumble of stupidities – here Murphy is very close to the spirit of Voltaire's *Philosophical Dictionary*, which also provides a deliberately literal reading of Christian myths, the better to ridicule them. The word 'lingo' completes the demystification of the Holy Word, reducing the sacred text which emanates from the deity to a vague jargon, just good enough to make an impression on men; by the end of this prologue, it has been stripped of any privileged status.

In the second movement of his tirade, JPW at last starts on the specific question of the 'I-am-who-am syndrome':

> God taking his stroll in the Garden, as we were told, and passing by innocent Adam, he would nod and say (*He nods and winks.*) 'I am who am.' And that was fine until one day, Adam, rather in the manner of Newton, was sitting under a tree and an apple fell on his head, jolting him into thought. 'Whatever can he mean, said Adam, 'I am who am'?' And he waited until the next time God came strolling by, and he said, 'Excuse me' — or whatever they said in those days. 'I must find out.' And he put the question to God. But God said, 'Out, out!' 'I only asked', said Adam, but God said 'Out!' And, naturally, after such rude, abrupt and despotic eviction, the wind was taken out of Adam's intellectual sails: not surprising that he was not up to pursuing the matter. Which is a pity. Because, the funny thing, God had got it wrong. Because what does it mean, 'I am who am'? It means this is me and that's that. This is me and I am stuck with it. You see? Limiting. What God should have been saying of course, was 'I am who may be'. Which is a different thing, which makes sense — both for us and for God — which means, I am the possible, or if you prefer, I am the impossible (211).

Fintan O'Toole has remarked that the passage from 'I-am-who-am' to 'I-am-who-may-be' — from a tautological formulation to an open-ended one — expresses the thrust of Murphy's theatre as a whole, which aims at leaving the prewritten text of the old world for a new world in the making, a world of endless, as yet undefined possibilities.[5] Such is the meaning of the 'magic' to which JPW ultimately resorts in order to change apparently unchangeable natural laws, and sing in another man's voice.

Rewriting certain key Biblical episodes in his own way, JPW *de facto* brings about the shift from the old world to a new one, as yet unexplored. In one sweeping movement, and with characteristic casualness, his speech knits together a variety of myths: Adam driven out of Eden; Moses to whom God effectively says 'I am who am' as He hands him the Tables of the Law; even Newton whose incongruous presence here is due only to the cliché which associates him with an apple, the same fruit of knowledge as that which Adam was forbidden to taste. Such a speech ideally exemplifies the aesthetic implications of the 'I-am-who-may-be' frame of mind, since here Murphy takes every liberty with the text *par excellence*, the most fixed, granitic word — the Biblical Word itself. This burlesque rewriting is a way of invalidating a world in which speech can only be interpreted with reference to a system of set ideas, and is always turned into a 'stereotype' — 'carved in stone', just like the Ten Commandments on the Tables of the Law. Although he thinks he is addressing the Irish man, JPW is alone on stage when he speaks these lines, which thereby lose their theoretical dimension and become a sort of magic incantation to change the rules of the game, using words to escape the omnipotence of words. It paves the way for the final climactic moment of the play – JPW's magic song, which transgresses all the laws of the old world.

Magic, such as JPW defines it, is merely the refusal to consider that things are settled once and for all – the refusal to abide by the text, any text, not least the classic text of Marlowe's *Dr Faustus* which JPW burlesques:

> **JPW:** You are going to ask me what is magic. In a nutshell, the rearrangement and redirection of the orbits or trajectories of dynamatological whirlings, i.e., simply new mind over old matter. This night I'll conjure. If man can bend a spoon with beady steadfast eye, I'll sing like Gigli or I'll die (238).

The Faustian paradigm acquires its full potential here, as Faust damns himself forever in his attempt to act magically, and transgress the natural laws by making the impossible possible. In the Elizabethan context, the art of magic defies the divine order to impose its own laws, and Faust, who will not repent, inexorably damns himself. In *Gigli*, however, it is perhaps singing itself, more than magic, which constitutes absolute transgression. A song supports a text which echoes the original text of the Bible, but at the same time it is the instrument of the disappearance of that text. Both the Irish man and JPW insist that it is quite unnecessary to understand the words in order to enjoy the music, and indeed all the songs played during the show are sung in foreign languages, either Italian or French. Besides, lyrical singers tend to alter the vowels to produce a beautiful sound, especially in the high register of their voices, so that above the E natural it is practically impossible to distinguish between the various vowels: thus the intelligibility of the text is compromised, and the voice becomes almost instrumental. In his essay entitled *La voix du diable* (*The Devil's Voice*), the French historian Michel Poizat recalls that both Christianity and Islam were originally wary of music and singing, before they started to encourage it:

> Those two religions ... detect the face of the devil behind the transgression of the divine law which singing and music tend to commit – a transgression of that law of language which governs every individual and which the figure of the Word-God deifies. Indeed song and music tend either to dissolve language, to make it indistinguishable, or to exceed it, thereby engendering that lyrical *jouissance* which exceeds the experience of merely listening to the Word-God; the latter then finds itself confined in a place where it is bound to appear flawed, since an 'excess' of *jouissance*, or 'another' form of *jouissance*, takes hold of the subject.[6]

Thus the singing voice breaks free from the linguistic order, to the profit of an immediate, eminently sacrilegious *jouissance*. Singing engulfs the meaning of the text, thereby endangering the communal order, whose stability depends on the respect for the Law and for the Word which has dictated it. When he starts singing, JPW commits the ultimate transgression which frees him from the old world and its verbal foundations, and it is he, the smooth talker of the play, who dares to come face to face with the sacred without the mediation of the Text.

Indeed, while singing is transgressive in the context of religious orthodoxy, which only recognizes the law of the Word-God, it is considered as a privileged means of access to God in the mystical conception of religious praxis:

> Contrary to the 'orthodox' worshipper who postpones the promised enjoyment of God until after death and salvation, and who therefore conforms to the divine law to earn this salvation, the mystic wants to enjoy God now. His sacred project, then, is the transgression of the law of the Word, which he considers only as the ineffective human expression, or the debasement, of a divine law which transcends it. Whatever participates in such a transgression thus participates in the divine essence: voice and music are defined as its privileged instruments.[7]

JPW's spiritual adventure takes place at the crossroads of those two contradictory approaches: it is precisely because his singing is transgressive, and forces him to break free from the old world which has lost touch with the sacred, that it enables him to apprehend something of the *mysterium tremendum*, the unknowable which lies beyond the abyss and remains completely indefinite in the strange, elusive final scene:

> **JPW:** ... (*Orchestral introduction begins again*): Abyss sighted! All my worldly goods I leave to nuns! Leeep! (*Leap.*) pluh-unnge! (*Plunge. And a sigh of relief.*) Aah! Rebirth of ideals, return of self-esteem, future known.
>
> On cue, he sings the aria to its conclusion and collapses. (Gigli's voice; the recording he made solo, without bass and chorus.) JPW on the floor. The church clock chiming six a.m.
>
> **JPW:** Mama? Mama? Do not leave me in this dark (239).

The final moments of the play provide both resolution and a sense of redemption for JPW, but no revelation in the traditional sense of the word: nothing is explained, and JPW's final cue playfully echoes the feeling of the mystified audience as Murphy changes the rules of the game and suddenly flaunts the conventions of realism just before curtain fall. While the Irish man's speech is ventriloquized by Gigli's autobiographical voice, and fossilized into a pre-written text, JPW constantly works at subverting texts, playing with words and thus jerking the stereotype – the dead text – alive. He thus changes the text of the play itself, from a realistic to a fantastic one, when he sings with Gigli's singing voice – another case of ventriloquism, but one which entails not perpetual return to the old text, but radical novelty. When the aria 'O Paradiso' is heard again after JPW's final exit, it is no longer ironic, but expresses infinite possibility.

---

[1] Pierre Legendre, *L'inestimable objet de la transmission: Etude sur le principe généalogique en Occident* (Paris: Fayard, 2004): 75. Translation by author.

[2] Mircea Eliade, *Mythes, rêves et mystères* (Paris: Gallimard, 1957): 243. Translation by author.

[3] Tom Murphy, *Plays: Three* (London: Methuen, 1994): 238. Further quotations from *The Gigli Concert* will be referenced in the text.

[4] Nicholas Grene, 'Talking it through: *The Gigli Concert* and *Bailegangaire*', *Talking About Tom Murphy*, ed. Nicholas Grene (Dublin: Carysfort Press, 2002): 68.

[5] Fintan O'Toole, *Tom Murphy: The Politics of Magic,* 2nd ed. (London: Nick Hern Books, 1994): 219-21.

[6] Michel Poizat, *La voix du diable: La jouissance lyrique sacrée* (Paris: Métailié, 1991): 158. Translation by author.

[7] Poizat, 159.

10 | Spatializing the Renewal of Female Subjectivity in Marie Jones's *Women on the Verge of HRT*

Mária Kurdi

The upsurge of Irish drama by women during the last two decades is not only spectacular but has earned a well assured place for some authors and new masterpieces in the national canon. *The Field Day Anthology of Irish Writing V* contains a selection of contemporary works by female playwrights, which can be seen as representative of the thematically and technically varied and challenging achievement of this body of literature. The selection, edited by Anna McMullan and Caroline Williams, considers such perspectives as gender and ethnicity in mapping the terrain. Their critical introduction emphasizes that

> Women's writing for the theatre has contributed towards the diversity of models of theatrical practice, towards the search for new audiences, and towards the reworking of concepts of the family, of gender roles and of the nation, clearing a space in this art which has been so closely associated with 'the national identity' for the cultural representation of the complexity and diversity of women's lives and the expression of their creativity.[1]

The playwrights negotiate a male-dominated tradition by representing particular constraints of gender identity and culturally overdetermined images of femininity as well as inherited prejudices and restrictive stereotypes, highlighting also the manner of their perpetuation in the patriarchal society. It is through alternative, at times quite radically altered, ways of writing for the stage that they tap into the discourses, narratives, and practices which define or impact on the place and positioning of women in the various domains of social life in Ireland, both north and south of the border.

By foregrounding the intersection of internal and external worlds, theatrical space carries the potential to become a site for exploring the stages and processes of female self-construction and (re)gaining subjectivity. Several plays by Irish women deploy the conventions of setting and location strategically, underscoring the permeability of borders and the transformational function of edges and margins, evoking the psychic by the physical. In this way, they destabilize mimetic forms and those aspects of realistic dramaturgy, which imply the fixity of gender roles as well as the relations they are based on and which they reproduce in turn. One play included in the *Field Day V* selection, *Women on the Verge of HRT* (1995) by Marie Jones, addresses the delicate issue of women's experience of menopausal changes. This essay will discuss the links between space, gender and subjectivity in Jones's dramatic representation of her female protagonists' engagement with, and their interrogation of, the discourse of ageing with its embedded gender-bias. My understanding of the multifaceted role of space is informed, in the first place, by Joanne Tompkins's introduction to the special issue of *Modern Drama* on geographies in theatre. She contends that theatre space is 'most frequently studied in terms of the metaphoric meaning of a play's setting, rendered on stage by the interrelation of a number of "locations"' and she refers to the intersection of spatial studies with time and the body.[2] In addition, my analysis benefits from the inquiry of Gay McAuley, who argues that 'the way the space is conceived and organized, the kinds of space that are shown and/or evoked, the values and events associated with them are always of fundamental importance in the meaning conveyed' by a drama.[3]

Jones's earlier plays about women were written for the Charabanc Theatre Company in the 1980s, when she and fellow-members created their texts by closely studying the life of women and families in Northern Ireland during the Troubles. Written after the Charabanc connection, *The Hamster Wheel* (1990) re-examines the traditional obligation of women to look after sick or disabled people in the family or the larger community. Her subsequent play, *Women on the Verge of HRT*, is novel in that it is completely devoid of political images and the theme of related tensions. Nevertheless, aspects of politics emerge covertly since the play re-appropriates the search for individual freedom and forms of resistance to prevailing norms, and connects to the Jones canon through links with the immediately preceding one-man show entitled *A Night in November* (1994). In that work the male protagonist, Kenneth McCallister, sets out on a kind of spiritual journey. The centuries-old motif of the journey, expressed in countless literary pieces in many genres, in which the hero encounters the Other, is, in fact, a confrontation with the self, understood as the cultural self in modern times.[4] *A Night in November* manipulates this complex paradigm in the context of the postcolonial divisions and sectarian hostilities of Jones's home territory, Belfast. By the closing scene

Kenneth has progressed from narrow-minded tribalism to embracing a more inclusive and individualized sense of identity, the Protestant reconciled with the Irish side in him. *Women on the Verge of HRT* tackles borders and barriers, cultural, linguistic and personal, even more transgressively, reinforced by its setting in markedly different locations in each of its two acts. As indicated by the title itself, its female protagonists are travellers like Kenneth, but their trajectory is gender-specific: they have reached a crucial stage in life, menopause, and now are facing its othering and self-alienating implications.

At the beginning of *Women on the Verge of HRT,* the protagonists, Vera and Anna, have already gone from Belfast to Donegal, leaving their everyday lives behind. Act I takes place in The Viking House Hotel opened by the famous crooner Daniel O'Donnell in 1993, where he welcomes his numerous fans annually to a tea party. Act II happens outside, on the beach of the bay in the small hours of the following day. The contrasting locations accommodate a significant shift from the characters' socially determined view of the biological changes that undermine their confidence in being sexually attractive to a more individual perception. On the other hand, they spatialize the women's increasing need to redefine their femininity on new grounds.

In Act I, the bedroom setting is a recognizable social space. It is in a hotel where people have assembled for the tea party, which has become a regular event in contemporary Irish popular culture. A short film presented before the play itself begins reminds the audience of this. The event is heavily gendered, with the great majority of the participants being older women. This locates Jones's protagonists according to their place in the culture and explains, at least to an extent, why they seek this form of pastime. Vera ironically observes that ladies like themselves are 'just a big mass of middle-aged nobodies',[5] suggesting that the party may well turn out to be nothing but an occasion to face their mirror images in the other participants and become further alerted to the narrowing of the social space they inhabit. The comparatively small, unhomely hotel room where they are placed during the whole of Act I represents physical as well as ontological confinement. In addition, the obtrusive presence of a pair of narrow, convent-style single beds, which Vera and Anna will occupy for the night, marks out the room as an oppressively gendered arena, exposing the women's shared loneliness and that they are without sexual partners.

To quote Mary Russo, 'the cultural constructs of femininity and Womanness' and their normative power, which operate within the mechanism of the symbolic order,[6] render ageing women invisible once they do not fit the coercive, homogenizing ideal any more. Having internalized this through the usual ways of gender programming, Vera and Anna are portrayed experiencing their body as a site of uncertainty and humiliation. Their comments testify to an increasing measure of the 'tension, ambiguity, and duality' that characterize a 'woman's modalities of bodily comportment, motility, and spatiality' and underlie the tendency of thinking of her body as an object.[7] Vera's story about visiting the C&A clothing store expresses the feeling that it is hardly possible, even for herself, to have an unmediated, untainted view of her body: 'I stood in the changing room ... and I didn't know what to buy. I just stood there looking in the mirror and I says; Vera, you don't know what you are supposed to look like anymore' (13).

The conventional perception of menopause is that it is a kind of failure, which maintains a negative view of ageing. The protagonists' condition as women nearing menopause is almost a pathology, shaping their attitudes in ways that alienate them from their own personal history because of its being inscribed on the surface of the body. Vera envisages a male doctor who shrugs his shoulders while attributing her emotional instability to the biological change without as much as taking a closer look at her. For her part, Anna describes her own menopausal symptoms through the lens of her dismayed husband and other people, barely mentioning how they really affect herself:

> Well, there's the flushes for a start. I used to flare up like a beetroot. God. Dead embarrassing in company. It used to drive Marty mad. And then he would whisper to whoever was in our company 'It's the change.' He wouldn't even use the word. He might as well as been saying leprosy (19).

Influenced as well as manipulated by recycled images and categories, the protagonists feel on the verge of self-abnegation as they lose the foundations of their womanhood and its cultural meaning. Their experience is deeper than merely being on the verge of considering the hormone replacement tablet as a possible remedy for the feeling and diagnosis of being different.

Vera and Anna's conversation, which revolves around the problem of ageing and a corollary of related anxieties, foregrounds an even more subtle kind of imprisonment. They are restricted by the discursive space regulated and made available to them through the categorizing practices of the patriarchal culture they live in. This is made manifest through their persistent use of a received vocabulary, their habitual choice of stereotypes and clichés to refer to the signs and consequences of menopause, which are current in the operations of the symbolic system of language 'indebted to, induced and imposed by the social realm' as Julia Kristeva expounds.[8] Vera underscores the deficiencies and limitations of the discourse of ageing with regard to women, finding it embarrassing to speak about sex and men, as it might make her ridiculous in a society which has not developed an adequate language to deal with these aspects of older women's lives. For want of the latter, she describes their situation by punctuating her talk with expressions and spatial metaphors, which visualize a certain ongoing tendency in the public mind to devalue women, especially when they are no longer young. References to commodification and exchange rates complicate the prospect of being soon thrown 'on the sexual scrap heap' like a disused article or on having to 'book into a sex hospice' (5) because of being forced to retire from a life still sexually active. Furthermore, Vera compares older women's attempts to find a male partner to last minute 'panic buying', which may easily result in 'grab[bing] something you don't want', and warns Anna that 'whether you like it or not we have passed our sell-by date' (5, 13). Anna, in turn, rehashes clichés that are rooted in the centuries-old tendency of disciplining women: 'you put up and shut up ... Most women accept that they get old' (15). There is another side to the protagonists' talk, especially to Vera's, however. While undoubtedly reflecting an amount of tension and ambiguity, it seasons despair with humour by drawing on the rich potential inherent in language to transgress the boundaries of register and style, and expose the absurdities of patriarchal logic.

Considering their non-verbal communication, Vera and Anna seem to represent contrasted ways of responding to their overdetermined personal experience of sexual marginalization, which has much to do with their respective social positions in terms of marital status. Vera is divorced and single, whereas Anna is a married woman. Vera, following the conventions, distinguishes Anna from herself on the grounds of the positive fact that she, at least, has a permanent relationship with a man in her life, her husband. On the surface, their physical movements underscore this difference. In the Dubbeljoint production where the playwright herself was playing the role of Vera, it was her restless coming and going from room to bathroom and back that offered a telling contrast to Anna's calm sitting or lying in the one place for most of the time. Yet the action reveals even more subtle implications of the protagonists' attitude to the changes that threaten women with the passing of time, and demonstrates that they are not so much antithetical as complementary characters. Discussing varieties of female protest against the pressures created by the conventional construction of femininity, Susan Bordo claims that 'the language of femininity to protest the conditions of the female world' usually involves the ambiguity of conforming to the ideals of the patriarchal culture and memorizes 'the feel and conviction of lack'.[9] In *Women on the Verge of HRT,* this is brought home by having Vera and Anna unwittingly reinforce aspects of the biased social treatment of and commentary on ageing as gendered phenomena. Jones exposes Vera's application of expensive facial creams and wearing a kind of nightdress that cost a fortune as a means to resist as well as combat the inevitable effects of corporeal changes. This way, however, she merely succumbs to the seductive discourse of fashion which promises that the signs of ageing can be erased through complying with the cultural expectation that 'women constantly work on the transformation of their body' to improve it.[10]

Anna's escape mechanisms are a voluminous novel about other people's love affairs, and the admiration of the crooner, Daniel, whose romantic songs and kindness as host are a treasured source of consolation for her, keeps her going. Her evasiveness about her own problem is a silent protest against the stifling of her voice following her attempts to be open and speak honestly with her husband:

> I had a few drinks on me one night and I said, 'Marty, why do you never make love to me anymore?' and he got up and walked out of the room and didn't speak for about a week. Too frightened in case I brought it up again. So I never. So that's that' (16)

Because of her husband's indifference, Anna resorts to complacent notions about marriage as social convenience, which may even include some meagre compensation for a restricted sense of freedom. In terms of Bordo's analysis, the attitudes of both Vera and Anna reflect traditional ways of normalizing and disciplining the female body in the patriarchal society. Thus, the conventionally posited difference between the single and the married woman on the threshold of menopause is thoroughly relativized by Jones. Adding to the overall irony, their host, the singer is a middle-aged person himself, whose songs evoke nostalgic memories rather than vital emotions, and his parties are occasions to boost his fame at least as much as offer genuine entertainment for his female guests.

Yet the pop singer's hotel in Kincasslagh constitutes a crucial staging post on the journey of Vera and Anna, because it allows them to confront the self-alienating implications of their situation more acutely than before. This is possible because it differs from the everyday social reality they have left behind, and opens up a new space, a performance space. Early in the play, the protagonists seek to use the alternative languages of song and dance, though within the four walls of the bedroom, this underscores the ambiguity inherent in their respective protests articulated through the symbolic system and its practices. When they break out dancing, they enjoy liberation only for some seconds. With the sense of frustration looming not far behind, the attempt at non-verbal self-expression comes to a sudden end, with Vera exclaiming how split she is between the impulse to move and the thoughts that press her down. Not unlike Friel's Mundy sisters in *Dancing at Lughnasa*, Vera and Anna are in need of an alternative performance space to refashion their subjectivity, away from the gender-specific claustrophobia and discursive parameters of their predicament.

The hotel, which is set in a coastal part of Donegal known for its alluring beauty, may become permeable by values other than narrowly understood social realities. To explore this aspect, Jones uses a third character in the drama, the bar waiter, whose name, Fergal, is originally associated with choice. He acts as mediator between outside and inside, and is also a surrogate for his employer, Daniel, whose style of singing he vividly brings to stage, by means perhaps of a record-player in actual productions, to enhance the magic of performance. The enchanting landscape with the sea appears to be a surreal, longed-for place in the song which Fergal presents in the spirit and manner of Daniel, walking among the audience. This implies crossing the boundary between conventionally distinct spaces in the theatre and complicates the theatrical situation, opening up multiple levels of reality.[11] The performance gives voice to and transcends the gap between dreams and actual situation, inspiring Vera and Anna, both audience and characters here, to explore forces beyond the symbolic realm. Anna remarks that '[w]hen you have all this around you it does help you to see into yourself', and Vera's concluding song claims space for the free articulation of desires and needs through the transforming power of the imagination: 'I want to be the one in the story / The one who has fallen in love' (13, 20).

It is just an alternative territory that the setting of Act II of *Women on the Verge of HRT* represents. In sharp contrast with the earlier physical confinement, the characters reappear on the shore of the sea shortly before dawn, the time of mysterious transformation, in a liminal space opening up toward distances, suggesting freedom and possibility. The offstage ruling presence and influence of the male singer is replaced by that of the wailing ghost of the Banshee, a solitary female spirit widely associated with mourning. Discussing the role and meaning of this supernatural figure in Irish folklore, Patricia Lysaght claims that the Banshee haunts the living by her lamentations and cries of grief, supposed to signal approaching death to the community so that people, especially certain families, should prepare themselves for loss. The Banshee's favourite time of haunting is 'the dark or grey hours: midnight, dawn and dusk', while she prefers to dwell in places near water, where the sound travels easily, and there may be natural formations like strange-looking pieces of rock.[12] These mythical links with the landscape are rendered visible by the non-naturalistic *mise-en-scène* of the second act of the play. Furthermore, a version of the Banshee's 'tale of difference' involving her ruthless betrayal by a male fairy called the Pooka once she had grown old makes Vera recognize her as a fellow victim of marginalization and stereotyping: 'She could have been just like us. [...] You were not born a banshee. They made you a banshee' (22). Margaret Llewellyn-Jones suggests that the spirit's wailing performs the displaced voice of Vera and Anna, whose sexual identity is threatened by annihilation during menopause. In this sense, the Banshee acts as 'a harbinger of death'.[13]

Throughout the centuries, folklore images and figures are known to have developed socio-historically determined variants. As with the complexity of the female figures representing the country in the Irish cultural tradition, the role of the Banshee in *Women on the Verge* is not the foreboding of loss exclusively, but may well be connected with a more ancient dimension of inherited beliefs. Lysaght clarifies that the origin of the Banshee goes back to the mythical sovereignty goddess, who symbolizes the land itself and its power to bestow identity; therefore the songs and stories about her 'were always tinged with pride of the homeland'. Drawing on such a genealogy, Lysaght concludes that the Banshee remained a kind of guardian or patron 'concerned with the fortunes of her people'.[14] This function is evoked in other Irish texts, such as Anne Devlin's *After Easter* (1994), where the central female character is haunted by a Banshee-like apparition on her journey towards greater self-awareness, involving death and rebirth.

Jones's strategy situates her woman protagonists in the Banshee-controlled-and-protected mythical borderline space between land and sea, where they are both audience and performers in a series of fast-moving, imaginary scenes. This part of the drama displays heightened theatricality, manifesting the drive towards the latent energies of the semiotic and maternal which characterizes a lot of women's drama, carrying the potential to 'explode the symbolic'.[15] The Banshee's grotesque screams introduce an action which, being outside social rules and normalizing discourses, transforms the shoreline into a pluralized space of performance, establishing the world of the carnival. Fergal's former role of mediator between inside and outside becomes stretched; he enacts an androgynous shape-shifter or trickster who transgresses gender, space, and time to impersonate offstage characters. Writing about the female grotesque, Russo claims that 'the masks and voices of carnival resist, exaggerate, and destabilize the distinctions and boundaries that mark and maintain ... organized society' and in women's literature, the carnivalesque suggests 'a redeployment or counterproduction of culture, knowledge, and pleasure'.[16] Accordingly, the ruptures, discontinuity, and confusion which underpin this mode as it operates in the second act of *Women on the Verge of HRT* dramatize and articulate the women's encounter with the deeper layers of their selves and their interior experience as experienced through intuitions and revelations. Male and female stereotypes are questioned, problematizing the rigidities of their construction, illuminating the artificiality of their juxtaposition and being contrasted with each other.

It turns out that having neglected to redefine her relationship with her husband after their children grew up, Vera herself does not match the idea of the unjustly abandoned woman. Played by the shape-shifter Susie, the much younger second wife appears to be very different from the image of the irresponsible seductress when she speaks about marrying an older man so as to avoid her mother's fate of coming to feel herself ugly and invisible at the side of a husband of her own age group. Brought also to stage, Dessie, Vera's ex-husband, confesses that he was put on a diet by his young wife, which shows him a somewhat pathetic case rather than a triumphant conqueror of female hearts. Fergal presents a song about a man who 'had a terrible time meetin' weemin' (27), which indicates that a kind of male invisibility also exists. Stella, whose husband Vera might have flirted with, enters the scene in the guise of the jealous woman. However, her anxieties prove to derive largely from self-centeredness, expressed in grieving over not looking the same as she was when her husband wrote romantic love poems to her. Her husband, in turn, ill-fits the role of born womanizer, blaming his wife for making him into a hopeless 'loveaholic' and even 'an addict' by her emotional demands (32). The renewed hope of Anna about the reconciliation of married partners is shattered when she is pushed to see that the masculinity of her indifferent husband is probably even more damaged than her female identity. Their imaginary debate reveals that he escapes to pornographic literature as a substitute for the revitalization of his marital lovelife and just dreams about sex with the girls in the pictures. In her comments on the play, Imelda Foley rightly asserts that there is 'a shared isolation and a mutual pact of silent acceptance and despair in the lives of Anna and Marty'.[17]

The fast changing, randomly structured scenes, in which, as Anna McMullan writes, 'hidden assumptions and attitudes [are] brought to the surface and exposed',[18] effectively recontextualize established categories and expected forms of gender behaviour. Nonetheless, they make unmistakable reference to the various cultural manipulations of the body, paralleling the protagonists' experience of being treated on the basis of bodily changes and in view of a coercive social ideal. Older and younger figures, male and female, conjured up by the carnival seem to be conditioned by rules that operate 'directly through bodily discourse: through images that tell us what clothes, body shape, facial expression, movements, and behaviour are required'.[19] The eye-opening new knowledge about the power of the discourse of the body and its concomitant destructive potential, facilitates the rebirth of Vera and Anna as viewers with renewed ways of perceiving. They gain insight into what Bordo calls 'the contemporary preoccupation with appearance [...] in our narcissistic and visually oriented culture' (91-2), and realize that it reasserts the existing norms by means of media images, advertisements and dictates of fashion. Every time someone turns it on, Vera remarks, 'on the telly there's another gorgeous girl with her mouth wrapped round a bar of chocolate' (8) to reify the audience's received values and prescribe their private interests and needs. In this context the protagonists' self-consciousness verging on self-abnegation proves to be rooted in having internalized the falsities circulated by the communication systems of a fundamentally consumerist culture.

Through the manipulations of Fergal, the alter ego of Daniel, the final scene unmasks the pop-singer's world of entertainment as itself being continuous with the deceit underlying the culture of the day. After playing the romantic lover to Vera by pandering to her emotional needs and saying he has seen into her soul, Fergal suddenly vanishes, which deconstructs his as well as Daniel's magic. With the trickster's disappearance into the void the carnival comes to an end, but the usual order is by no means restored. In fact it is the state of having cast off self-deprecating prejudices and self-deceiving illusions that makes possible the woman protagonists' transformation into individuals who have their own perspective and belief in themselves, comparable with Kenneth's epiphany at the end of his journey in *A Night in November*. The playwright represents this interior change by creating a complex stage image through the interaction of visual and aural effects. Anna's exclamation of anger at the trickster's disappearance invokes the wailing of the Banshee immediately followed by flute music and the breaking of day, replacing crisis with celebration under the new sun, a new light. The 'Finale Song' is the women's own song, which they perform directly to the audience as Fergal/Daniel did earlier, with the difference that they call on the audience also to act, to resist sexual devaluation and being controlled by constraining and repressive social norms:

> So come on sisters
> Don't let them win
> We may be over forty
> But we can still sin, sin, sin, sin (40).

Creating its own imaginative space, the concluding scene of *Women on the Verge* is an expression of the Kristevan concept of *jouissance* which, as Aston explains, involves joy and ecstasy over the finding of meaning.[20] In this case, Vera and Anna celebrate unrestrained female re-embodiment and resolution to reject and combat the threats of invisibility. The repetition of 'sin' in their song exposes and ridicules the negative connotation of free sexual expression by women over forty and close to or already past menopause.

Lysaght characterizes the tradition of the Banshee as a dual one, not at all surprising in the Irish context, accommodating attitudes to both life and death.[21] Jones's play reinforces the ancient function of the mythical female Banshee in securing identity, according this precedence over the role of announcing death and loss, which it assumed during the centuries of troubled modern history. This emphasis demonstrates that the meanings imposed under the patriarchal conditions can be overwritten by a more personal and flexible view of women's ageing, which admits difference without the pressure to feel traumatized by it. Not accidentally, one might remark, did *Banshee* become the title of the magazine launched by the feminist society called Irish Women United in 1975. In the second act of Jones's play the unavoidable 'verge' ceases to be a space of 'cracking' and entrapment, but re-emerges as a site of empowerment for Vera and Anna, confirming Luce Irigaray's suggestion made in *Je, tu, nous* that 'what is often defined as the end of a woman's life is for her just as much an opportunity'.[22] The feminine journey of self-discovery that functions as the structuring motif in the play leads the middle-aged protagonists from an acute sense of being objectified to the renewal of their subjectivity.

In her work *Technologies of Gender*, feminist theoretician Teresa de Lauretis interrogates the modes of an alternative construction of gender and argues for the necessity of 'a movement from the space represented by/in a representation, by/in a discourse, by/in a sex-gender system, to the space not represented yet implied (unseen) in them'.[23] Jones's *Women on the Verge of HRT* dramatizes a comparable kind of movement, transposing its women characters from a setting of physical and discursive confinement to one of boundless liminality and free-moving imagination, figuring the possibility to reconstruct and represent their female identity in the face of fossilized ideologies and preconceptions. Dissenting from the mimetic and the symbolic, the experimental strategies of the play, through the subversion of prevailing gender stereotypes and awareness of the cultural sensitivities associated with it, clear a space for new perspectives on ageing.[24]

---

[1] Anna McMullan and Caroline Williams, 'Contemporary Women Playwrights', *The Field Day Anthology of Irish Writing* Vol. V: *Irish Women's Writing and Traditions*, ed. Angela Bourke, et al (Cork: Cork University Press, 2002): 1246.

[2] Joanne Tompkins, 'Space and the Geographies of Theatre: Introduction', *Modern Drama* 46 (2003): 537-38.

[3] Gay McAuley, *Space in Performance: Making Meaning in the Theatre* (Ann Arbor: The University of Michigan Press, 1999): 32.

[4] Una Chaudhuri, *Staging Place: The Geography of Modern Drama* (Ann Arbor: The University of Michigan Press, 1997): 138-39.

[5] Marie Jones, *Women on the Verge of HRT* (London: French, 1999): 7. Subsequent references appear parenthetically in the text.

[6] Mary Russo, *The Female Grotesque: Risk, Excess and Modernity* (London: Routledge, 1994): 54.

[7] Stanton B. Garner, Jr, 'Bodied Spaces: Phenomenology and Performance', *Contemporary Drama* (Ithaca: Cornell University Press, 1994): 201.

[8] Kelly Oliver, ed., *The Portable Kristeva* (New York: Columbia University Press, 1997): 43.

[9] Susan Bordo, 'The Body and the Reproduction of Femininity', *Writing on the Body*, eds Katie Conboy, Nadia Medina, and Sarah Stanbury (New York: Columbia University Press, 1997): 99.

[10] Bordo, 98.

[11] See McAuley, *Space in Performance*, 270.

[12] Patricia Lysaght, *A Pocket Book of the Banshee* (Dublin: O'Brien, 1998): 10, 52, 59-60.

[13] Margaret Llewellyn-Jones, *Contemporary Irish Drama and Cultural Identity* (Bristol UK: Intellect, 2002): 77.

[14] Lysaght, 1, 92.

[15] Elaine Aston, *An Introduction to Feminism and Theatre* (London: Routledge, 1995): 53.

[16] Russo, *The Female Grotesque*, 62.

[17] Imelda Foley, *The Girls in the Big Picture: Gender in Contemporary Ulster Theatre* (Belfast: Blackstaff Press, 2003): 53.
[18] Anna McMullan, 'Gender, Authorship and Performance in Selected Plays by Contemporary Irish Women Playwrights: Mary Elizabeth Burke-Kennedy, Marie Jones, Marina Carr, Emma Donoghue', *Theatre Stuff*, ed. Eamonn Jordan (Dublin: Carysfort, 2000): 41.
[19] Bordo, 94.
[20] Aston, 56.
[21] Lysaght, 7.
[22] Luce Irigaray, *Je, tu, nous: Toward a Culture of Difference*, trans. Alison Martin (London: Routledge, 1993): 115.
[23] Teresa De Lauretis, *Technologies of Gender: Essays on Theory, Film, and Fiction* (Bloomington, Indiana: Indiana University Press, 1987): 26.
[24] In the course of revising and expanding the present paper I greatly profited from the discussion it generated at the IASIL Conference in Galway in July 2004, especially from the remarks and comments of Enrica Cerquoni, who chaired, and Melissa Sihra, who acted as respondent to the panel entitled 'Gender and space in Irish theatre: past, present and future (im)possibilites.'

11 | The Present through the Prism of the Past: Frank McGuinness's *Dolly West's Kitchen*

Donald E. Morse

Frank McGuinness's *Dolly West's Kitchen* premiered at the 1999 Dublin Theatre Festival. The play focuses on the several tensions created by Ireland's neutrality during World War II – a subject much neglected in contemporary Irish drama. As Atom Egoyan said of his remarkable film, *Ararat,* this play 'is not so much about the past as it is about the present. It is about the responsibilities of people living now'.[1] If, as Fintan O'Toole contends, 'you cannot write 1950s kitchen comedies about 1990s Ireland'[2], then in *Dolly West's Kitchen* McGuinness daringly asserts that you can write a 1990 kitchen drama about 1940s Ireland. The kitchen, that ubiquitous symbol of Irish domesticity, family, and safety, as well as the setting for innumerable popular comedies on the twentieth century Irish stage, particularly at the Abbey Theatre, here becomes re-visioned. By harshly lighting and sharply defining the kitchen with its central table surrounded by space suggestive of house, garden, seaside, and, later, of the Belfast Blitz, the set designed for the Abbey production created a visual image of uneasy domesticity with the possibilities of intrusion and danger as the series of concentric circles comprising the table, the kitchen, the house, and the immediate surround, extends by implication to include the island of Ireland isolated in a landscape of a world at war. In this setting, interrelated questions involving Irish history and neutrality including those of identity, gender, and nationality urgently arise as family history and personal relations replace the abstractions of war and neutrality.

McGuinness describes himself quite accurately as 'a writer involved with politics'.[3] But his 'plays are political not in an *agit prop* sense, but in the wider sense of concern with how humans carry out the eternally challenging task of living, in private and public'.[4] As reflected in his plays, this political involvement results in a dual rather than unitary vision— perhaps one fostered by his early life lived in physical proximity to the border of Northern Ireland. The full title of *Observe the Sons of Ulster Marching Towards the Somme* (1985), his play best known in Ireland, for instance, registers both the historical calamity for Northern Ireland of the murderous Battle of the Somme and, at the same time, the compassionate neutrality of the southern Irish playwright observing the event. It might be well to recall that both Northern Ireland and the Republic remember the year 1916 as a terrible year of martyrdom, but the one commemorates slaughtered Ulster regiments at the Somme, while the other memorializes decimated Dublin irregulars at the GPO. Within this context, McGuinness's portrayal of the Ulster soldiers who fought and died at the Somme is remarkably empathetic. '*Observe the Sons of Ulster* ... sympathizes profoundly with an alien point of view,' as Christopher Murray argues.[5] Additionally, the play succeeds by tightly focusing on only eight volunteers. 'No extraneous characters are admitted; no representatives of church, state or even officer class' (Murray, 204). *Someone Who'll Watch Over Me* (1992) is even more severely limited in its focus by concentrating on three captives held prisoner in Lebanon).

Seen against the background of these and other, earlier McGuinness plays, the cast of *Dolly West's Kitchen* appears almost expansive, including as it does a most memorable, larger-than-life, and slightly Rabelaisian or Wyfe of Bath-like mother, Rima West, her family of three siblings, her son-in-law, a servant girl, and one British and two American soldiers. If Eamonn Jordan's contention is correct that in his earlier plays 'confinement is McGuinness's greatest theme'[6], then in *Dolly West's Kitchen* that theme becomes muted except for two of the Irish characters, Esther and Ned, who remain throughout physically confined in Ireland and emotionally confined in their loveless marriage. All the other characters escape confinement at one time or another: Dolly left Ireland to live and work in Italy before the Rise of Fascism, for instance. While a case can be made for her choosing 'confinement' after the war by agreeing to go with Alec to an uncongenial England, the fact that she goes knowing exactly what she will face and how she will meet it, suggests that her adventuresome spirit and personality remain, like Rima's, unconfined. The others also escape. Anna heads for New York with Jamie, and Justin plans to go to Italy with Marco. Although each of these pairings is fraught with known difficulty and abounding in unknown danger, none could be said to represent confinement.

Yet a change in theme hardly accounts for the varied reception of *Dolly West's Kitchen* in Dublin and London. Nor does the 'tightening' of the over-all production that director Patrick Mason undertook for the London venue as a result of Dublin criticism. While various possible changes in production do account for some of this shift, they cannot account for all. '[T]he Dublin reviews [of *Dolly West's Kitchen*] were unfavourable and negative, whereas in London it received many positive reviews,' reports Hiroko Mikami[7] and had a fairly long run. Such disparity of critical and audience response points to attitudes that I would like to examine briefly. First, there was and remains today a division between the predominant Irish and predominant British (and American) attitude towards Irish neutrality during World War II. Second, in 1999 when the play premiered, there was a considerable difference in attitude towards and experience of overtly gay characters in British and American theatre and television contrasted with Irish theatre and television. Third and most important: *Dolly West's Kitchen* shares with some other recent Irish plays, such as Brian Friel's *Translations* (1980) or McGuinness's own *Observe the Sons of Ulster*, a complexity – some might say a confusion – arising out of employing what appears to be a clearly identifiable historical setting in a play that is neither 'a documentary narrative or a traditional history lesson'.[8] McGuinness did not write a historical drama faithfully based on life lived during World War II in the neutral Ireland of 1943-1945. Instead, his is a play *of* history, made for the purpose of providing a contemporary audience with the means for 'disentangling the contradictions of the present by placing them at a distance' to borrow Fintan O'Toole's phrase and for the parallel purpose of seeing more clearly certain contemporary topics including asylum-seeking and sexual preference in a historical perspective.[9]

History and *Dolly West's Kitchen*

Although *Dolly West's Kitchen* is not a history lesson, it bears a definite complex relation to historical events. For instance, in 1938 de Valera retrieved the 'Treaty ports' that then made possible Ireland's declaration of neutrality.[10] In *Dolly West's Kitchen*, Justin hotly defends de Valera's action in ways that reflect the view of many Irish people at the time: 'That's what they [the British] want. The ports of our free neutral country. It's for them they want us in this war'.[11] This is part of the historical record. Some other references in the play, however, are to events unlikely to have been historically well known to the people living in Buncrana in the early years of the war. The most obvious and perhaps most complex of these is the reference to Hitler's attempt to annihilate the Jews.

>**Rima**: (*to Alec*) How's the war going to shape?
>**Alec:** It's touch and go ...
>**Rima:** And the Jews?
>*Silence.*
>Is it as bad –
>**Alec:** It's worse, I think. We don't know –
>**Rima:** We do.

Silence.
If any country should have opened the door to any people facing what they are facing – Ireland –
Alex: It might not be as bad –
Rima: We did nothing to save them.
Alec: Ireland's a neutral country (48-9).

During the war, Irish censorship forbade any story that might have been pro or contra England or Germany and, therefore, such references to Irish neutrality and the holocaust might appear anachronistic. Clair Wills observes that 'the lifting of censorship and the sudden circulation in Ireland of stories of atrocity ... [including] pictures and newsreels of Buchenwald' occurred only with the death of Hitler and de Valera's notorious condolence visit to the German legation in Dublin.[12] Solely at the end of the war did the Irish people learn of the death camps from public or official sources. Other unofficial and mostly non-print sources did, however, spread hearsay about Hitler's plans for exterminating the Jews. But while one must be cautious about identifying completely what the censors allowed to appear in print with what people knew,[13] the ferocity and magnitude of Hitler's megalomaniac efforts were not fully realized until after the war. Yet Rima's comment that 'If any country should have opened the door to any people facing what they are facing – Ireland – ' while only partially historically correct, would nevertheless have had an immediate and powerful resonance with Irish audiences in 1999 preoccupied as many people were with the several controversies over the various asylum seekers then in Ireland. The Irish debate on giving asylum to refugees has a long and often bitter history. Prominent in that history is the 1975 and 1976 refusal of the Irish government to resettle any Vietnamese and the 1979 offer by the government of one hundred resettlement places for the Vietnamese Boat People when 'the Episcopal Commission for Emigrants (IECED), in the person of Bishop Eamon Casey, demanded 1,000 resettlement places'.[14] Another crisis occurred immediately before McGuinness wrote the play when the political debate raged and numerous political speeches were made, many of which could be termed 'racist'. Irish audiences could hardly avoid bringing remnants of this debate to their experience of *Dolly West's Kitchen* (see Sheridan, 2004).[8]

Kurt Vonnegut once remarked that the only benefit of his experience fighting against the Germans in World War II was that it enabled him to converse with veterans from any war anywhere and any time as an equal. Justin in *Dolly West's Kitchen* proves the representative Irish soldier who sits out World War II as an Irish neutral and so has no such right to converse as an equal with those who fought. But McGuinness uses the figure of Justin additionally to explore other sides of Ireland itself during the Emergency. One non-Irish critic, in examining Justin and his role in the play, suggests that there exists 'a sense of shame, which is crystallized in the image of a backer of Nazism, [which] is never to be blotted out of the national memory. It is possible that this memory might have affected the Irish reception of the play ...' (Mikami, 154). Yet both the character and situation portrayed in the play proves far more complex than any such simple identification of Justin with the Nazis. As a so-called 'backer of Nazism' Justin is motivated by the prospect of England losing the war following the familiar reasoning of 'the enemy of my enemy' becomes my friend: '[This war]'s not a shower of Paddies with sticks and stones,' he throws at Alec, the English officer. 'It's the full might of Hitler's army. And you are going to lose the war. Germany will win the war. The might of Hitler's army will win the war.' (36-37) Justin's speech shocks non-Irish audiences – certainly, it seemed to shock the international audience at the 1999 Dublin Theatre Festival – both by its assertion of Germany's might and by its use of the second person pronoun, 'you' that emphasizes not just Irish neutrality but also the distance separating the Irish and the combatants. This distance becomes even greater as Justin's speech elicits an immediate reply by Alec:

> Then God help you, Justin ... and God help all of us about this table. There are millions dying because of the might of Hitler's army. And their sacrifice might save your skin, but I call what they're suffering a damned sight worse than whatever you and your people have suffered. God save Ireland, isn't that one of your country's battle cries? Do you know who will save Ireland this time? English conscripts, Welsh miners, Scottish shipbuilders, Irish navvies – that's who'll save Ireland (37)

McGuinness gives this, the most eloquent speech in the play, to a British soldier. Later after the war is over, it is the Americans who confront the Irish with the disgrace of their being neutral and unengaged while others were fighting and dying. Jamie taunts Ned by boasting 'We knew how to win a war rather than sit on the sidelines shitting ourselves' (79). Ned's immediate physically violent response is to 'flatten [...] Jamie ... [and t]hey fight fiercely, destroying the garden' (79). Marco, in turn, accuses Justin of 'holding the fort back in dear old Ireland. What a waste of time that was, for there was no one coming near you. You always knew you were safe so you let us suffer for you' (77). This, too, is answered first by physical violence as Justin strikes Marco followed not by political argument, but one couched in terms of human relationships and responsibility: 'I have spent over a year not knowing anything about you. I have been waiting and willing you to come back to me. And to bring you back I would have done anything a man dared have done – I swear that,' declares Justin (77).

That 'sense of shame' the non-Irish critic postulates, and which these speeches by the American soldiers attempt to elicit had historically only limited application to Ireland. According to Terence Brown:

> When in 1940 Professor Michael Tierney ... recorded that neutrality afforded Ireland 'the nightmarish satisfaction of looking on in

comparative safety at horrors we can do nothing to prevent' most Irish people would have agreed with his sentiments and would have seen little reason to forsake that comparative safety for the overwhelming risks to their young state that political and military partisanship would involve. And nothing that happened in subsequent years would have changed their minds. A minority however thought such safety ignoble, believing that to remain a spectator in such desperate times was to place Ireland in grave moral jeopardy.... Most people [in Ireland] simply supported neutrality as the only sane policy in a world gone mad and got on with their lives as best they might.[15]

Officially neutral, Ireland nevertheless did exhibit 'telling signs of partiality' (Brown, 172) such as repatriating Allied airmen shot down over Ireland, while interning German airmen similarly shot down for the duration of the war. Many of the latter remain buried in the German cemetery in County Wicklow.

If the West and especially Britain, as epitomized by – say – Winston Churchill, saw Irish neutrality as a political and moral failure comparable to a failure of manhood, then *Dolly West's Kitchen* challenges such attitudes not primarily from within their historical period of World War II, but from today's perspective, which recognizes not only the limitations of Irish neutrality, which isolated Ireland culturally, intellectually, and politically, but also its considerable long-lasting positive value. Declan Kiberd, among others, argues that 'When Ireland entered the United Nations after World War Two, its position of non-alignment between the superpowers became a model for other emerging states.'[16] As Irish Commemoration Day 2004 with its many veterans of various UN peacekeeping efforts illustrated, to be non-aligned did not mean to be non-involved. Moreover, the issue of Irish neutrality remains alive today although 'usually dodged around' (Wills, 45) in terms of Ireland's role within the various European Union security and defence arrangements. Clair Wills, after examining Irish neutrality throughout the twentieth century, concludes '[a]mbivalence continues to haunt the politics of Irish neutrality' (144) – an ambivalence reflected in *Dolly West's Kitchen*.

Sexuality and Neutrality

Justin in uniform at the head of the table, as 'the man of the house' (10), the head of the family in place of his previously-absent and now-dead father, acts with a kind of authoritarian swagger reminiscent of Il Duce, from whose Italy Dolly fled.[17] Justin's character also bears a crucial resemblance to Justin Cavey in Elizabeth Bowen's short story, 'Summer Night' – a story that also takes place in neutral Ireland during the war. McGuinness's Justin, like Bowen's, 'becomes prone, like a perverse person in love, to expose all his own piques, crotchets, and weaknesses'.[18] In portraying Justin as gay, however, McGuinness adds a complication not present in Bowen's story. Historical attitudes towards gender and sexuality become updated from the 1940s to the 1990s in the play as McGuinness attempts to clarify the contemporary topic of gender by viewing it from a historical perspective.

Justin and Marco's gay identity within the historical context could have provided a metaphor for neutral Ireland as a failure of manhood but McGuinness rejects such simplicities along with their implications for either his play or Ireland. Attitudes typical of both 1940s Ireland and the United States are, however, amply illustrated by Marco's sadistic story of how his mother attempted to 'cure' him of being a 'cissy' by forcing him to eat his sketches of dresses that he'd made at age seven:

> She poured ketchup on every page, salt and lots of pepper. She made me eat them one by one until I vomited. I thought it was blood, the red coming up my throat (60).

Marco's parents' action, along with their values and attitudes, appear typical of the time and Justin would almost certainly have encountered such or similar ones as well. Marco concludes his cruel story by exclaiming:

> I hate her. I hate him. My mother. My father. Don't lose your hatred? Remember. I am fighting this war because of hatred ... Don't lose your hatred. I told you. Hatred brought me to you' (60).

While Marco may have survived the viciousness of his parents through hatred, that hatred proves insufficient to sustain him through the horrors of war and its aftermath. The surface simplicity of his outrageous character hides depths of hurt and sorrow that his experience in the war accentuates into paranoia.

Rima in accepting Justin's sexuality reflects values and attitudes of the late twentieth-century west that would be unlikely to have existed in early 1940s Ireland. Although her action in inviting American soldiers home emphasizes the importance of traditional Irish hospitality and may be seen as unexceptional for the time, her inviting the outrageous Marco remains well beyond the social pale. Such action emphasizes that McGuinness is not writing historical or sociological drama, but focusing instead on conflicting loyalties, values, and assumptions, on 'how humans carry out the eternally challenging task of living, in private and public' (Lojek, viii). Helen Lojek, writing of the captives in *Someone Who'll Watch Over Me* fantasizing about inviting their captors to party with them, suggests that the scene 'reminds us how different the world would be if we all drank and sang together' (Lojek, 131). In *Dolly West's Kitchen* a similar situation obtains as the combatants and non-combatants, the Americans, British, and Irish, the straight and the gay find themselves thrown together into the one social pot through Rima's machinations. They can continue with their old antagonisms or become open to new possibilities. Like the three captives in *Someone Who'll Watch Over Me,* those in Dolly's kitchen find, during their meal and after, their stereotypes of the other challenged, with such stereotypes either damaged or refuted. New possibilities – however slim or fragile – begin to appear and with them hope for a future different from the past.

Hiding in his Donegal closet, Justin reacts incredulously and proceeds with caution in his first conversations with the flagrant Marco, the New York Queen.

> **Justin:** A right gathering of the Allies.
> **Marco:** Boys together – that's right.
> **Justin:** You've crossed the border.
> **Marco:** Hasn't everyone?

To which Justin, who cannot believe he may have heard two sexual *double entendres* in as many phrases, replies, 'I beg your pardon.' (28)

In their second exchange, framed by the various couples exiting to the beach arm-in-arm, Marco turns to Justin and says, 'I shall refuse your arm, young man. I do not trust men in uniform.' And this time Justin does at last ask the right question: 'What the hell are you?' Not *who* are you but *what* are you? (29). Followed by another good question: 'Where exactly are you from?' He is not looking for a street address nor does he get one in Marco's reply: 'Paradise' (29). A reply destined for irony as the war changes everything.

Identity and the Cost of War and the Cost of Neutrality

The hideous cost of the war in terms of human physical, psychological, emotional, and spiritual loss, so painfully apparent in the last scene of *Dolly West's Kitchen* that takes place after the war, knits together the play's various strands. The war spared no one. Neither neutrality nor engagement saved anyone from hurt. All the characters were damaged in or by the war and none achieves his or her dream of post-war peace and happiness. Parallel to the individual stories lie those of history. Later events begin to intrude on the post-war mid-century meal. This time the echoes are of the Northern Irish 'Troubles' that will dominate more than a quarter century of Irish history north and south. Dolly, attempting to get Alec to communicate asks him to 'tell me what you saw.' To which Alec replies, 'Children. Dead Children. Burned off the face of the earth. Millions. They saved us. The innocent. I walk through this town – '

> **Dolly:** Buncrana.
> **Alec:** That's never known a war. That's never lost its young. I hope it never does.
> **Dolly:** If we ever do, it will be our own doing.
> **Alec:** Would you do that to each other?

Dolly: Alec, after what you've seen do you not know what we're all capable of doing? (83)

Dolly West's Kitchen thus concludes in dramatic irony as the audience knows that in a few short years the North will become the site of vicious internecine warfare culminating in the Omagh bombing suggested in Alec's question that later events make rhetorical: 'Would you do that to each other?'

'Is the War Over?'

Dolly West's Kitchen focuses on Irish neutrality, which the Irish theatre denied by ignoring, but does so within the context of three-quarters of twentieth-century Irish history from the founding of the Free State through what might be the last violent gasp of the 'Troubles' in the North. Rejecting both the documentary narrative and traditional history lesson, McGuinness brings into play overlapping layers of history that enable audiences to see more clearly – because from a historical perspective – both current events and such contemporary issues as political neutrality, individual identity, and gender. The issue of national identity raised acutely through Irish neutrality becomes compounded with individual identity raised acutely through gender – both issues having 'previously been demonized or denied'.[19] Nicholas Grene might have been speaking of *Dolly West's Kitchen* when he argues that

> Playwrights from Synge to Murphy have sought to enlarge the awareness of what constituted the nation by going out to the neglected and forgotten, unexpressed underclasses who deserved a voice. The spirit of McGuinness's [...] work, though comparable in its purpose of dramatic recuperation, is different in its need to cross over politically to engage with what has previously been demonized or denied (244-45).

But the struggle to achieve national and individual identity comes at a high price as seen in the verbal and visual imagery of the play's last scene. That earlier series of concentric circles comprising the table in the kitchen within the house, the immediate surround, the island of Ireland, a world momentarily not at war has been broken. As Esther trenchantly observes 'this war has changed us all. What are we now ...?' (75) The intimate first circle of the table centred in the kitchen has shrunk through the natural, because inevitable, breaking of the chain of generation – Rima is dead and buried – and through the also natural, because continuously and consistently ambiguous, relationship of Ned and Esther symbolized in his staying outside the kitchen in the garden with their daughter in the pram. The removal of Alec and Dolly to outside the kitchen is not, however, natural since caused by the war and their attempt to deal with its aftermath. There is every indication that Dolly will survive in the hostile environment of England, but little to assure that Alec will.

Joan FitzPatrick Dean's observation of McGuinness's earlier plays that the 'emphasis typically falls on the paradoxes of identity and freedom, essence and existence'[20] aptly applies to the conclusion of *Dolly West's Kitchen*. The paradox in the last scene may be seen in this small band of survivors who affirm what they are able to affirm within the limits of their freedom, which is, in turn, at least partially defined by their individual identities and their relationships with one another, however uncertain they might be. In the kitchen, Justin declares his and the others' identity in their relationships as he repeats the wedding ceremony vow as a kind of grace before the meal: 'For richer or poorer – in sickness and in health – till death us do part' (85), words to which the experience of war and waiting have given a particular urgency. Juxtaposed to this sacramental verbal imagery, the physical imagery present in the locations of the several couples emphasizes the variety and kind of commitment in their relationships. At the head of the table, Esther as the eldest carves the lamb while her husband Ned, along with Alec and Dolly stay close to but clearly apart from the kitchen group. Esther and Ned, the only married couple present, have never been close. Esther summarizes their relationship: 'I had married the best of men. I didn't love him, I still don't. But he is still the best of men' (75). In the kitchen, Marco sits beside Justin unable to let him out of his sight for fear he will then die as in his nightmares where 'all my dreams are red' (76). Their relationship goes from violent to reconciliation. Jamie sits with '*Anna behind him, her arms round him*' (85) displaying the engagement ring she has just shown to the town of Buncrana preparatory to leaving it for New York. If the Americans have done the fighting in the war, it now falls to the Irish, Justin and Anna to sustain them in the war's aftermath. 'They're like children .... They've had a bad dream. We have to comfort them,' asserts Ned (73). Neutrality, it appears, does indeed have positive survival values.

If the losses of war and the ordeal of waiting appear over at the end of *Dolly West's Kitchen,* still those in the audience know that such experiences and horrors will be repeated again and again and again. The twentieth century began by being proclaimed the Century of the Child, 'as Ellen Key hopefully called it in its opening years that turned into the century of Moloch, the eater of children'.[21] The number of dead from that Century of Wars exceeded that of all the dead from all previous wars. The following century appears thus far to fare no better.

More specifically for an Irish audience, however, is the knowledge that just fourteen short months before *Dolly West's Kitchen* premiered at the Dublin Theatre Festival, the horrendous Omagh bombing took place that left twenty-nine dead and 350 injured. That explosion, as bad as any wartime bombing, echoes throughout this play, especially under its penultimate line: 'Is the war over?' (85) as the horrific past becomes a metaphor for the murderous present. Countering this terrible contemporary overlay of the Omagh bombing on the historical depiction of lives damaged by World War II is all the ancient, overtly sacramental visual and verbal imagery of the play's last moments: the breaking of bread, the drinking of wine, and the partaking of the sacrificial lamb. Although everyone can no longer sit together at the table, still all of them – combatants and neutrals, straight and gay, Americans, British, and Irish, young and old – come as close together as they are able. In this ritualized last scene, McGuinness appears to suggest that a new life could be built on the ruins of the old were the price paid in disrupted, damaged lives, as well as in lives sacrificed, to be acknowledged. Nationally and individually, there remains the need to assimilate the past while at the same time exorcising its demons. Only then might the war – all wars – be truly over and peace be assured. To Alec's twice repeated question of 'Is the war over?' all Dolly West – or Frank McGuinness or any of us – can answer lies in her curtain line 'I hope so' (85). Her words resonate with a contemporary audience living in a world continuously at war, for which Irish neutrality in World War II and even the Last Just War itself have now become metaphors. What Terence Brown said of Stewart Parker's *Northern Star* (1984), McGuinness's *Observe the Sons of Ulster Marching Towards the Somme*, and Brendan Kennelly's long poem, *Cromwell* (1983) is equally true of *Dolly West's Kitchen* in that such works 'may be an indication of a developing openness to new interpretations of Ireland's past and present experience. What they unquestionably reveal is the vital energy of contemporary Irish art in its engagement at fundamental levels with crises of identity, violence and historical consciousness' (246).

---

[1] Atom Egoyan, 'Poetic Licence and the Incarnation of History', *University of Toronto Quarterly* 73.3 (2004): 883.

[2] Fintan O'Toole, 'Hidden Charges', *The Irish Times* 25 October 1994. Reprinted in O'Toole, *Critical Moments*, 134.

[3] Richard Pine, 'Frank McGuinness: A Profile', *ILS* 10.1 (1991): 29.

[4] Helen Lojek (ed.), *The Theatre of Frank McGuinness: Stages of Mutability* (Dublin: Carysfort, 2002): viii.

[5] Christopher Murray, *Twentieth-Century Irish Drama: Mirror up to Nation* (Manchester: Manchester University Press, 1997): 206. Nicholas Grene also emphasises McGuinness's extraordinary empathy. In another setting, he points out that in Ireland 'the imagination of anything other than being Catholic and nationalist becomes genuinely difficult' (1999: 242).

[6] Eamonn Jordan, *Theatre Stuff: Critical Essays on Contemporary Irish Theatre* (Dublin: Carysfort Press, 2000): 195.

[7] Hiroko Mikami, *Frank McGuinness and His Theatre of Paradox* (Gerrards Cross: Colin Smythe, 2002): 154.

[8] Anthony Roche, *Contemporary Irish Drama: From Beckett to McGuinness* (Dublin: Gill & Macmillan, 1994): 266.

[9] Fintan O'Toole, *Tom Murphy: The Politics of Magic*, rev. ed. (Dublin: New Island, 1987): 113.

[10] David Fitzpatrick, 'Ireland Since 1870', *The Oxford History of Ireland* (Oxford: Oxford University Press, 1989): 224.

[11] Frank McGuinness, *Dolly West's Kitchen* (London: Faber and Faber, 1999): 36. Earlier, in the opening scene of the play, Esther refers to the same ports but with sexual overtones: 'Buncrana is a port. Our beloved leader, De Valera, has warned this part of the country they might invade us for our ports, coming at us from all sides, the English, the Germans and the Yanks' (5). In similar fashion, she adds an overtone of 'neuter' to neutral when referring sarcastically to her husband, Ned: 'An excellent man. An excellent soldier. Defending Ireland from invasion, a neutral man in a neutral army protecting his neutral wife' (4).

[12] ClairWills, 2004, 124.

[13] I am indebted to John DeVitt for this cautionary observation (conversation July 2004 at IASIL, Galway).

[14] Kathy Sheridan, 'Turning a Haven into a Home'. *The Irish Times* 14 August 2004: W5.

[15] Terence Brown, *Ireland: A Social and Cultural History 1922-2002* (London: Harper Perennial, 2004): 172-73, 175.

[16] Declan Kiberd, *Inventing Ireland* (London: Vintage, 1996): 558.

[17] Sensing the danger to all foreigners, such as herself, Dolly left her beloved Italy only to find repeated in small the prejudice against foreigners she had already experienced from the Italians in her brother's chauvinistic insularity that, in turn, represents a negative part of Irish neutrality, 8-12.

[18] Bowen, Elizabeth, 'Summer Night', *The Collected Stories of Elizabeth Bowen* (London: Cape, 1980): 589.

[19] Nicholas Grene, *The Politics of Irish Drama: Plays in Context from Boucicault to Friel* (Cambridge: Cambridge University Press, 1999): 245.

[20] Joan FitzPatrick Dean, *Riot and Great Anger: Stage Censorship in Twentieth-Century Ireland* (Madison, WI: University of Wisconsin Press, 2004): 144.

[21] Van Wyck Brooks, *The Writer in America* (New York: Avon, 1953): 159.

12 | 'Grow a Mermaid': a Subtext for Marina Carr's Dramatic Works

Mika Funahashi

Marina Carr was first recognized as one of the most talented contemporary Irish playwrights with the success of her tragic family drama, *The Mai* (1994), and her subsequent two plays, *Portia Coughlan* (1996) and *By the Bog of Cats...* (1998). In these plays, Carr stages the potential dangers engendered in the family. In her theatre, the home is not a safe zone; it is a space of entrapment from which no family member can easily escape.

In 1994, the year of *The Mai*'s premiere at the Peacock Theatre, Carr's short story, 'Grow a Mermaid' appeared in the *Sunday Tribune*, and was included in *The Hennessy Book of Irish Fiction* in the following year. The plot is quite similar to *The Mai*: a child's mother builds a house on a lake during the child's father's long absence, and drowns herself after his leaving them again. Creating a mermaid in her mind, the child uses this fantasy as an escape from the dangerous grip of her mother, who literally nearly suffocates the child. The story ends with the child swimming deeper into the pool, following the mermaid's tail. Whether it is real or a dream is ambiguous.

Over the past decade, numerous studies have been devoted to Marina Carr, but little attention has been given to this story although 'Grow a Mermaid' is of great significance as the nucleus of Carr's plays. The mother in 'Grow a Mermaid' inflicts physical violence on the children, as revenge on her husband. Strangely, the child rather enjoys the affliction as a routine game, and what each episode reveals is the process of dream formation: how the child comes to create an alternative world in her dream. Another noteworthy point to observe is the detachment with which the child describes her mother's death in the story: the grief of the bereaved child is not fully dealt with in the narrative. In her dramatised work, Carr develops the motif and goes further into the subconscious of the female characters. Through comparing Carr's theatrical world with this short story, this essay will investigate how Carr developed each motif and character in her dramatized work, with a focus on the wounds caused by the mother.

The damage, which can be caused by a mother to her children, is a recurrent theme in a loose 'trilogy' focusing on female protagonists -- *The Mai*, *Portia Coughlan*, and *By the Bog of Cats*.... It can also be traced in Carr's two more recent works with a male protagonist, *On Raftery's Hill* (2000) and *Ariel* (2002). The domineering destructive power of Red Raftery, staged in *On Raftery's Hill*, is the most extreme example. It is as if the lives of his three offspring are confined in a claustrophobic cell, where their vulnerability is exposed and their voices are stifled. The disclosure of ongoing incest between Red Raftery and his first daughter Dinah is unnerving, but not a shock. The most horrendous disclosure is that her dead mother made Dinah go to her father's bed. This is not to say that the trauma of Carr's characters is caused mainly by their mothers, but in her trilogy, she analyses the relationship between mother and daughter more thoroughly. What is remarkable about these three works is the heart-piercing pain of each female protagonist, through the loss of a loved one or nostalgia for someone gone. This is also the case with The Mai's daughter Millie who narrates the story of her dead mother. The hidden wounds of each woman are disclosed with such intensity it induces us to experience their pain.

'Grow a Mermaid' is an intriguing but relatively short story of only nine pages, divided into fourteen sections. The main character is a female child living in the countryside with her mother, her little brother and her grandmother. The characters have no names, simply 'the child' or 'the child's mother', except for Grandma Blaize. The narrative is mostly in the past tense, except for the closing two sections and two in the middle, which are in the present tense. There are many small episodes or incidents in 'Grow a Mermaid', as in a jigsaw puzzle. What each episode reveals is the process of how the child comes to create an alternative world in her dreams. It gives us some insights into Carr's theatre where we come to encounter many characters, mainly female, who cling obstinately to their fantasies. Through analyzing the mechanism of dream formation, the hidden meaning of the story will surface.

The story's title 'Grow a Mermaid' sounds like an eye-catching advert. In fact, it derives from an advertisement the child found in a magazine. The first section gives us many hints on how to consider this story. Although Carr uses a third-person narrative structure, the narrative is definitely operated through the child's perspective. To show the characteristic tone of the story, here is the first section in full.

> The child leaned across the blue formica table and read the advertisement, her grubby little fingers leaving snail tracks under the

words – GROW YOUR OWN MERMAID. The child looked at the words in amazement, read it again, slowly, more carefully this time. The same. Underneath the caption was an ink drawing of a tiny mermaid in a fish bowl, waving and smiling up from the page. Behind her was a sea-horse. He too was smiling. The child, bewitched by the mermaid's smile, smiled back and waved shyly to the tiny beautiful fish woman. Send 25 cents, the advertisement said, and we will send you mermaid and sea-horse seeds. You put them into water and they grow and can even talk to you. The child imagined waking up at night and going to the fishbowl for a chat with the mermaid. What would mermaids talk about, the child wondered.[1]

This is a mesmerizing opening with the same gripping power that we find in Carr's plays. Even though this advertisement appears very outlandish, I believe it was not created from the sheer imagination of the child, nor by Carr herself, but was inspired by a real product for children, probably made in the United States in the 1960s. It was an educational toy for science learning. If you got such a product, you would have seen not a mermaid but microorganisms, or a certain kind of plankton with tiny transparent bodies that could sustain their lives in special water for some weeks, and die or eventually disappear.

It is noteworthy that Carr uses here a narrative technique which she makes use of in her theatre. For example, Millie's first narration begins with 'When I was eleven The Mai sent me into the butcher's to buy a needle and thread.'[2] Just as the first line of the mermaid advertisement affects the child, Millie's statement causes doubt in the audience, because of its sheer strangeness, and induces them to listen to her story more attentively. What narrator Millie does next is to transform what initially seemed strange into the familiar and usual; with small pieces of incidental but particular information, she gradually constructs a picture of what actually happened five years ago when her father left them. This is a narrative skill Carr adopted from the storytelling tradition of local legend, and she applies the same method in a far more dramatic way in *By the Bog of Cats...* as, for example, in the Ghost Fancier's appearance in the opening scene. In the development of her theatrical work from plays such as *Low in the Dark* to *By the Bog of Cats...*, Marina Carr's narration-based theatre shifts into a more action-based drama. One of the prominent features of this short story is the graphic verbal description. This is an appropriate choice since this short story is from the child's point of view, which naturally restricts the author's vocabulary.

The use of meta-fiction can be seen in 'Grow a Mermaid'. More precisely, this story is a meta-fantasy. As seen in the quotation above, Carr not only uses this narrative technique to start her story, but also analyses its effects on the reader, the child: the words of the advert sow the seeds of the concept of a mermaid in the child's mind. The child's wish to 'send away for a mermaid' was thwarted by the mother, although the child saw that the mother herself 'was bewitched by the little mermaid' (256). In a paradoxical way, having failed to get those seeds in reality, the child begins to grow a mermaid in her mind.

'Grow a Mermaid' deals with child abuse by the mother. There are three episodes where the mother inflicts physical violence on her children: twice on the female child and once on her little brother. Her violent physical force is first introduced in the third section, the longest in the story, where we can see how the seeds of a mermaid take root in the child's mind. The child's mother, just like The Mai, is building a house on the lake, wishing her husband would 'come back, for good this time' (257). It has become their habit to sleep together, talking for hours about how they will decorate the house. However, all the decisions are made by the mother; she wants the music room for her husband and 'windows everywhere' (257). She whispers her plans that the child's room 'will be all in yellow', 'with a yellow sink and yellow curtains, yellow presses and a yellow carpet' (257). The child says nothing though she does not like that colour: 'She wanted her room blue and green, like a mermaid's room. It didn't matter; she'd pull the blue and green from an invisible string, the way Grandma Blaize did, and then the mermaid would arrive' (257).

The child learns the trick of imagining another world from Grandma Blaize. Although she has the same name as Portia Coughlan's vile-tongued grandmother, Grandma Blaize of this story resembles other personae. Her habitual 'fossicking for some long forgotten thing' (255) and the strong rejection of the real world reminds us of Shalome Raftery, the demented old lady of *On Raftery's Hill*. She can also be read as the archetype of Grandma Fraochlán of *The Mai*, with such noticeable attributes as an opium pipe and her fighting with the ghost. Grandma Blaize's ghost of Syracuse is not her father but the husband who left her thirty years ago. The fossicking is the sign of Grandma Blaize's being 'on the descent', stepping 'into the other world', and the child imagines 'that Grandma Blaize was pulling open a door with a magic thread, a door on somewhere else, anywhere, but away from here' (256). The 'magic thread' reminds us of the strange opening line of Millie's first narration while leading us into the second: 'The Mai set about looking for that magic thread that would stitch us together again and she found it at Owl Lake' (*Mai*, 14). However, I shall leave this thread for later discussion.

In bed beside her mother, the child is visualizing the mermaid thanks to the trick she learned from Grandma Blaize. Out of darkness, at the same time as the mother's words, comes the light: yellow, the brightest colour of all emerges like the rising sun. Then, against the yellow, the child brings in blue and green. The contrast of the two colours makes a vibrant picture. In the spectrum, blue is the complementary colour of yellow; these two colours are complete opposites, but placed side by side create exciting effects. What the mother and the child are doing here in the dark is another creation, not with paintbrushes but with their words. Enrica

Cerquoni has pointed out 'Carr's strong visual consciousness': referring to Patrick Mason's words, she draws our attention to Carr's power as 'image-maker, as creator of striking pictures that illuminate the stage and ... animate the inner stage of the audience's imagination'.[3]

The nocturnal talk about the colourful plans for the future house, however, takes a sudden dramatic turn: the mother's deadly holding of the child under the quilt. Over the child's struggling movements to breathe, the mother's whispering voice is heard through the covering quilt, saying 'that bastard!' 'all I've done for him' and 'this is how he repays me' (257). Unmistakably, the mother is intentionally suffocating the child, as revenge on her husband, and her words strongly remind us of Euripides' Medea. These vengeful words come into her 'croon[ing]' voice singing 'My little darling', while the child 'lay there soaked in sweat, with the mother's damp face on her neck,' finally she 'fought back a scream' (257). There is no mention of the mother's grip loosening. That means the child's 'scream' has no effect on her mother.

In this episode, no sounds are uttered from the child until her last scream, as specifically shown in the description: 'The child would try to put her hand outside the covers to get a bit of cool air on it and the child's mother would grab it and pull it back into the slick heat of the bed.' (257) What impresses us is her movement of the body without voice. Ominously, almost as a strange bad joke to invite the child into eternal sleep, the child hears Grandma Blaize singing 'The Connemara Lullaby'. (257) It is relevant here to quote from Elaine Scarry's statement about physical pain or torture:

> One aspect of great pain ... is that it is to the individual experiencing it overwhelmingly present, more emphatically real than any other human experience, and yet is almost invisible to anyone else, unfelt, and unknown. Even prolonged, agonized human screams ... convey only a limited dimension of the sufferer's experience. It may be for this reason that images of the human scream recur fairly often in the visual arts, which for the most part avoid depictions of auditory experience. The very failure to convey the sound makes these representations arresting and accurate; the open mouth with no sound reaching anyone in the sketches, paintings, or film stills of Grünewald, Stanzione, Munch, Bacon, Bergman, or Eisenstein.[4]

Like the works of art or films mentioned by Scarry, the child's scream, in its true meaning, has and is no sound at all. She screams in vain, for however long or high-pitched she may scream her agonizing cry does not reach anybody. Her silent scream surely leads us to Hester Swaine's long wail after killing her loving daughter Josie, or Millie's closing narration. Such screams are the last resort for people suffering pain, but as in Scarry's argument, it rather reveals the gap between a person in pain and their listeners. In her theatre, especially in her trilogy plays, Marina Carr is successful in staging such moments. On the other hand in 'Grow a Mermaid' the child's pain is literally covered up, as her cry for help is muffled under a quilt, pressed hard by her mother. This gives the impression of the child sinking deeper into the bottomless dark pit. However, Grandma's lullaby, again in a paradoxical way, gives a cue to the child to escape; that is to dive into the imaginary underworld of the mermaid.

We are invited into this whole new world. Following the advertisement's instructions, the child starts to grow a mermaid: with the water fetched from the lake, she uses a Tupperware box for the container. The following procedure is like a cookbook recipe: 'then pour in the mermaid seeds and stir it all gently' (257). The child dreams of meeting the mermaid the next day, who will sing for her 'about castles and whales and turtles and whole cities and families who lived under the sea' (257). This vision of a happy world has a festivity similar to that in Disney's animated film, *The Little Mermaid* (1989), especially with the strong resonance from its most joyful hit song 'Under the Sea'. We may also note in passing that Disney's mermaid is called Ariel, the same as the daughter to be killed and sunk in the lake by her father in *Ariel*. The child imagines what she will tell the mermaid: about school, her friend Martina, and about the time 'they saw a balloon in the sky and chased it for hours' (257). This happy moment with the child chasing the balloon with her friend creates another visionary picture in the reader's mind. Now under the sea, she has the sky above her, which gives the child vast space to play around in. A stark contrast is apparent. After the dark, humid, claustrophobic nightmarish struggle for life with the mother, the child has a refreshing time with the mermaid. Paradoxically, in this fantasy, she can take a deep breath under the water.

Here, once again we should return to the scene of their talk about the house, to reconsider one thing. The dominant feature of this long narrative is the mother's whispering voice. Deliberately, Carr uses the same phrase three times, 'the child's mother' whispered' (256-57), and its variation 'her mother whispered' (257) to amplify the atmosphere. Taking into consideration that the plans for the house are their secret, and most probably that the mother must be taking great care not to disturb the younger male child's sleep, and yet the total effect is quite ominous. She sounds like she is suffering from anoxia, lack of air. Her act of suffocating the child seemed to be a sudden eruption of violence. However, it can be also recognized as the last stage of her progressively intoxicated state, which drives her to put the child into the same condition. Constructing the new house and making plans for it, literally and figuratively, is her desperate struggle for survival. With the child beside her in bed, she too tries to build up the fantasy. Yet, the flickering recognition of her husband's substantial absence urges her into abuse, or in its original meaning, to misuse the child. Thus, the child's struggle for air could be read also as a reflection of the desperate state of the mother's entrapment without hope of escape.

There are other things to note. The child recounts the last words of the husband of Grandma Blaize as he 'stepped out the door one day 'to get a breath of fresh air' and never came back' (*Mermaid*, 258). If a symbolic reading is possible, this remark suggests that Grandma's husband also felt anoxia, but he left successfully. This induces us to another darker reading of the mother's suffering: that it is not only caused by the absence of her husband. What is troubling her most is not voiced, but there is a strong possibility that she also wants to escape from that entrapment, that small unit of family ties — the home. Yet, she knows that she cannot be permitted to go anywhere, except into the lake. The irony is the way she chooses to die: drowning herself is just a continuation of the struggle of her life, that is, a gradual deprivation of oxygen.

In the fifth section, the child is chastised severely by the mother with a wooden hanger, because she 'ate sweets belonging to her sick brother' (258). Through the torture by her mother, the child dreams of a man with a pitchfork who lives under the sea. This imagined man is suggestive of her surrogate father. She imagines him as a pacifying being who watches over her with the power to soothe her suffering. In the following section her father actually returns, and he does not betray or contradict that otherworldly figure with such magical power that the child dreamed of. Her father's sojourn is described as an interlude or a magical show, too brief to be believed as real when it is over. The abruptness of his leaving impresses us more strongly than his return. There is another interesting point to note: for that short period of time only, this man appears with such a festive aura. When he returns 'for good this time' after the child's mother's death, the child's eyes are sour and critical against him: 'He skulks along the lake shore with his weak old whingy eyes. "He pisses tears," the child whispers to the mermaid and they both laugh in the silent house.' (261) He no longer possesses the former mesmerizing power for the children; or rather the child is released from his spell.

The child's disillusion with the father derives from both the death of her mother and his presence remaining instead of her. Although there is no mention of it, the child must have guessed correctly why he left them again and what made her mother walk finally into the lake. Carr provides certain clues in a small episode where the child finds 'a box of magazines' of 'lurid fat women's gees' in the father's cupboard (263), and his announcement, too adult to make to the children: 'In memory of your dear mother I'm going to remain celibate for six months.' (262) The child's look of disgust at him indicates this, and these verbal pictures of the father are certainly reflections of the child's feelings. The way in which the child of the story describes her father is the exact opposite of the romanticized figure Bláth of the legend of Owl Lake, in *The Mai*. Manipulating the child's point of view, Carr deconstructs the legend, and dismantles the fantastic cover of Bláth's belated lament for Coillte, whom he abandons just as Robert does. In this way, 'Grow a Mermaid' reveals the dark possibility of the effects of a displaced fantasy. This story also gives an insight into what is left out in *The Mai*: how each day constitutes a constant battle of words between Millie and Robert.

Returning to the scene describing the mother's chastising of the child, it seems that the child rather enjoys the punishment by her mother. The child 'wavered, looked away, treasuring the small rebellion', and even after she sees 'a whiff of anger coming off' her mother, still she 'half-yielded'; but finally she 'surrendered' to swear she will never do it again, only because she 'valued the unwelted slivers of her chubby torso' (259). However, at this stage, we come to understand fully how violently the child is tortured by the mother. The child's rebellious heart goes on to the limit so that her body feels like it is splintered into pieces. The passage closing this section is very significant:

> The child's mother gathered her up in her fat, still young arms. The child counted her breaths, slowly, carefully. They matched her mother's footsteps on the stairs. A mermaid would die in this house, the child thought (259).

Literally, the mother picks up the torn pieces of the child, while the child counts her own breath as if to check life is still going on inside her body. This can be read also as the sign of anoxic troubles the child herself experiences. Similar symptoms appear in the final abusive episode, which happens just after the child's father leaves them again:

> The child's mother knocked the child's brother's head through the glass door. The child counted her breaths, sharp and shallow. Her brother looked at her as the child's mother held him while the doctor cleaned the wound (260).

We should note that the mother embraces each of her children after she inflicts the violence, as if trying to undo what she has done.

This image surely leads us to the final cry of Hester Swane, in the closing of *By the Bog of Cats...*, holding her daughter Josie in her arms, after killing her. However, the comparison seems to end here. We cannot hear such a cry uttered by the mother of this story. Even though *By the Bog of Cats...* is a re-working of *The Medea*, as Carr herself admits 'The plot is completely *Medea*'[5]: what drives Hester to kill her child is not the vengeful feelings against her lover Carthage. *By the Bog of Cats...* reveals the full dimension of longing and true affection within Hester for her mother and her daughter. It is most important to point out that Hester never shows any signs of abusing her child, even though she herself suffered from her mother's physical violence occasionally.[6] The mother of 'Grow a Mermaid' appears to act much more like Medea, in abusing her children. However, we should note that the inner feelings of the mother are not revealed clearly and this mainly derives from the use of the child's limited point of view.

The darkest image can be seen in the eleventh section describing 'the real funeral' (262) where she mourns her mother. The child sings 'My Darling Clementine', strumming her guitar, watching the mother's dead body being dragged up from the lake with a pulley. From the child's 'vantage point', her mother is 'not unlike the mermaid' (262). This scene parallels the opening of Act II of *Portia Coughlan*, but we come to notice that the child's singing is not real at all, but a sheer imaginative creation: 'It wasn't real, none of it. Strumming her tiny guitar in the reeds was, with her mother skimmin' towards her stinkin' of goose scream and the bullin' moon.' (262) This meta-fictional narrative seems to suggest the child's detachment as author. Eilis Ní Dhuibhne's discussion about Millie of *The Mai* is useful here: '[Story] allows the narrator to control the chaos of past experience and to achieve an understanding of it. But the cost of this control is distance. Drama depends on the opposite, total engagement. When Millie stops narrating she starts to be.'[7] What we see in this story of the child is not understanding. She is making a picture of her mother, just as she did with the mermaid. More importantly, due to the use of a meta-fiction narrative, the behaviour of the child at this funeral does not resemble a mourner; she is rather enjoying the funeral. However, there is another possibility to take into consideration: the child's feeling of detachment can be an ordinary reaction of a child at the death of parents. Throughout the story, the child's actual age is never mentioned, but we should notice a surrealistic feature that the child never grows old after her mother's death, as appears in the second last section beginning, 'The child sleeps for twenty years.' (263)

Now the child has long forgotten the mermaid, and she throws her mother's wedding ring into a dustbin. This should be read as her farewell to the dead mother and her fantasy of married life. Yet, the following end section describes the child swimming deeper into the pool where she finally meets the mermaid, with these concluding lines:

> 'At last, you've come at last,' the child says. The mermaid smiles, that smile of years ago at the blue formica table. The child braces herself for the watery descent. The mermaid's tail lights the way (263).

The playful light tones describing the underwater world are a beguiling feature. Even though her last descent looks refreshing, this is a fantasy to cover up the suffocation of her mother's last moment. Her watery descent behind the mermaid follows the same path her mother trod. Another reading must also be possible: it is the child's mother herself that is chasing the mermaid into the water. This reading is valid, taking into consideration that the mother's building of a new house is exactly what the child does in reality; she is growing a mermaid on a larger scale. We see the same childlike tendency not in Millie but in her mother The Mai. The closing line of the third section, 'The child slept as the mermaid grew away out in the dark at the edge of the child's dream' (*Mermaid*, 258) closely resembles The Mai's remark about her house: 'these days I think it's the kind of house you'd see in the corner of a dream – dark, formless, strangely inviting ... It's the kind of house you build when you've nowhere left to go.' (*Mai*, 51)

The open-ended nature of the story also suggests the everlasting reality of the child's entrapment with the dead mother's memories, like Millie's final narration in *The Mai*. The narrator, Millie, is not a child but a thirty-year-old unmarried woman with a child. She dreams of water all the time. Her dream has lost the mermaid. Her recurrent nightmare of a struggle for air, or wrestling with a black swan that is trying to drag her under the water, reminds us of the dangers we see in 'Grow a Mermaid': the ultimate being that the child never recognizes the perilous water she is trapped in. However, a playful light style is prominent in the story. This is created mainly by use of the child's point of view, who is enjoying herself in creating this narrative, reminiscent of the similar excitement seen in a child when piecing together a jigsaw puzzle.

To conclude, there is one more issue to consider. This jigsaw puzzle feature also suggests the fragmented body and mind of the child severely damaged, which is illustrated in the scene of the mother's gathering up the body of the child. Elaine Scarry's consideration of physical pain is helpful here again; she points out 'its obliteration of the contents of consciousness', and continues thus: 'In torture, this world dissolution, acknowledged in confession, is ... resulting cancellation of all parts of the room as well as all parts of the larger world that can be bodied forth in the torturer's action and speech.'[8] Considering her statement, we should recognize that the child's creation of an alternative world in 'Grow a Mermaid' is a beguiling mask, which covers up the total cancellation of any world beyond the torture of life.

From the materials of 'Grow a Mermaid', Marina Carr creates in her play, *The Mai*, a patchwork quilt with many colourful episodes and multiple voices of female characters, each of whom originates in one or more of the three female characters of the story. To mention just one example, Beck's story of meeting her father is a happier version of dismantling the imagined father figure. What combines each female experience is not the fanciful 'magic thread' in Millie's second narration, but what was originally contained in Millie's first narration of her mother's request: 'Millie, would you ever run up to the butcher's and get me a needle and thread.' (*The Mai*, 13) What seemed odd but memorable at the beginning becomes more touching in the final scene. When the play begins, the audience is as ignorant as eleven-year-old Millie, who cannot understand the full dimension of her mother's bleeding pain inside, which wants to be stitched together.

The structure of *The Mai*, especially with Carr's manipulation of time at its closing, has a great effect upon the audience. The closing scene between The Mai and Millie is placed just after Millie's narration about her nightmare of struggle in water, ending with these lines: 'The Mai at the window again. The Mai at the window again, and it goes on and on till I succumb and linger among them there in that dead silent world that tore our hearts out for a song' (*The Mai*, 71). Here again, we should remember Scarry's argument: 'the open mouth with no sound reaching anyone ... coincides with the way in which pain engulfs the one in pain but remains unsensed by anyone else'.[9] All through the closing dialogue, the audience must keep that vivid image of Millie's heart-wrenching cry, that is as belated as that of Bláth, as that of the father of 'Grow a Mermaid' and as that of every character in this play. The Mai's agonies of pain, unheard fully during her lifetime, become visible and voiced on stage by Millie, and are communicated at last to the audience, as the shared experience of theatre.

---

[1] Marina Carr, 'Grow a Mermaid', *The Brandon Book of Irish Short Stories*, ed. Steve MacDonogh (An Daingean: Brandon, 1998): 255.

[2] Marina Carr, *The Mai* (Oldcastle: Gallery Press, 1995): 13. Subsequent references included parenthetically in the text.

[3] Enrica Cerquoni, '"One bog, many bogs": Theatrical space, visual image and meaning in some productions of Marina Carr's *By the Bog of Cats...*', *The Theatre of Marina Carr: 'Before rules was made'*, eds. Cathy Leeney and Anna McMullan (Dublin: Carysfort Press, 2003): 177.

[4] Elaine Scarry, *The Body in Pain: The Making and Unmaking of the World* (Oxford: Oxford University Press, 1985): 51-2.

[5] Marina Carr, 'Marina Carr Interview', *Reading the Future: Irish Writers in Conversation with Mike Murphy*, ed. Clíodhna Ní Anluan (Dublin: Lilliput Press, 2001): 51.

[6] This reading is based on *By the Bog of Cats...* (Oldcastle: Gallery Press, 1998). For Faber's *Marina Carr: Plays 1* (1999), Carr rewrote most of the lines referring to the physical violence of Hester's mother, Big Josie Swane. Minimizing the original characterization of Big Josie made the agonies of her daughter Hester rather pointless.

[7] Eilis Ní Dhuibhne, 'Playing the Story: Narrative Techniques in *The Mai*', *The Theatre of Marina Carr: 'Before rules was made'*, eds. Cathy Leeney and Anna McMullan (Dublin: Carysfort Press, 2003): 73.

[8] Scarry, 54.

[9] Scarry, 52.

13 | Beyond Ryanga: The Image of Africa in Contemporary Irish Theatre

Jason King

Throughout Europe it is 'the Irish [who] are the closest people to Africa', declares Old Man, one of the protagonists of George Seremba's *Napoleon of the Nile* (23).[1] This ideal of cultural proximity and sense of historical affinity between the peoples of Ireland and Africa has been dramatized in a number of recent Irish theatrical productions, most prominently in Brian Friel's *Dancing at Lughnasa* (1990). As is often argued, it is the disgraced former missionary Father Jack's reminiscences about his experiences in the leper colony of Ryanga, Uganda, that serves to provide an objective correlative in the play for pre-modern Ireland's vitality and more integral sense of community at the point of its demise, as the celebration of the Lughnasa festival and recourse to 'ritual ... dancing ... [and] ceremony' (Friel, 40) become compensatory gestures for the disintegration of a traditional, rural way of life 'after the industrial revolution had finally caught up with Ballybeg' (59). *Dancing at Lughnasa* uses its master-image of dancing to link the suppressed harvest festival practices of a pre-Christian Ireland with the equivalent African rites of celebration, notes Nicholas Grene (265). According to Declan Kiberd, it is Father Jack who comes to embody this ideal of intercultural connection and decolonization after 'going native' (Friel, 39) and becoming exposed 'to the counterclaims of the local culture ... in ways which suggest how deep the analogies between Celtic Ireland and contemporary Africa might be' (Kiberd, 1999: 143). Indeed, for Kiberd it is precisely the conflation of 'colonized traditional societies' in Father Jack's imagination and his inability 'to distinguish between Irish harvest festivals and African tribal practices' (611) that infuses the play with a politically progressive dimension: as a dramatic exemplification of the 'idea that [Ireland] contained both First World and Third World realities' (143). Thus, while some commentators have cautioned against presupposing a direct form of 'equivalence between the Africa and Donegal of the play' (Jordan, xliv; also see O'Toole, 95-6), it is still remarkable the degree of critical acquiescence about Friel's portrayal of the Irish-African intercultural encounter, in which his underlying 'analogy between Celtic Ireland and contemporary Africa' is assumed to be relatively unproblematic.

Since *Dancing at Lughnasa* was first performed in 1990, however, the primary setting for Irish and African cultural interaction has shifted from the scenario of Irish missionaries in Uganda to the increasing arrival of African immigrants, often asylum seekers and refugees, into Ireland itself. The predominant impetus for intercultural contact is less to be found in vestigial forms of ritual than in the cultural exchanges between African migrants and members of the Irish host society. It might prove salutary to consider, then, that shortly before Brian Friel began plotting the return of his Irish missionary from Uganda in the late 1980s, the Ugandan born playwright and Irish theatre practitioner George Seremba was being persecuted, shot at, and tortured in his native land, as reflected both in his autobiographical play *Come Good Rain* (1993) and in his performance as a Ugandan refugee in Ireland, the protagonist Joseph Omara, in Donal O'Kelly's play *Asylum! Asylum!* (1996).[2] In his work as both a playwright and an actor, George Seremba brings a very different angle of vision to the interrelation between Ireland and Uganda from that of Father Jack in *Dancing at Lughnasa*: one which substitutes Friel's celebration of intercultural ritual, dancing, and ceremony for the eruption of political violence as the predominant symptom of colonial modernity that links both Africa and Europe in their respective plays. Similarly, if the return of Fr. Jack, carrying into the household Ryangan customs represents 'the pagan affirmation of his native Lughnasa' (Pine, 271) in Friel's work, then the same Irish missionary tradition is also invoked as a point of contact between Ireland and Africa in Charlie O'Neill's play *Hurl* (2003). For O'Neill, however, Friel's affirmation of pagan customs becomes reconceived as a pretext for reverse migration. Thus, the protagonist of *Hurl*, a de-frocked and 'dishevelled priest' named Lofty, or 'Father Bernard Joseph McMahon' (O'Neill, 1), has returned from his missionary work in Sierra Leone in disgrace, like Father Jack in *Dancing at Lughnasa* before him, to an unsettling retirement, only to find that his many African charges have followed him in tow, to apply for asylum in Ireland as the literal and spiritual descendants of the 'hundreds of Irish emigrants who went there' (O'Neill, 5) in the first place.[3] Most crudely put, the Africans are here because the Irish were there, even if under the pretext of providing spiritual salvation rather than founding colonial settlements.

Whatever the dramatic force of Friel's 'analogy between Celtic Ireland and contemporary Africa', their interconnection is reconceived from a spiritual to a geopolitical nexus in the eyes of Donal O'Kelly, Charlie O'Neill, and George Seremba, as coeval cultural entities which are bound together in contemporaneous spatial and temporal relation with one another. More specifically, it is my contention that these playwrights significantly reconfigure the colonial relationship between the Irish missionary and the African migrant into a metaphor for Irish-African intercultural relations that are focalized in geopolitical rather than spiritual terms. About his education by Irish missionaries, the Sudanese refugee character Old Man in Seremba's play *Napoleon of the Nile* recalls that: 'We used to have a St. Patrick's Day parade at school' replete with 'shamrocks and pipes. In the middle of Africa. I love the Irish, but talk about neo-colonial overtones.' (Seremba, 24) Despite its neo-colonial overtones, however, the figure of the Irish and European missionary would also appear to be rehabilitated in these plays: from a paternalist educator intent on the deracination of African culture, to a colonial intermediary who offers a means of escape from the threat of persecution and ultimately a pathway to the west.

This reconfiguration of the colonial relationship between the Irish missionary and the African migrant from the promise of spiritual to the provision of geopolitical salvation marks the narrative trajectory of *Come Good Rain*, and appears implicit in the plotlines of *Asylum! Asylum!* and *Hurl*. Each of these plays thus transfigures the spiritual imperative of Ireland's missionary legacy from the spread of Christianity, the education of the African natives, and the inculcation within them of a Roman Catholic world view into a geo-political imperative to open migratory corridors and provide a place of refuge for those Africans who have been either imperilled or impoverished by the collapse of the imperial social order in which Ireland through its missionaries was implicated. By contrast, *Dancing at Lughnasa* simply substitutes one spiritual imperative for another. The process of Irish and African intercultural exchange that it dramatizes never moves beyond what Declan Kiberd terms 'the level of the spirit' (49). Indeed, although the historical present of *Dancing at Lughnasa* is set in the 1960s or 1970s, the narrator Michael does not recognize any sense of geo-political obligation towards the descendants of those Africans whom Father Jack has left behind, in a Ryanga now engulfed by the cataclysmic violence of the Idi Amin and Milton Obote regimes. By hypostatizing the spiritual, Friel pre-empts any geo-political interrelation between Ireland and Africa from becoming recognizable in the play.

Thus, beyond Ryanga, it is the dramatic works of George Seremba and Donal O'Kelly, in particular, that serve to remind an Irish audience that Uganda and the rest of Africa continue to exist in a contemporaneous spatial, social, and political relationship with Ireland long after its missionaries have left the continent, to which the Irish still have some obligation in the moment of the historical present. Implicitly their dramatic works destabilize Brian Friel's analogous sensibility between 'Celtic Ireland and contemporary Africa' with a more current set of images of the geo-political *asymmetry* that divides Ireland, Uganda, and other

African nations into postcolonial states that exist at very different removes from the polarizing effects of globalization. By conjunctively reading the works of O'Kelly and Seremba alongside each other, one can begin to reconstruct imaginatively a refugee's journey from Uganda to Ireland in its entirety, and to bridge over these incommensurate cultural entities that bind his or her world together. Through their sympathetic portrayal of Ugandan migrant protagonists, these plays encourage Irish audiences to look beyond Friel's Ryanga to a more contemporaneous image of the African in Irish theatre: one that takes shape against the backdrop of global socio-economic disparities in which the Irish themselves are implicated.

The question, however, of whether Irish theatre is receptive to external cultural influence or even capable of representing the polarizing effects of globalization has engendered increasing critical debate. Recent Irish theatre criticism has grappled with the impact of globalization, for example, on the development and reception of Irish theatrical forms, and questioned the adequacy of postcolonial theory to provide an interpretive framework that situates Irish theatre production in relation to contemporary social reality. Shaun Richards has thus suggested that while much postcolonial Irish theatre criticism remains fixated on the construction of binary forms of identity in Irish drama that reflect the British imperial legacy in Ireland, a more pertinent question for theatre scholars in the era of globalization might be the extent to which Irish drama has engaged with the integration of the Irish state into the world capitalist system (2004).[4] Similarly, Patrick Lonergan argues that the influence of globalization in Irish theatre is most readily apparent in the enhancement of 'mobility' across the Irish theatre industry as a whole. According to Lonergan, 'mobility has become the dominant value throughout the globalizing world, in sometimes shockingly different ways'. Irish 'theatres and writers have achieved success by seeking freedom from impediments to their mobility', he adds, whereas for 'the refugee who has spent thousands of dollars to be stowed away in a truck bound for Ireland ... inhibition of mobility signifies disadvantage' (22-3). Implicit in Lonergan's argument, however, is the identification of Irish theatre with the beneficiaries of globalization rather than its victims, the idea that 'globalization has created opportunities for Irish theatre companies and writers to tour and produce new work abroad' (20) in place of any sense of responsibility to represent the adverse effects of globalizing social processes on those who have felt them most directly, such as asylum seekers and refugees. And yet, their arrival in Ireland represents a more obvious face of globalization than the peregrinations of the Irish theatre diaspora, and should occupy a more prominent place in the emergent critique of globalization and Irish theatre that is too often preoccupied with the reception of Irish plays abroad.

Postcolonial critics and globalization theorists of Irish theatre also appear curiously insulated from the wider debate about the development of intercultural theatre in both an Irish and international context. Surprisingly few Irish theatre scholars have engaged, for example, with the theoretical perspectives on the production of intercultural theatre developed by critics like Patrice Pavis and Rustom Bharucha, let alone considered what the contours of an Irish form of interculturalism would look like in specific theatre practice. One exception is Brian Singleton, who has traced the origins of intercultural theatre in Ireland to the modernist aesthetic of W.B. Yeats, especially as exemplified in *Cathleen Ni Houlihan* (1902). 'Yeats's plan for a new indigenous Irish theatre looked to Ireland's pre-colonial myths and legends for his subject', Singleton writes, 'but also to the classical nō plays of Japan for his dramaturgical construction' (628).

Elsewhere I have examined the emergence of more contemporary Irish intercultural theatrical forms and practices in relation to the portrayal of immigrants on the Irish stage (King, 2005). The impetus for contemporary Irish intercultural drama has developed, I have suggested, in the space of imaginative overlap that has opened up between Irish historical memories of migration and the experiences of immigrants in Ireland now, which has become a recurrent narrative conceit in a number of recent Irish plays. From the dramatization of Irish historical memories of migration, the contours and core values of a specifically Irish form of interculturalism thus becomes imaginable both in theoretical perspective and in contemporary theatre practice. Here I want to extend and refine that argument further. More specifically, I want to suggest that the imaginative recuperation of the missionary experience in Irish theatre illuminates one particular aspect of Irish historical memory, which brings into sympathetic alignment the arrival of the African migrant with what Ronit Lentin has described as 'the return of the national repressed' (233). Thus, whether it be through their symbolic adoption of 'black babies', or the provision of education and inculcation of Irish norms and values abroad, Irish missionary activities in Africa became a metaphor in recent Irish theatrical productions for the neo-colonial relationship in which the image of the African in Ireland takes shape under the shadow of Irish historical memory.

The geo-political interconnection between Irish missionary history and the arrival of African migrants in Ireland only becomes evident, however, in a conjunctive reading of the plays of George Seremba and Donal O'Kelly alongside one another, rather than in either of their individual texts. In *Come Good Rain*, George Seremba recalls the cause of his displacement from Uganda to Canada and then Ireland as a result of his personal experience of abduction, interrogation, torture, botched execution and escape with the help of Catholic missionaries. In his performance in Donal O'Kelly's play *Asylum! Asylum!*, Seremba also recounts the experiences of

Joseph Omara, a refugee in Ireland, who was forced by the Ugandan military to watch while his father and four other prisoners were 'placed in a pit' that was 'covered with logs' (O'Kelly, 114) and then set alight before he could flee from the country.[5] About his performance in *Asylum! Asylum!*, Seremba has said, 'it was fantastic for me because there were some cross-currents between it and *Come Good Rain*. As in *Come Good Rain,* I was watching it from within, the whole trauma unfolding,' he adds, as Joseph 'is made to pile up the logs for the ghastly crime, the ghastly murder, really, of his father. So, for myself, the joy was in part that someone from a very different country had the ability to empathize with that sort of situation, and to actually think that it would make theatrical material.'[6]

Thus, in his various roles as a playwright, an actor in *Asylum! Asylum!*, and a cultural commentator, George Seremba has developed these cross-currents and created a composite narrative of a refugee's movements from Africa to Ireland in each of its consecutive stages: from the experience of persecution in Uganda, through the process of displacement, to the moment of arrival in Ireland and the refugee's subsequent reception by members of the Irish host society. About his own life story that is recorded in *Come Good Rain*, Seremba recalls that it 'is a very autobiographical play'.

> It is about growing up and coming of age in Uganda in the era of Milton Obote and Idi Amin, who were two dictators in succession almost. The play itself and its pivotal moment revolves around this one day, in fact, one evening: December 10th, 1980. Uganda had gone through eight years of Idi Amin, who was deposed in 1979. After he was finally overthrown, there was a brief period of peace – it was as if the nation had resurrected. Pretty soon after that, one started to see the clouds gather that would lead ominously to the return of Obote.
>
> When I returned to Uganda in December 1980, on the eve of the election on December 10, I was at the campus of Makerere University, and I could see that it was a very polarized campus. The men who picked me up that night, that evening, from the university campus, were, it turned out, members of what was known as the G Branch, which was military intelligence. They summarily tortured me and interrogated me, and then took me for more interrogation and more torture at the office of the chief of staff of the army, who was Obote's right hand man. It was there that the die was cast, as one would say, because we got into his office at half past nine that evening, and by eleven o'clock I had been sentenced and I was in the Namanve Forest on the outskirts of the city: where the shooting, what turned out to be a botched execution, happened. I believe it was meant as a lesson to those who harbored similar ideas of the kind of Uganda they would be operating in. So, in the end, I think that in the play, to me, there is obviously the historical background which I have

been dwelling on, but it is also very much a story of a celebration of that ability to triumph against all those odds. There is an element of poetic justice in it. It is definitely a celebration of the spirit of humanity, and how sometimes those who are prepared to lose their life actually cling to it.[7]

There in embryo is the substance of George Seremba's claim for asylum as well as the plotline of *Come Good Rain*, in the performance of which he would play the roles of thirty one separate characters to tell both his own and his 'country's story' (111). In order to tell his story, George Seremba claims,

> painful memories were dredged out of my subconscious. Each bullet, each pause, each gun had to be expressed differently. Each bullet had to sting and hurt, enter the body, leave or stay the same way it did, together with all the shrapnel, on the night of the 10th of December 1980. It had to be a one man show, with a musician to accompany me, through the tears and raptures, as I relived the horror on my therapeutic voyage (11).

Seremba's re-enactment of these 'painful memories dredged out of his subconscious' has both aesthetic and political applications: for like every asylum seeker before a refugee tribunal, he has to become both the author and object of his own narrative of persecution and traumatic displacement, in which his ability to relive the horror and to communicate its effects in an expressive fashion will determine the credibility of his claim, and whether or not he is allowed to stay.[8] This is precisely what Fintan O'Toole credits Seremba with in his 'extraordinary re-enactment of his own torture and attempted murder by the Ugandan secret police [in] *Come Good Rain*': namely, his ability 'to take the piece far beyond the realms of artistic imagery' and make it appear 'inescapably real' (O'Toole, 328). The sheer difficulty of making such 'painful memories' seem 'inescapably real' to a sceptical audience of Irish immigration officials also provides the basic plotline of Donal O'Kelly's play *Asylum! Asylum!*, in which George Seremba was cast in the part of the Ugandan refugee Joseph Omara.

One aesthetic strategy that Seremba employs in *Come Good Rain* to make his 'painful memories' seem 'inescapably real' to the audience is to acquaint it with the effects of violence and progressive feelings of disembodiment that result from the experience of torture. Throughout his performance, he increasingly emphasizes the spectacle of the body in pain. Thus, as Seremba re-enacts his experience of being shot and left for dead in the Namanve Forest, an increasing disjunction becomes apparent between his disembodied perceptions of the self and the overwhelming sensations of pain being inflicted upon the body as it is blasted with six bullets and then a rocket propelled grenade in rapid succession. Ric Knowles notes, for example, that Seremba's 'narrative is marked by the language of self-alienation' (23): for 'as he undergoes his torture and intended murder, Seremba moves between first-person references to the self and a third-person account of what is happening to 'the body,' as bullets hit 'the leg,' 'the left arm,' 'the right thigh,' and 'the head'.... As one soldier aims a rocket-propelled grenade at him, [Seremba recalls that] 'I stared at him in disbelief. Oh God, there goes the rest of the body.' (Knowles, 23) By substituting pronouns for the definite article, in other words, Seremba communicates his own sense of *disembodiment* and thereby makes his audience feel intimately acquainted with the experience of torture by sharing its detached perspective, as not just the object of but also a spectator and witness to the spectacle of the suffering 'husk that was my body' (Seremba, 47). Even his stage directions are intended to draw the audience in to this experience of progressive disembodiment through torture when, after 'the fifth shot is fired,' the script reads that 'the familiar and by now comparatively tame sound of another bullet is heard.' (Seremba, 45) Like George Seremba in the Namanve Forest, the audience too is drawn into the inescapable reality of the experience of torture, by having to normalize its perception of the effects of violence upon the body in pain, as 'familiar and by now comparatively tame'.

In this way, the audience is not only forced to bear witness to George Seremba's experience of persecution and traumatic displacement, but it also becomes the potential vehicle of his salvation. Modupe Olagun argues that although *Come Good Rain* 'foregrounds the continuities' between the murderous regimes of Milton Obote and Idi Amin 'within a broad historical matrix, ... the hero of the play is neither of these two strongmen' but rather the 'men and women who rescue George' (441) after he is shot at considerable risk to themselves. Indeed, Seremba acknowledges that the reason that he wrote the play was because 'it was already commissioned by [my rescuers,] the people of Bweyogerere village – [and that] fulfilling it was going to be [my] thank-you note to them and to [my] family as well as to all [of my] valuable friends.' (10) Thus, 'Seremba's hero in the play is the human(itarian) community' as a whole, Olagun suggests (445), whereas Seremba himself pays tribute to 'the so-called African extended human family' (153) for whom the audience by its 'collective nature' (11) stands in as a potential humanitarian community in the making.

The point here, however, is that Seremba's conception of the 'so-called African extended human family' is sufficiently broad to also include those Catholic missionaries who play a vital role in facilitating his escape from Uganda. Thus, at the very end of the narrative, it is a group of Catholic missionaries, and Brother Andrew, in particular, who not only 'promise help' but make possible Seremba's escape 'across the border' (53). As Seremba recounts: 'Photographs are taken. A new identity card is issued and stamped ... I'm also listed as a postulant, a Brother in the making so to speak. The card also calls for a brand new story.' (54) In other words, as in the case of so many refugees, these Catholic missionaries help fabricate a new identity for George Seremba in order to traffic him out of Uganda. Seremba thus reconfigures the image of the 'triumphalist Catholic missionary' (Kiberd, 47) from that of a spiritual intercessor, as the transmitter and receptacle of spiritual value, into a human trafficker of sorts. Not only that, but to facilitate his flight, Seremba is disguised as a missionary, thereby completely inverting the experience of Father Jack, who, in 'going native', seeks to emulate African cultural norms. By contrast, George Seremba adopts the mannerisms of a Catholic postulant in order to reverse the trajectory of inter-cultural contact that the Catholic Church established in Uganda, and to gain access to the west. Ultimately, the missionaries in *Come Good Rain* offer a means of escape from the threat of persecution and political violence, because they tend to the needs of the African body as much as the immortal soul.

Thus, George Seremba inverts the whole paradigm of 'conversion' at the heart of missionary history from a spiritual to a geo-political setting, whereby those former missionary harvesters of African souls now actively engage in breaking down borders in order to deliver their charges to safety in Europe and North America. As A.B.K Kasozi writes in *The Social Origins of Violence in Uganda*: by the 1970s and 1980s Uganda's Catholic missions like Father Jack's in Ryanga had become perceived as 'places of refuge and hope to the surrounding communities ... to which many exiles fled before proceeding elsewhere' (160). That those missionaries who traffic humans in the name of God are the heroes of our time is one of the more provocative ideas communicated in *Come Good Rain*. Indeed, it is precisely this idea that Irish Minister for Justice, Equality, and Law Reform, Michael McDowell, has sought to exorcise when he publicly 'questioned ... the information given by Nigerians who applied for asylum [in Ireland claiming] that they had been given money by unknown Irish priests to help flee Nigeria' (Liam Reid, *The Irish Times* 28 March 2005).

In Donal O'Kelly's play *Asylum! Asylum!*, it is not an Irish missionary but a 'just retired sacristan, in his late sixties' (114), Bill Gaughran, who offers shelter and a place of refuge to the Ugandan refugee Joseph Omara after the Irish state has failed to deport him. The play thus represents the obverse of Ireland's missionary tradition in which the sacristan comes to embody the enactment of Christian teaching in a local Irish rather than exotic African setting. Although not a defrocked priest like Lofty in *Hurl*, or disgraced like Friel's Father Jack, Bill Gaughran is also forced into retirement and protests that he 'didn't jump... [but] was pushed' (115). 'The oul biddies in the church won't know what to be doing', his friend Boylan cajoles, because 'they all fancied you in that slinky black soutane. 'Big Black Bill' ... that's what they called you.' In retirement, Bill Gaughran discovers himself to be the paterfamilias of a deeply dysfunctional household in which his daughter Mary, an immigration solicitor, and his son Leo, an immigration officer, both come into conflict over his decision to invite Joseph Omara into their home; their professional interests become reinforced by a sense of sibling rivalry. On the surface, the subsequent love interest and interracial romance that develops between Joseph and Mary would seem to symbolize the reconstitution of the traditional Irish family through the provision of hospitality to the outsider, and the reinvention of a cultural ideal of welcoming the stranger that is deeply embedded in Ireland's Christian heritage. *Asylum! Asylum!* thus encapsulates both the figure of the refugee as well as Irish ideals of hospitality and exclusion within the same Gaughran family household which becomes a microcosm for Ireland's response to its so-called refugee crisis.

More specifically, the play offsets a hospitable Irish self-image in pitting Joseph Omara against Leo Gaughran and Pillar Boylan, both of them ambitious Irish immigration officers who seek to deport Joseph as part of a larger project of sweeping expulsions and boundary consolidation ironically code-named 'Operation Sweep' (153). Both their project and *Asylum! Asylum!* culminates, then, in a sequence of spasms of anti-immigrant violence that links Leo's eye-witness account of the conflagration of an immigrant hostel in Berlin in magical realist fashion with Joseph's forcible deportation from Ireland: as symbolic manifestations of the same underlying 'pressure from Europe. Pressure for expulsions. Pressure for asylum rejections. Pressure to stop immigration' (138).

Whether or not this represents a bald-faced allegory of Ireland's reception of asylum seekers and refugees or a more nuanced and sophisticated treatment of the subject to some extent depends upon one's interpretation of the genre of the play. In response to the original production of *Asylum! Asylum!* at Dublin's Peacock Theatre in 1994, Victor Merriman criticized its staging within 'a proscenium format, where the pull of the conventions of theatrical realism diluted its impact' (290), while Fintan O'Toole questioned the 'perception that a play which has a direct and urgent political content must adopt the most immediate and direct of [naturalist] forms' (*Critical Moments* 127). In performance, *Asylum! Asylum!* 'is most effective ... when it is most strange', according to O'Toole, because in these moments it enables the audience to comprehend the sense 'of estrangement that Joseph is made to feel. The aesthetics and the politics reinforce each other.' (128) Like Merriman, however, O'Toole argued that the original production of *Asylum! Asylum!* faltered to the extent that it was 'hedged around by naturalist conventions that simply' could not convey Joseph's experience of disorientation and 'the way the world looks from the outside'. Victor Merriman attempted a more expressionist treatment, on the other hand, in his own production of the play in 1997, which featured George Seremba, 'in order to open up the theatrical playfulness of the script's Irish/African encounters, and to enable the magic realist ending to emerge more fully' (290). Like in *Come Good Rain*, the artistic challenge in *Asylum! Asylum!* is to engender sympathy for the African immigrant by transforming the cultural incongruity of the play's 'Irish/African encounter' into a matter of aesthetic and political concern.

Where *Asylum! Asylum!* differs from *Come Good Rain*, however, is in its emphasis on the remembrance of trauma rather than its portrayal outright. More specifically, O'Kelly's play foregrounds the difficulties that refugees have in conveying their experiences of persecution, and the politics of storytelling that delimits and underpins Ireland's refugee hearings and asylum debate. The Irish asylum debate is an unequal contest, he suggests, between the occasional strategic duplicity of the would-be migrant, on the one hand, and the institutional disingenuousness of the Irish host society that would seek to reject his or her claims without, at the same time, disavowing its traditionally congenial and hospitable self-image as an open and welcoming place. The play's underlying sense of conflict is predicated, in other words, upon this contestation of narratives as a vehicle of a wider social and political struggle that pits the individual figure of the asylum seeker against the preconceptions and hostile attitudes of the Irish host society.

The play's underlying sense of dramatic irony thus hinges on a discrepancy between the immigration officers' perceptions of Joseph as a 'chancer' (124), a story-teller, and a master of 'the immigrant's twist and turns' (145), – 'Heart-wrenching stories like his [are] being trotted out at every point of entry… the same scam all over Europe' (144), Leo declares – and the inference the audience draws that he is a genuine refugee. For although Joseph Omara admits to having been a 'small-time smuggler' (151) and petty criminal in Uganda, he bears obvious physical and mental injuries (123); suffers from post-traumatic stress disorder (128-29); and he recalls his experience of persecution with a sense of immediacy and candour punctuated by sporadic recollections of horror that Fintan O'Toole describes as a compelling 'evocation of the nightmare of torture' (127). When confronted by Leo and Pillar with the threat of imminent deportation, Joseph visualizes the scene of horror that is transfixed in his memory and frozen in time. 'Come to Uganda with me!' he implores. 'Come to the schoolyard. I'll show you a pit! There is smell of smoke!' he avows, to which Pillar replies: 'Nothing but the same old yarn! We don't believe you! You're a chancer!' (163) The politics of storytelling and recitation and reception of refugee narratives thus becomes one of the primary sites of conflict in the play.

Underlying these conflicting narratives of immigrant duplicity and the memory of terror, however, are the geo-political imperatives of globalization to stem population movements and secure borders. 'It only takes one leaky section in the walls of Fortress Europe and the flood of immigrants will pour in and swamp the continent', declares Pillar. Ireland's points of entry, in particular, he adds, need to be 'plugged' (153). Joseph's adversaries thus articulate their mission in terms of disaster prevention and national self-preservation; they envision themselves metaphorically to be a bulwark against a rising tide of migrants. Behind their calamitous metaphors of fluidity, however, lies the starker, socio-economic parlance of limited resources, unemployment, imminent overpopulation, and the prevailing assumption that 'there's no room for anybody else ... [Europe's] full up' (120). Indeed, according to Pillar, the ultimate 'criterion for enforcement of [Ireland's] immigration barrier' (165) is, quite simply: 'survival ... survival of the fittest ... [For] everybody knows it's a jungle out there.' (167) Ireland's immigration policy and a discourse of Social Darwinism thus coalesce into explicitly linked manifestations of a prevailing ideology of natural selection.

More to the point, this ideology of natural selection and global discourse of Social Darwinism frame a more localized form of conflict between the figure of the African immigrant and contradictory ideals of Irish humanitarianism and inhospitality. The tension between these humanitarian and hostile responses of Irish society towards African migrants tends to be resolved to their detriment, as those characters who extend hospitality, like the retired sacristan Bill Gaughran, or Lofty in *Hurl*, become associated with a sense of obsolescence in each of their respective plays. *Asylum! Asylum!* and *Hurl* thus make visible the interconnection between global inequality and more localized forms of struggle, like that of Joseph Omara, within a singular frame of reference. Joseph's struggle becomes emblematic of the masses of African migrants, in other words, who have been dislocated by the social, economic, and political processes of globalization in which Ireland and Europe are implicated. In the end, he is forcibly deported from Ireland, but his friends and companions become politicized in the process and so the conclusion of the play is somewhat open-ended, charged with the possibility that further deportations might be disrupted if Irish people engage in acts of civil disobedience to prevent them.

In conclusion, O'Kelly's depiction of deportation would seem to anticipate the fate of some of the cast members of another recent Irish theatrical production that has also explored the interconnections between Irish missionaries and African migrants, by conflating the two of them together in the character of a black St. Patrick: the protagonist in Calypso's 'multicultural musical' (Crawley, 20 March, 2003) entitled 'Mixing It On The Mountain' that was performed over the course of the St. Patrick's Festival in 2003. 'It's never referred to, the fact that our Patrick is Nigerian', declared the play's director Bairbre Ní Chaoimh, but in casting a Nigerian to play the role of Ireland's patron saint and first missionary she was clearly 'playing fast and loose' with the nation's foundational myth, in order 'to reflect the changing face of contemporary Ireland' (Crawley, 17 March, 2003). The play thus featured a mixed cast of professional Irish actors and unaccompanied minors, with the former performing in the role of Celtic raiders and slave traders whose captives were played by child asylum seekers in the care of the state, with whom Calypso has been working for several years in its 'Tower of Babel' project.[9] Such members of the 'Tower of Babel' are also enrolled in Irish schools, where their presence in some ways represents an inversion of the Irish missionary tradition, as the African recipients of an Irish education on Irish rather than African soil. Since their appearance in 'Mixing It On The Mountain' in 2003, many of them have performed in a variety of intercultural theatrical spectacles, including on *The Late Late Show*, during the 'Bloomsday' centenary in 2004, and for Ireland's former President Mary Robinson, and yet, several have received deportation notices in the past year.

The experience of these African immigrants thus points up a profound ideological contradiction between the Irish self-image of a hospitable and welcoming nation of 'saints and scholars', and the geo-political reality of its renunciation of its missionary legacy and refusal to recognize any corresponding obligation to maintain access and provide a place of refuge for its former African charges. Whether it be through the sport of Hurling or Ireland's missionary legacy as a whole, both become re-imagined as metaphors in contemporary Irish drama for the transculturation of Irish norms and values in the people of Africa, for whom the Irish are 'still responsible' (O'Neill, 11) after the decline of their spiritual empire. The image of the African thus becomes transformed in the works of George Seremba, Donal O'Kelly, and Charlie O'Neill from a passive recipient of Irish cultural and spiritual values into a more active migrant who must cross the global and geopolitical threshold of Ireland's 'immigration barrier' in order to participate in Irish society.

Ultimately, in both *Come Good Rain* and *Asylum! Asylum!*, George Seremba and Donal O'Kelly celebrate the spontaneous formation of humanitarian communities in response to specific incidents of suffering as the impetus for heroism in their respective plays. The Irish arts community and wider public could take their lead from these dramatic works to transform themselves into one such humanitarian community in the making, dedicated to the expansion of the moral imagination of Irish society. 'You sometimes wonder', claims George Seremba, 'whether some of those people on the planes that take people back to Nigeria ... went through exactly what I did, or something similar to it, and perhaps ... were not endowed with the ability to say what happened, or to be believed?' 'It speaks a lot to the kind of responsibility that one has if you are lucky enough to have the gift of storytelling, particularly through drama,' he adds.[10] That responsibility extends from the dramatist to the audience and wider Irish public to ensure that deportation is not the only end imaginable for vulnerable African immigrants, such as the members of the 'Tower of Babel', in Irish society. More than most Irish dramatists, Seremba and O'Kelly have pointed the way forward beyond Brian Friel's Ryanga towards a geopolitical rather than spiritual ideal of interculturalism in Ireland. And yet, the conversion of the image of the African from the object of spiritual salvation to the agent of social change that their plays insist upon is only fitfully realized in the world offstage.

---

[1] I am grateful to George Seremba for sending me a draft copy of 'Napoleon of the Nile'.

[2] George Seremba himself has lived on both sides of the global divide, having arrived in Ireland not as an asylum seeker from Uganda but as an internationally acclaimed playwright from Canada, when *Come Good Rain* was commissioned for the Galway Festival in 1995, after which he was invited to perform in the second run of Donal O'Kelly's play *Asylum! Asylum!* (1997). He is now an immigrant in Ireland, enrolled as a PhD student in Irish Theatre and Film Studies at the Samuel Beckett School of Drama, Trinity College Dublin. In 2005, he was nominated for an ESB-*Irish Times* theatre award for best male performance in the South African Athol Fugard's play *Master Harold and the Boys* that was mounted by Calypso Productions.

[3] I am grateful to Tríona Ní Dhuibhir of Barabbas for making the unpublished script of *Hurl* that I have cited available to me.

[4] This argument has been further developed by Shaun Richards in '"To me, here is more like there": Towards a New Paradigm for Irish Theatre Criticism', unpublished paper presented at the IASIL (International Association for the Study of Irish Literature) conference, held at Charles University, Prague, 25-28 July 2005.

[5] O'Kelly notes that Joseph Omara's horrific experiences in Uganda were actually based upon a 'real event', though adapted 'with some license': 'an incident in Bucoro, Gulu District, Northern Uganda, reported in [an] Amnesty International Report, December 1991, where five prisoners were placed in a pit, the pit covered with logs, and a fire lit on top of the logs', 114.

[6] Interview with George Seremba conducted by author, Thursday, 14 April 2005, Irish Film Institute.

[7] Jason King, 'Canadian, Irish, and Ugandan Theatre Links: An Interview with George Seremba', *Canadian Journal of Irish Studies* 31. 1 (Spring 2005): 113-14.

[8] Elsewhere I have argued that refugee narratives are especially resistant to the construction of an expressive autobiographical persona as well as the conventions of naturalism, which are often required of them on a performative level by immigration officials in order to verify their imputed claims of a well-founded fear of persecution, even though the experiences of trauma and displacement do not readily lend themselves to fluid and seamless recollection. Jason King, 'Biographies of Displacement', *New Voices in Irish Criticism*, eds Fionnuala Dillane and Ronan Kelly, vol. 4 (Dublin: Four Courts, 2003).

[9] According to Bairbre Ní Chaoimh, 'the Tower of Babel project is a series of drama and music workshops which we facilitate on a weekly basis in the hall of O'Connell's Christian Brothers' School in Dublin for a group of young people

from Ireland, Nigeria, Angola, Kosovo, Palestine, Macedonia and Vietnam. The group includes some refugees here in Ireland with their families and a number of Unaccompanied Minors living in hostels who are in the care of the Health Boards', 3.

[10] Jason King, 'Canadian, Irish, and Ugandan Theatre Links: An Interview with George Seremba', 114.

14 | Nation and Myth in the Age of the Celtic Tiger: Muide Éire?

Lisa Fitzpatrick

In Declan Hughes's 2003 play *Shiver*, two of the characters develop an internet company called '51st State'. Conceived as a cyber representation of the New Ireland, its slogan is 'Neither here nor there, but that space between' (Hughes, 38). The American investors the developers target, however, are bewildered by the concept and insistent that the website contain recognizably Irish material, such as poetry by Seamus Heaney. Frustrated by this retrogressive attitude, one of the founders, Jenny, denounces Heaney and all that he stands for. 'That's what we've had enough of', she proclaims; 'dead mammies and peeling potatoes and farms and bogs and fucking... all that old tweedy fucking [...] Seamus Heaney is made of tweed' (Hughes, 43). The scene comically exposes the discontinuity between international perceptions and images of Ireland, based largely on its literature and marketing, and the globalized, affluent Ireland imagined by Jenny and her colleagues. Her reductive litany of pastoral themes seems centuries removed from the dot-com 51st State, an idealized, pseudo-American zone of post-industrial, post-modern capitalism that is, as the slogan states, 'neither here nor there'.

The re-imagining of Ireland and Irish identity in recent years, linked to both the globalization of the economy and the country's embrace of European integration, is being expressed in theatrical performance and in dramaturgy in a range of ways. *Shiver* is one of a number of plays that represents the shift from a homeland of mammies and tweed and potatoes and bogs to a curiously featureless, sterilized, suburban nowhere. This unidentifiable space is given a range of physical expressions on stage, including the traditional spaces of the domestic interior, the local pub and, less commonly, spaces of the Irish emigrant abroad. But the traditional domestic spaces tend now to be overtly theatrical rather than naturalistic, are physically invaded by other spaces and times, or exist in a featureless landscape, isolated from external society. Key dramatic narratives of the

1960s to the 1980s of intergenerational conflict and emigration, which functioned to communicate shared experience and cultural identity, are becoming obsolete or are being re-imagined as narratives of wealth and power and choice. Both Malachy McKenna's *Tillsonburg* (2000), and Gerry Stembridge's *That Was Then* (2002), set in rural Ontario and London respectively, perform this revision. The Irish characters are abroad, but they are not emigrants. In *Tillsonburg,* the Irish characters are students, in Canada for the summer before returning home to university. Their freedom and affluence is the envy of a local Canadian boy. In *That Was Then*, Irish Noel owns tower blocks in London, and visits often. But he lives in Ireland with his young, glamorous second wife. In these texts, the Irish presence in two major sites of Irish immigration is reworked, to obscure a recent history of poverty and disenfranchisement. Such experiences are now displaced in the media onto the body of the Other: the new Irish, economic migrants and refugees.

Viewed retrospectively, the changes in Irish dramaturgy have been gradual, and have manifested themselves in a number of ways, which includes not only the obsolescence of certain narrative tropes, but also the parodying of genres such as the Peasant Play, and a range of experiments in language and dialect. But this essay focuses specifically on another aspect: the search for a binding mythology with which to express and unify conceptions of Irish identity for the contemporary stage. The turning to classical mythology is apparent from the mid-1980s. In 1984-1985 there were three *Antigones*, and two new translations of *Medea* were performed in 1991. These are only five of many translations of classical plays by Seamus Heaney, Colin Teevan, Brendan Kennelly, and others, in addition to numerous adaptations. More recently, there has been a resurgence of interest in the possibilities of Irish mythology as material for theatre – often with limited success. But while the translations of the 1980s and early 1990s are read as commenting upon Irish society[1], the contemporary adaptations are more problematic. Both texts discussed here – Sebastian Barry's *Hinterland* and Marina Carr's *Ariel* – received a mixed critical response. Yet if the texts fail, they do so in ways that expose gaps in critical scholarship and conventions of interpretation, and reveal a need for new frameworks to reflect and address the functions of theatre in the new Ireland. Fintan O'Toole raises this question, and first identifies the links between these two very different plays, in his review of the 2002 premiere of *Ariel* at the Abbey Theatre.

> The society that gave form and meaning to the work of [earlier playwrights] is in disarray. Playwrights such as Carr and Sebastian Barry, whose recent work, *Hinterland*, bears many resemblances to *Ariel*, have to start almost from scratch. They have to find a way to make their own private myths fuse with the public world they now inhabit. This is a journey into unmapped territory... (*Critical Moments* 188).

O'Toole here identifies social disunity as a key difficulty for Irish dramatists, in seeking to stage plays in a national theatre that was founded expressly to represent the truth about the Irish nation and character. In contemporary society, where economic globalization and European federalization have put the concept of nation-state under pressure, Julia Kristeva argues, we are 'for the first time confronted with the following situation: we must live with different people while relying on our personal moral codes, without the assistance of a set that would include our particularities while transcending them'.[2] Yet in the absence of shared moral codes, shared mythologies – other than individualistic ones – become problematic, perhaps impossible.

The theoretical basis this essay proposes for this new generation of Irish writing is the postnational, a term that requires some definition. Its relationship to postcolonialism, particularly in the light of contemporary Irish drama's revision of the relationship with England, also demands discussion. The term 'postnationalism' was first used in a clearly defined sense by Richard Kearney, Jürgen Habermas, and Deirdre Curtin during the 1990s[3], reporting on a radical development in the contemporary European legal, social, and political landscape. Habermas and Curtin point out that economic globalization and the federalization of the European Union are rendering obsolete the basis of European law and politics: the democratic nation state. Democratic self-determination – the business of the modern nation state – can only come about, Habermas argues, when a number of people who have been

> thrown together with each other...with the help [of the idea of the nation], construct a new form of collective identity beyond their inherited loyalties to village, family, place, or clan. The cultural symbolism of 'a people' secures its own particular character, its 'spirit of the people', in the presumed commonalities of descent, language, and history, and in this way generates a unity, even if only [as Anderson reminds us] an imaginary one' (64).

It is the loss of these commonalities that O'Toole refers to when he writes of society being in disarray.

The changes in stage representations of Irish life have therefore not come about simply because the cottage in Ballybeg has been replaced with a semi-detached in Naas. There are a number of plays written in the early 1990s and set in contemporary urban middle-class Dublin, where the setting is still a recognizable performed Ireland. Such plays rehearse familiar, canonical themes of emigration, the dead on stage, and the re-enactment or disclosure of trauma and loss, so common in Irish dramaturgy. The cathartic revelation of a past familial or personal trauma conventionally functioned as a signifier for the national trauma: the father-son conflict opening itself to interpretation as a microcosmic representation of the rupturing of linguistic and historical continuity, for example. To make appeal to Barthes' theory of myth, such micro-narratives endlessly work and rework a meta-narrative[4] of Irish history, creating a myth of a timeless, ahistorical nation and its struggle to come into being. This nationalist and, later, postcolonialist reading of Irish culture positions the intrusion of the past into the present – in the shape of the dead on stage or of repressed trauma – as a cathartic release of historical grief, with the personal and familial functioning as the national in microcosm. The repression rather than resolution of the trauma associated with colonization, famine and loss of language, is thus posited to recur endlessly in mythologized form, never quite resolving itself satisfactorily and requiring constant iteration. These myths upon which Irish national identity is founded, summarized by Corkery in terms of religion, nationalism and the land, and by Deane as a meta-narrative composed of competing micronarratives, are dismissed contemptuously by Jenny as dead mammies, potatoes, farms and bogs. These shifts in dramatic convention – away from writing the family or village as the nation in microcosm, away from the repression and recovery of trauma – are significant because the presence of trauma has been essential in postcolonial theory generally and in postcolonial readings of Irish drama and literature. The absence of trauma reinforces the suggestion that Irish culture is entering a *post*-postcolonial phase.

Postnationalism, though it is contemporaneous with economic globalization and late capitalism, has an historical relationship to postcoloniality in its Irish manifestation. In fact, Declan Kiberd uses the term in *Inventing Ireland* to describe 'a project of perpetual translation' in his discussion of translating tradition. By linking the term postnational to authors normally defined as postcolonial – including Friel, who is deeply involved in a postcolonial interpretation of Irish history and culture – Kiberd implies that postnationalism is an essential aspect of postcoloniality, because postcolonialism maps Ireland onto a global grid of former colonies and so transcends national boundaries. Such an assertion, however, oversimplifies the concept of postnationalism. Postnationalism is not simply and unproblematically an historical stage proceeding from the cultural and romantic nationalisms of the nineteenth and twentieth centuries. Nor can it be easily subsumed into postcolonial theory. Kiberd's argument that nationalism cedes to a pan-national solidarity in opposition to colonialism is not borne out by the historical evidence[5]. Furthermore, this argument could be made of many other cultural forces, most of which are pan-European and so link the country tightly to the former imperial powers: Roman Catholicism, urbanization, and modernity for example. These are all transnational experiences, and all map Ireland onto a grid of Western industrialized nations, but they are not necessarily postnational.

However, although postnationalism is not an aspect of postcolonialism, in the Irish context it is to some extent rooted in postcolonial theory and the processes of decolonization. Friel's dramas and the Field Day project, not in themselves postnational, nonetheless foster an awareness of diversity, nurtured by postcolonial readings of Irish culture. As such, they have helped create the conditions for the contemporary representation of the fragmentation of Irish identity. A comparison of Frank McGuinness's 1985 *Observe the Sons of Ulster* and Sebastian Barry's 1995 *The Steward of Christendom* illustrates this progression. McGuinness's play essentially argues for a national identity inclusive enough to incorporate the Orange tradition, deliberately writing the Battle of the Somme into Irish history. But McGuinness's map of Irish identity, while it includes both nationalism and loyalism, does not interrogate the customary identification of these political stances with Catholicism and Protestantism respectively. Barry, however, writes a history of Irish Catholic loyalism, so disrupting the conception of a unified Catholic, nationalist identity. Both plays can be read and interpreted as postcolonial works, but Barry's disrupts a tendency in Irish postcolonial scholarship to read Irish postcoloniality in a binary colonizer-colonized model. Although his representation is of an historical Ireland, its interrogation of the relationship with England hints at an emerging self-confident concept of Irishness, which is essentially post-postcolonial. Postnational, in the sense in which it is emerging in contemporary Irish culture and theatre, has roots in revisionist historiography but points firmly towards the present and the future. With its increasingly multi-cultural, multi-ethnic face and largely affluent native population, this new conception of Irishness largely or entirely disregards the existence of Northern Ireland; in this too, it moves away from postcolonial readings of Ireland.

Yet despite all of the above, 'postnationalism' is not synonymous with 'post-nationalism', in the sense of nationalism becoming obsolete or losing its popular appeal (for if obsolete, it certainly retains its popularity). If anything, nationalism in its narrowest manifestation as tribalism appears to be gaining ground in Europe. Thus, the process of European federalization masks twin contradictory impulses. In re-imagining the state as a region of Europe, the issue of economic viability of that state becomes less immediate, allowing for the emergence of tiny statelets that can survive as economic units within the larger system of the EU. Thus, as nations become increasingly identified as regions within a larger entity, increasing possibilities for multinational, multi-ethnic conceptions of identity, there is a simultaneous impulse away from multi-national structures towards the historically conceived, ethnically specific, Habermasian 'pre-political' community. Hence a dialectic: beyond the nation, towards a regional identity in accepting a place in a broad multicultural community, and back from the nation in the sense of a retreat into smaller and therefore seemingly more secure ethnic or social units, placing the local and the global in confrontation. Habermas and Kearney explore the artistic manifestation of this dialectic.

Both of these scholars characterize postnationalism in its artistic manifestation primarily as a globalization of culture that, in addition to producing a levelling of difference, also gives rise to 'a remarkable dialectic between levelling and creative differentiation' (Habermas, 75). Kearney argues 'The drift towards a more global understanding of identity calls for a countervailing move to retrieve a sense of local belonging' (Kearney, 102). This is true of both *Ariel* and *Hinterland*, where the dramatic agon of the international texts is framed with local dialect, references, and histories. Both plays are contemporary tragedies that draw upon political events in their attempts to represent contemporary culture and identity. They are chosen from a range of possible examples of plays that point simultaneously both to a continued desire for a meta-narrative that explains the present, and to the unsustainability of such a meta-narrative.

At first glance, these two works share only a protagonist who is a prominent politician. *Ariel* is a sweeping tragedy, borrowing the story of the *Oresteia* and incorporating references, in Carr's signature style, to multiple other texts. The plot details the crimes of a wealthy businessman, Fermoy Fitzgerald, who believes he speaks to God, and who murders his beloved eldest child, Ariel, because he believes that God demands that sacrifice as the price of worldly success. Duly elected to the Dáil, Fermoy is set to become Taoiseach when his wife Frances discovers what he has done and stabs him to death. Their younger daughter, Elaine, kills her mother to avenge her father. Barry's *Hinterland* is a portrait of a disgraced Irish politician, an apparently thinly veiled study of former Taoiseach Charles Haughey, incorporating fictionalized versions of Haughey's mistress, Terry Keane, and the ghost of his deputy, Brian Lenihan. While *Ariel* borrows from classical mythology, *Hinterland* attempts the opposite: using material from the social world, it seeks to turn that material into myth.

In *Ariel*, unlike Carr's other plays in which the scope of the myth or legend that the dramatic action broadly describes is domestic and familial, the tragic source material overwhelms the local story. The themes of the *Oresteia* are too vast, and stretch far beyond the concept of blood sacrifice; but even the blood sacrifice itself in *Ariel* has a small and selfish return, and cannot easily be likened to Agamemnon's sacrifice of Iphigenia. The sacrifice of Iphigenia in the classical tragedy is demanded by the gods for victory at Troy; the fate of the city-state hangs on Agamemnon's actions. The sacrifice of a child also recalls the Biblical story of Abraham and Isaac, another myth in which the future of a nation is at stake. Like Abraham and Agamemnon, Fermoy hears the voice of God demanding Ariel be offered up to him; there is also the suggestion of a miracle child, akin to Isaac who was born when Sarah was too old to bear children (Genesis 20-22). But Abraham's God proves his existence by sparing Isaac's life, and Agamemnon's sacrifice secures the defeat of Troy.

Fermoy's Dionysian deity with his turquoise skin and vermilion mouth never appears, however, so that in the end even Fermoy is unsure he exists. His conversations with God, therefore, are deluded rather than connotative of the scope of his greatness. Furthermore, for a deity so alarming and beautiful, Fermoy's God offers very little, and Fermoy's greatest ambitions are depressingly banal.

Despite the gorgeousness of the language and the grim eccentric cast of characters, the mythical structure of *Ariel* breaks down. The weakest points are, paradoxically, both those where the characters are most of the naturalistic world, and those where the action is closest to the mythic. Thus, Fermoy's television interview reveals a mundane protagonist that detracts from the fabulous figure who walks with God[6]. Conversely, Elaine's character works best as a brooding hobgoblin. When she speaks as Electra, justifying her father's murder of her sister, she becomes merely irritating. The strongest dramatic moments and dialogue are those that take place in the indeterminate space between the natural and the supernatural, a space in Carr's work that is always characterized by the grotesque. Friedrich Dürrenmatt writes that 'The grotesque is the uttermost element in stylization, a way of making something suddenly vivid, and for that very reason capable of assimilating questions of the time and even more the present itself, without being propaganda or journalism.'[7]

The grotesque elements in *Ariel*, when present, open gaps in the text through which another level of meaning is revealed. The opening scenes of the play show Frances breast-feeding her ten-year-old son, while the grim Aunt Sarah looks on. Sarah foretells disaster in these first scenes, when the characters dismiss the cake she has made – 'swear ud was Versailles yees were brough up in' (12) – and is a lingering, malign presence observing the disaster unfold. Towards the end of the play, her own grisly history as an accomplice in the murder of her sister, is revealed. In such moments, the sacrifice of Ariel takes on new and more complex significance, becoming a demonic act in pursuit of foul ambition, reversing the normative meaning of the act. Fermoy's election platform makes his vision of society clear:

> aqual wages, crèches in the workplace, no ceilin on the women, the pace process, a leg up for the poor, the handicapped, the refugees, the tinkers, the tachers, the candlestick makers. In Sparta they were left on the side a the hill and that's where I'll lave them when I've the reins ... Migh surprise ya to know how many agrays wud me (*Ariel*, 18).

Fermoy's rejection of community responsibility for the weak strips classical tragedy of its public function, and of Hegelian interpretations as a conflict of opposing forces, each in themselves essentially good. Furthermore, at the level of local mythologies, the sacrifice in the *Oresteia* fails to signify. Irish dramatic (and nationalist) tradition is familiar with the sacrifice of a son for the sake of the nation; such sacrifices appear in legend, in the writings of revolutionary figures, and in the plays of the dramatic canon. But nowhere is the sacrifice of a daughter mythologized. The daughter, on the contrary, has generally functioned as the symbol of the nation, Cathleen Ní Houlihan, who demands the blood of her sons and lovers; or as supportive daughter, girlfriend, wife, or mother of the nationalist hero. Thus Fermoy's killing of Ariel, which does not fit with these gendered conventions of Irish dramatic and critical practice, fails to communicate locally at the level of myth or of community.

In general in *Ariel*, the mythic structure fails by becoming incongruous. While it evokes a shared pan-European network of references drawing on classical myth and the Bible, it is unable to create new meaning in the gaps between the classical and Biblical intertexts and the localized dramatic action. In comparison, *Hinterland* seems to suffer from a reverse flaw: there is too little mythic material. Although Barry has said that this play uses a former statesman as a metaphor to explore a particular kind of Irish masculinity, and to examine the father-son relationship, the similarity of its central character to Haughey is overwhelming. The central protagonist, Johnny Silvester, a former political leader now disgraced and awaiting a summons to appear before a tribunal, sits at home in his Georgian mansion with his betrayed wife and broken son. He is visited by his former mistress, and by the ghost of his former deputy Cornelius, whom he betrayed. There is even a song Cornelius sings with him: *Rise Up Lovely Sweeney*, which recalls Haughey's personal anthem *Arise and Follow Charlie*. It is difficult to overcome the sense of the work as a fictionalized biography that never quite manages to focus the drama on the central question posed: is the protagonist a great man or a crook? The spectators' reactions to that question – at least in Ireland – are likely to be predicated on how they feel about the real-world character.

Barry does attempt to rework his historical material into a tragic landscape. But Silvester fails as a tragic hero not only because the audience sees Haughey, but more importantly because he refuses to act nobly at the end. In classical tragedy, the downfall of the hero is paradoxically his moment of greatness, and this convention recognizes tragedy as a public art form, which speaks to its audience about the nature of their world, and what it means to be human. It is a form of speech that relies upon a coherent shared system of values. The hero's moral qualities – quite different in the various examples of Oedipus, Hamlet, and Willy Loman – all powerfully express the contemporaneous understanding of the relationship between the individual and the universe, and draw the spectator into an emotional response. The conventions of the genre are thus intimately related to the relationships between the individual and the community. Here, however, is the great leader, saviour of his people, finally undone by his own hubris; but rather than accept the role of the scapegoat, and offer himself as purifying sacrifice, he twists and turns and lies in a repugnant abnegation of moral responsibility. He behaves like a man and not like a hero; but the frame of the dramatic action does not allow this to be the tragedy of an ordinary man.

Like *Ariel*, *Hinterland* involves the sacrifice of a child and, as in *Ariel*, the sacrifice fails to convey meaning at anything other than the personal level of the characters. Yet in *Hinterland*, unlike *Ariel*, the protagonist sacrifices a son. The failure of this act on stage further exposes the changes that have taken place in dramatic and genre conventions. Without a strong concept of nation and national identity, such sacrifices become meaningless; attempts to re-form them fail; the actions become signifiers signifying nothing.

Silvester's stunted relationship with his son Jack evokes one of the central tropes of Irish theatre, that of intergenerational conflict. The Oedipal struggle often functions as a microcosmic representation of the colonial relationship and struggle for independence – as it does in *Playboy of the Western World*, for example. But Barry presents, not the convention of the son who finally asserts his own adult masculinity either in action or by emigrating, but a damaged son who so pities his father that he takes the father's plight upon himself, and breaks beneath the burden. Therefore, although the mechanics of the relationship resemble that of, for example, Gar and Screwballs in *Philadelphia*, the outcome is utterly different. Jack fails to attain the status of manhood. He lives at home dependent upon his mother, is unable to cope with the world, and cannot emerge from the shadow of his hyper-masculine father. Silvester leads his country, conducts business ruthlessly, and keeps a mistress; Jack tends to animals, is asexual, and breaks down psychologically under the stress of his father's disgrace. In interview, Barry speaks of the play as an exploration of a particular kind of Irish masculinity. But in the relationship between Silvester and Jack there is a sense of strong leadership giving way to a void. Silvester, despite his corruption, achieves; Jack is paralysed. This shows, tellingly, a profound hesitation in the face of the future.

In the figure of Jack, Barry crystallizes certain debates and problems of contemporary Irish society. If the play explores types of masculinity, then Jack's withdrawal into madness represents a radical confusion at the proper role of men. Such confusion goes beyond realistic, social representations of a response to feminism and changing gender-roles, and is instead a profound confusion at the level of the mythic. In both nationalist and postcolonialist mythologizing, the masculine role has been to engage in a national struggle in defence of the Motherland/Bride. This role is prescribed and validated by a tradition that imagines cultural resistance and the struggle for independence as stretching from the heroes of 1916 back to Cúchulain, and is dramatized – both critically and uncritically – in key texts of the theatrical canon. Stripped of a nation or a coherent national identity, there is nothing to defend. Silvester leads the country into a prosperity of globalization that ironically creates his son's crisis of identity and self-destruction.

Both *Ariel* and *Hinterland* foreground the increasingly urgent gap between dramaturgy and criticism. Both engage with and disrupt dramatic conventions, by the offering of a daughter as a national sacrifice, and the portrayal of a son who is unable to emerge from the shadow of his father. Such shifts away from conventional representations of gender and intergenerational relationships require critical interpretations which postcolonial theory has not supplied. Finally, the problem of mythologizing a society that has so rapidly become a globalized region in a federalized Europe, creates obvious difficulties for dramatic form and for audience reception. Myths are built from individual acts, it is true; but those acts, to function at the level of myth, must take on a wider significance; must tap into a shared symbology or system of meaning. If they fail to do so, they remain random meaningless deeds.

Thus O'Toole's demand, that playwrights find a way 'to make their own private myths fuse with the public world' (188), might be posed instead as a series of questions. How is it possible to represent the absence of community in an art form that is inherently communal, both in its creation and its reception? How can the dramatist represent the absence of a shared mythology, without a shared mythology to ground the work? Mythologies are built, not given; and the Irish theatre is at a liminal point, in transition between national myths whose elements no longer function, and a new mythology that is either more local, more pan-national, or more likely, is simultaneously both.

The fracturing of traditional power bases in Irish society, and the discrediting of those bodies that traditionally represented respectability and morality, are only one aspect of a broader development. The concept of the nation state, on which modern Irish identity is founded, is becoming redundant in many ways. The absence of shared values, resulting as Kristeva notes in a mosaic of individual values finding an accommodation with each other, leaves little possibility for the development of a binding national mythology for the future. Both *Ariel* and *Hinterland* attempt a representation of a contemporary Ireland, in which extraordinary levels of social inequality, and corruption in public life, are tolerated, and the general population greedily welcomes the spoils. These revelations threaten a core assumption of shared nationhood, which is mutual responsibility; in Habermas's words: 'while remaining strangers to each other, members of the same nation feel responsible enough for one another that they are prepared to make "sacrifices"' (64). In these two plays, only one character is willing to sacrifice himself for another, and that is Silvester's son, whose gesture fails. In place of the nation and the community are the micro-communities of individuals who chose their allegiances to each other, based on any number of possible factors, but rarely those of inclusion and social integration. The space occupied is indeed 'neither here nor there, but some space in between': in between endlessly self-selecting micro-communities and the great, global marketplace; in between the conjoining of local legends and classical mythology in productions that look out past the boundaries of Ireland or seek to stage specific localities, and somewhere in between the endlessly contested yet secure Irish identity of the past and the threatening chaos of Habermas's postnational constellation.

---

[1] Tony Roche, 'Ireland's *Antigone*s: Tragedy North and South'. *Cultural Contexts and Literary Idioms* ed. Michael Kennelly. (Gerrards Cross: Colin Smythe, 1988), 221-251.

[2] Julia Kristeva, *Strangers to Ourselves* (New York: Columbia Univesity Press, 1991) 195.

[3] Fintan O'Toole uses the term in his essay 'Modernisation and Modernity', *Crane Bag* 9. 2 (1985), but does not offer any definition.

[4] In his General Introduction to the *Field Day Anthology*, Seamus Deane writes 'There is a story here, a meta-narrative, which is, we believe, hospitable to all the micro-narratives that, from time to time, have achieved prominence as the official version of the true history, political and literary, of the island's past and present.'

[5] Although some of those involved in the Irish military campaign for independence did commit themselves to independence struggles in other nations, many were angered by comparisons made between themselves (White Europeans) and other colonised peoples (Africans and South Asians), seeing these other races as essentially inferior.

[6] In the sense that the term is used by Tzvetan Todorov, in his structuralist study of the Fantastic as a literary genre.

[7] Friedrich Dürrenmatt, *Writings on Theatre and Drama*, trans. H.M. Waidson (London: Jonathan Cape, 1976) 57-8.

Bibliography

Abbey Theatre, *abbeyonehundred Commemorative Programme* (Dublin: Abbey Theatre, 2003).

Abe, Isoo, 'Country Life and Economic Problems', 'The Issues of Country and City', *Waseda Literature* (August 1916): 3-7.

Achilles, Jochen. '"Homesick for Abroad": The Transition from National to Cultural Identity in Contemporary Irish Drama', *Modern Drama* 38: 1 (1995): 438-449.

Adorno, Theodor W., 'Subject and Object', *The Adorno Reader*. Trans. Andrew Arato, and Eike Gebhardt, ed. Brian O'Connor (Oxford: Blackwell, 2000): 137-151.

--------, *Aesthetic Theory*. Trans. Robert Hullot-Kentor (London: The Athlone Press, 1999).

-------, *Mimima Moralia. Reflexionen aus dem beschädigten Leben* (Frankfurt: Suhrkamp, 1969).

-------, *Negative Dialectics*. Trans. E.B. Ashton (London: Routledge, 1996).

-------, *Noten zur Literatur* (Frankfurt: Suhrkamp, stw 355, 1998).

Akiba, Taro, *History of Japanese New Drama*, vol. 1 (Tokyo: Risosha, 1955).

Allen, Paul, Presenter, *Kaleidoscope*, BBC Radio 12 November 1985.

Anderson, Benedict, *Imagined Communities* (London: Verso Press, 1983).

Arnold, Matthew, *Lectures and Essays in Criticism* (Ann Arbor: University of Michigan, 1962).

Aston, Elaine, *An Introduction to Feminism and Theatre* (London: Routledge, 1995).

Ayling, Ronald, 'Juno and the Paycock: A Textual Study', *Modernist Studies* 2.1 (1976): 15-26.

-------, 'Sean O'Casey and the Abbey Theatre Company', *Irish University Review* 3.1 (1973): 5-16.

Ballagh, Robert, et al, 'Mining a rich heritage, or digging trenches?' *The Irish Times* 19 October 1994: Arts 12. Commentary by Robert Ballagh, Jennifer

Johnston, Declan Kiberd, Edna Longley, Martin Lynch, Chris McGimpsey, Philip Orr, and Vincent Woods.

Barczewski, Stephanie L., *'Myth and National Identity', Nineteenth Century Britain: The Legends of King Arthur and Robin Hood* (Oxford and New York: Oxford University Press, 2000).

Barone, Rosangela, 'Thomas Hardy e John Millington Synge: Alcune Affinita', *Annali della Facolta di Lingue e Letterture Straniere*, Universita di Bari 1-2 (1970-71): 6-32.

Barry, Kevin, Letter, *The Irish Times* 23 February 1985:19.

Barry, Sebastian, *The Steward of Christendom. Plays* (London: Methuen Drama, 1997).

Bédarida, Catherine, 'Les plaies de la guerre au Coeur de theater de Frank McGuinness', *Le Monde* 24 Mai 1996: Culture 27.

Benstock, Bernard, 'The Harvest Festival', *O'Casey Annual* 1 (1982): 224-28.

Bentley, Eric, ed., *The Theory of the Modern Stage* (London: Penguin, 1990).

-------, *In Search of Theater* (New York: Vintage Books, 1954).

Blythe, Ernest, *The Abbey Theatre* (Dublin: National Theatre Society, n.d, [1963]).

Bordo, Susan, 'The Body and the Reproduction of Femininity', *Writing on the Body*, eds Katie Conboy, Nadia Medina, and Sarah Stanbury (New York: Columbia University Press, 1997): 90-110.

Bowen, Elizabeth, *'Summer Night,'* The Collected Stories of Elizabeth Bowen (London: Cape, 1980): 583-608.

Brankin, Una, 'Marching towards a full house.' Undated and otherwise unidentified clipping. Lyric archives. [March or April, 1990].

Brooks, Van Wyck, *The Writer in America* (New York: Avon, 1953).

Brown, Terence, *Ireland: A Social and Cultural History 1922-2002* (London: Harper Perennial, 2004).

-------, *Ireland's Literature: Selected Essays* (Mullingar: Lilliput, 1998).

-------, Review of Sons of Ulster, *Fortnight* 18 March 1985.

Budick, Sanford, and Wolfgang Iser, eds, *Languages of the Unsayable. The Play of Negativity in Literature and Literary Theory* (Stanford: Stanford University Press, 1996)

Carr, Marina, 'Grow a mermaid', *The Brandon Book of Irish Short Stories*, ed. Steve MacDonogh (An Daingean: Brandon, 1998): 255-63.

-------, 'Marina Carr Interview', *Reading the Future: Irish Writers in Conversation with Mike Murphy*, ed. Clíodhna Ní Anluan (Dublin: Lilliput Press, 2001): 43-57.

-------, *Ariel* (Oldcastle: Gallery Press, 2002).

-------, *By the Bog of Cats...* (Oldcastle: Gallery Press, 1998).

-------, *Plays 1* (London: Faber, 1999).

-------, *The Mai* (Oldcastle: Gallery Press, 1995).

Castle, Gregory, *Modernism and the Celtic Revival* (Cambridge: Cambridge University Press, 2001).

Cerquoni, Enrica, '"One bog, many bogs": Theatrical space, visual image and meaning in some productions of Marina Carr's 'By the Bog of Cats', *The Theatre of Marina Carr: 'Before rules was made'*, eds Cathy Leeney, and Anna McMullan (Dublin: Carysfort Press, 2003): 172-99.

Chaudhuri, Una, Staging Place: *The Geography of Modern Drama* (Ann Arbor: The University of Michigan Press, 1997).

Clarke, Brenna Katz, and Harold Ferrer, *The Dublin Drama League 1919-1941*, (Dublin: Dolmen Press, 1979).

Clarke, Jocelyn, 'First night: Irish eyes are smiling after a tour de force', *The Tribune Magazine* 26 May 1996.

Clear the Stage. Television documentary about McGuinness. Prod. Fionnuala Sweeney, A Besom Production. BBC Northern Ireland, 1998.

Collini, Stefan, 'Genealogies of Englishness: Literary History and Cultural Criticism in Modern Britain', *Ideology and the Historians*, ed. Ciaran Brady (Dublin: The Lilliput Press, 1991): 1-76.

Colum, Padraic, *Three plays: The Land*, *The Fiddler's House* and *Thomas Muskerry* (Boston: Little, Brown, 1916).

Crawley, Peter, 'Getting the mix right in the new Ireland', *The Irish Times* 17 March, 2003.

-------, Review of 'Mixing It On The Mountain', *The Irish Times* 20 March, 2003.

Curtin, Deirdre, *Postnational Democracy: The European Union in search of a political philosophy* (The Hague and Boston: Kluwer Law International, 1997).

Cusack, Cyril, 'In the beginning was O'Casey', *Irish University Review* 10.1 (1980): 17-24.

Dantanus, Ulf, *Brian Friel. A Study* (London and New York: Faber and Faber, 1988).

De Jongh, Nicholas, 'Powerful topicality proves so haunting'. Otherwise unidentified clipping. Abbey Archives (1995).

De Lauretis, Teresa, *Technologies of Gender: Essays on Theory, Film, and Fiction* (Bloomington and Indianapolis: Indiana University Press, 1987).

De Paor, Aine, 'Druid in Oz', *Theatre Ireland* (Winter 1990-1991): 47.

Dean, Joan FitzPatrick, *Riot and Great Anger: Stage Censorship in Twentieth-Century Ireland* (Madison, WI: University of Wisconsin Press, 2004).

-------, 'Self-Dramatization in the Plays of Frank McGuinness,' *New Hibernia Review* 3.1 (1999): 97-110.

Deane, Seamus, 'General Introduction'. *The Field Day Anthology of Irish Writing* (Derry: Field Day, 1991).

Dezell, Maureen, 'Fighting Irish (on the side of the king)', *New York Times* 23 February 2003: 28.

Duke, Michael, 'Opening your eyes to war', *Fortnight* (March 2003).

Dürrenmatt, Friedrich, *Writings on Theatre and Drama*. Trans. H.M. Waidson (London: Jonathan Cape Ltd., 1976)

Edwards, Christopher, 'Protestant passion', *Spectator* 2 August 1986.

Egoyan, Atom, 'Poetic Licence and the Incarnation of History', *University of Toronto Quarterly 73.3 (2004): 886-905.*

Eliade, Mircea, *Mythes, rêves et mystères* (Paris: Gallimard, 1957).

Ellis-Fermor, Una, *The Irish Dramatic Movement*, 2nd ed. (London: Methuen, 1954).

Fallon, Gabriel, 'Afterword', *Irish University Review* 10.1 (1980): 159-61.

-------, *Sean O'Casey: The Man I Knew* (London: Routledge & Kegan Paul, 1965).

Ferrar, Harold, *Denis Johnston's Irish Theatre* (Dublin: Dolmen Press, 1973).

Fitzgerald, Charles, 'Face to face with Ulster', *Belfast Newsletter* March 1985.

Fitzpatrick, David, 'Ireland Since 1870', *The Oxford History of Ireland* (Oxford: Oxford University Press, 1989): 174-229.

Fitz-Simon, Christopher, *The Abbey Theatre: Ireland's National Theatre the First 100 Years* (London: Thames & Hudson Ltd., 2003).

Fitz-Simon, Christopher, and Sanford Sternlicht, eds, *New Plays from the Abbey Theatre 1993-1995* (Syracuse: Syracuse University Press, 1996).

Flannery, James W., *W.B. Yeats and the Idea of a Theatre: The Early Abbey Theatre in Theory and Practice* (New Haven and London: Yale University Press, 1976).

Fleming, Deborah, *A Man Who Does not Exist: The Irish Peasant in the Work of W.B. Yeats and J.M. Synge* (Ann Arbor: University of Michigan Press, 1995).

Foley, Imelda, *The Girls in the Big Picture: Gender in Contemporary Ulster Theatre* (Belfast: Blackstaff Press, 2003).

Foster, R.F., *W.B. Yeats: A Life: 2: The Arch-Poet 1915-1939* (Oxford: Oxford University Press, 2003).

Frazier, Adrian, *Behind the Scenes: Yeats, Horniman, and the Struggle for the Abbey Theatre* (Berkeley: University of California Press, 1990).

Fricker, Karen, 'Observe the Sons of Ulster', *Guardian Review* 13 February 2003.

-------, 'The Abbey Has Lost Touch with Its People', *The Guardian* 4 February 2004.

Friel, Brian, *Give Me Your Answer, Do!* (Oldcastle: Gallery Press, 1997).

-------, *Molly Sweeney* (London: Penguin, 1994).

-------, *Performances* (Oldcastle: Gallery Press, 2003).

-------, *Selected Plays* (London and Boston: Faber and Faber, 1990).

-------, *Selected Stories* (Oldcastle: Gallery Press, 1979).

-------, *Dancing at Lughnasa* (London: Faber and Faber, 1990).

Garner, Stanton B., Jr., 'Bodied Spaces: Phenomenology and Performance', *Richard Strauss and his World*, ed. Bryan Gilliam (Princeton: Princeton University Press, 1992).

Gilmore, Keith, 'Observe the Sons of Ulster at the Lyric', Down *Spectator* 13 February 2003.

Gomme, George Laurence, *The Village Community, with Special Reference to the Origin and Form of its Survivals in Britain* (London: Walter Scott, 1890).

Gray, Stephen, 'Review corner', *South Belfast News* 22 February 2003.

Gregory, Augusta, *Our Irish Theatre* [1913] (Gerrards Cross: Colin Smythe, 1972).

Grene, Nicholas, ed., *Talking About Tom Murphy* (Dublin: Carysfort Press, 2002).

-------, *The Politics of Irish Drama: Plays in Context from Boucicault to Friel* (Cambridge: Cambridge University Press, 1999).

Griffith, Arthur, 'All Ireland', *The United Irishman* 17 October 1903: 1.

Habermas, Jürgen, *The Postnational Constellation*. Trans. Max Pensky (Cambridge, Mass.: MIT Press, 2001)

Hamilton, Sheila, 'Why we love and kill', *Communist Party Weekly* 5 May 1990.

Hardy, Thomas, *The Life and Death of the Mayor of Casterbridge: A Story of a Man of Character*. New Wessex Edition (London: Macmillan, 1974).

-------, *The Well-Beloved. A Sketch of a Temperament* (London: MacMillan, 1927).

Harris, Peter, *Sean O'Casey's Letters and Autobiographies* (Trier: WVT, 2004).

Hasegawa, Seiya, 'On Looking at a Garden City in England', 'The Issues of Country and City', *Waseda Literature* (August 1916): 16-7.

Hayes, Dermott, 'Tony hero of late night metro drama', *Evening Herald* 23 May 1996.

Hill, Ian, 'Great portrayal of the "shallowness of governments and horrors of war"', *Newsletter* 13 February 2003.

Hoad, T.F., ed., *The Concise Oxford Dictionary of English Etymology* (Oxford: Oxford University Press, 1987).

Hogan, Robert, and Richard Burnham, *The Years of Sean O'Casey, 1921-1926* (New Jersey: University of Delaware Press, 1992).

Hogan, Robert, et al, *The Modern Irish Drama: A Documentary History* (Dublin: Dolmen Press; Gerrards Cross: Colin Smythe, 1975-1992). 6 vols.

Hogan, Robert, *The Experiments of Sean O'Casey* (New York: St Martin's Press, 1960).

Howe, Stephen, *Ireland and Empire: Colonial Legacies in Irish History and Culture* (London: Oxford University Press, 2000).

Hughes, Declan, *Shiver* (London: Methuen, 2003).

Hunt, Hugh, *The Abbey: Ireland's National Theatre 1904-1979* (Dublin: Gill and Macmillan, 1979).

Irigaray, Luce, *Je, tu, nous: Toward a Culture of Difference*. Trans. Alison Martin (New York and London: Routledge, 1993).

Jeffery, Keith, 'Under the blood-red hand', *Times Literary Supplement* (22 November 1985): 1326.

Johnston, Denis, 'Waiting for Beckett', *Irish Writing* (Spring 1956): 23-28.

Johnston, Jennifer, Letter. *The Irish Times* 23 February 1985: 19.

Jones, Marie, *Women on the Verge of HRT* (London: French, 1999).

Jordan, Eamonn, 'From Playground to Battleground: Metatheatricality in the Plays of Frank McGuinness', *Theatre Stuff: Critical Essays on Contemporary Irish Theatre*, Eamonn Jordan, ed. (Dublin: Carysfort Press, 2000): 194-208.

Jordan, Eamonn, ed., *Theatre Stuff: Critical Essays on Contemporary Irish Theatre* (Dublin: Carysfort Press, 2000).

Kasozi, A.B.K., *The Social Origins of Violence in Uganda* (Montreal: McGill-Queen's University Press; Kampala: Fountain Publishers, 1994-1999).

Kavanagh, Peter, *The Story of the Abbey Theatre* (New York: Devin-Adair, 1950; Orono, ME: National Poetry Foundation, University of Maine at Orono, 1984).

Kearney, Richard, *Postnationalist Ireland* (London and New York: Routledge, 1997).

Kiberd, Declan, *Inventing Ireland. The Literature of the Modern Nation* (London: Vintage, 1996).

-------, 'Strangers in their own Country: Multi-Culturalism in Ireland', *Multi-culturalism: The View from the Two Irelands*, eds Edna Longley, and Declan Kiberd (Cork: Cork University Press, 2001).

-------, Review of Patrick Mason's production of *Dancing at Lughnasa* (14 June 1999), *Irish Theatre Magazine* 1. 3 (Summer 1999).

Kilroy, Thomas, ed., *Sean O'Casey* (New Jersey: Prentice-Hall, 1975).

-------, 'Theatrical Text and Literary Text', *The Achievement of Brian Friel* (Gerrards Cross: Colin Smythe, 1993): 91-102.

King, Mary C. *The Drama of JM Synge* (London and New York: Fourth Estate & Syracuse University Press, 1986).

Kölnische Rundschau, 'Von Clownerie zum Totentanz', *Kölnische Rundschau* (Cologne) 15 June 1996).

Komisar, Lucy, '"Sons of Ulster Marching" amid a hellish war', 2002, http://www.american-reporter.com.

Kono, Yoshihiro, 'On Country Literature', *Waseda Literature* (February 1916): 39-50.

Kosok, Heinz, 'The Three Versions of Red Roses for Me', *O'Casey Annual* 1 (1982): 141-47.

Krause, David, and Robert Lowery, eds, *Sean O'Casey Centenary Essays* (Gerrards Cross: Colin Smythe, 1980).

Krause, David, 'Sean O'Casey', *The Massachusetts Review* 6.2 (1965): 233-251.

Kristeva, Julia, *Strangers to Ourselves*. Trans. Leon S. Roudiez (New York: Columbia UP, 1991).

Legendre, Pierre, *'L'inestimable objet de la transmission', Etude sur le principe généalogique en Occident* (Paris: Fayard, 1985, 2004).

Lentin, Ronit. 'Anti-racist responses to the racialization of Irishness: Disavowed multiculturalism and its discontents', *Racism and Anti-racism in Ireland*, eds, Ronit Lentin. and Robbie McVeigh (Belfast: Beyond the Pale, 2002).

Lévi-Strauss, Claude, *Structural Anthropology*. Trans. Claire Jacobson, and Brooke Grundfest Schoepf (London: Penguin, 1986).

Levitas, Ben, *The Theatre of Nation: Irish Drama and Cultural Nationalism 1890-1916* (Oxford: Clarendon Press, 2002).

Llewellyn-Jones, Margaret, *Contemporary Irish Drama and Cultural Identity* (Bristol: Intellect, 2002).

Lojek, Helen, ed., *The Theatre of Frank McGuinness: Stages of Mutability* (Dublin: Carysfort Press, 2002).

Lojek, Helen, 'Watching Over Frank McGuinness's Stereotypes,' *Modern Drama* 38 (1995): 348-61.

Lonergan, Patrick, 'Recent Irish Theatre: The Impact of Globalization', *New Voices in Irish Criticism*, eds Fionnuala Dillane, and Ronan Kelly, vol. 4 (Dublin: Four Courts, 2003).

Longley, Michael, Letter, *The Irish Times* 2 March 1985: 23.

Lowery, Robert, 'O'Casey Letters', *The Sean O'Casey Review* 1.2 (1975): 19-25.

Lysaght, Patricia, *A Pocket Book of the Banshee* (Dublin: O'Brien, 1998).

Mackintosh, Fiona, *Dying Acts: Death in Ancient Greek and Modern Irish Tragic Drama* (Cork: Cork University Press, 1994).

MacLiammóir, Micheál, *Theatre in Ireland*, 2nd ed. (Dublin: Cultural Relations Committee of Ireland, 1964).

Malone, Andrew E., *The Irish Drama* (London: Constable, 1929; New York: Benjamin Blom, 1965).

Mason, Patrick, 'Playing with Words: A Fantasy on the Themes of Theatre, the National Theatre, and Post-Modernism' [pamphlet] (Dublin: Royal Irish Academy, 2000).

Mathews, P.J., *Revival: The Abbey Theatre, Sinn Féin, the Gaelic League and the Co-operative Movement* (Cork: Cork University Press/Field Day, 2003).

Matsui, Shingen, ed., 'Tea Making House', *Selected Play Scripts by Shoyo* (Tokyo: Kikuya Publisher, 1915): 1-85.

Matsui, Shoyo, 'Commonising Theatre', *New Entertainment* (February 1920): 6-7.

McAuley, Gay, *Space in Performance: Making Meaning in the Theatre* (Ann Arbor: The University of Michigan Press, 1999).

McCann, Seán, ed.,*The Story of the Abbey Theatre* (London: New English Library, 1967).

McCormack, W.J., *Fool of the Family: A Life of J.M. Synge* (London: Weidenfeld & Nicolson, 2000).

-------, *The Silence of Barbara Synge* (Manchester: Manchester University Press, 2003).

McDiarmid, Lucy, *The Irish Art of Controversy* (Dublin: Lilliput Press, 2005).

McDonald, Ronan, *Tragedy and Irish Literature: Synge, O'Casey, Beckett* (Basingstoke: Palgrave, 2002).

McFadden, Grania, 'Southern discomfort on the road to the Somme', *The Telegraph* (Belfast) 5 August 1996: 16.

McGuinness, Frank, *Observe the Sons of Ulster Marching to the Somme* (London: Faber and Faber, 1986).

-------, 'An Irishman's theatre', *Studies on the contemporary Irish theatre*, eds, Jacqueline Genet, and Elisabeth Hellegourac'h (Caen, France: GDR D'Etudes Anglo-Irlandaises du CNRS, 1991): 57-66.

-------, *Dolly West's Kitchen* (London: Faber and Faber, 1999).

McKenna, Bernard, *Rupture, Representation, and the Refashioning of Identity in Drama from the North of Ireland, 1969-1994* (Westport, CT: Praeger, 2003).

McKeone, Marion, 'Irish culture just packs in the French', *Sunday Business Post* 26 May 1996: Agenda 26.

McMinn, Joe, 'Language, literature and cultural identity: Irish and Anglo-Irish', *Styles of belonging: the cultural identities of Ulster*, eds Jean Lundy, and Aodán MacPóilin (Belfast: Lagan Press, 1996): 46-53.

McMullan, Anna, and Caroline Williams, 'Contemporary Women Playwrights', *The Field Day Anthology of Irish Writing* Vol. V: *Irish Women's Writing and Traditions,* ed. Angela Bourke, et al, (Cork: Cork University Press in association with Field Day, 2002): 1234-46.

McMullan, Anna, 'Gender, Authorship and Performance in Selected Plays by Contemporary Irish Women Playwrights: Mary Elizabeth Burke-Kennedy, Marie Jones, Marina Carr, Emma Donoghue', *Theatre Stuff*, ed. Eamonn Jordan (Dublin: Carysfort Press, 2000): 34-46.

McNally, Frank, 'Orangemen are invited down an untraditional route to the Aras', *The Irish Times* 11 July 1998: 1.

Mercier, Vivian, *Modern Irish literature: Sources and founders*, ed. Eilis Dillon (Oxford: Clarendon, 1994).

Mikami, Hiroko, *Frank McGuinness and His Theatre of Paradox* (Gerrards Cross: Colin Smythe, 2002).

Mikhail, E.H., ed. *The Abbey Theatre: Interviews and Recollections* (London: Macmillan, 1988).

Morash, Chris, '"Something's Missing": Theatre and the Republic of Ireland Act', *Writing in the Irish Republic: Literature, Culture, Politics 1949-1999*, ed. Ray Ryan (Basingstoke: Macmillan, 2000).

-------, *A History of Irish Theatre 1601-2000* (Cambridge: Cambridge University Press, 2002).

Murphy, Tom, *Plays: Three* (London: Methuen; London: Jonathan Cape, 1995).

-------, *Too Late For Logic* (London: Methuen, 1990).

Murray, Christopher, ed., *Brian Friel: Essays, Diaries, Interviews: 1964-1999* (London and New York: Faber and Faber, 1999).

-------, *Sean O'Casey: Writer at Work* (Dublin: Gill and Macmillan, 2004).

-------, *Twentieth-Century Irish Drama: Mirror up to Nation* (Manchester: Manchester University Press, 1997).

Myers, Kevin, 'An Irishman's diary', *The Irish Times* 22 October 1994: 15.

Ness, Fiona, 'Artistic Director to Quit Abbey Next Year', *The Sunday Business Post*, 4 July 2004.

Nesti, Robert, 'Waiting for God-knows-what', 2002, http://www.baywindows.com.

Ní Chaoimh, Bairbre 'Programme Note' for *Mixing It On The Mountain*, Calypso Productions (March 2003).

Ní Dhuibhne, Eilis, 'Playing the Story: Narrative Techniques in The Mai', *The Theatre of Marina Carr: 'Before rules was made'*, eds Cathy Leeney, and Anna McMullan (Dublin: Carysfort Press, 2003): 65-77.

Nietzsche, Friedrich, *Twilight of the Idols and The Anti-Christ*. Trans. R.J. Hollingdale (London: Penguin, 2003).

Nightingale, Benedict, 'Recognising the Somme total', *The Times* 22 August 1995.

Nowlan, David, 'Letter, *The Irish Times* 28 February 1985.

-------, 'Observe the Sons of Ulster Marching toward the Somme at the Peacock', *The Irish Times* 19 February 1985: 10.

'Observe the Sons of Ulster Marching Towards the Somme', *North Belfast News* 22 February 2003.

Ó hAodha, Micheál, ed., *The O'Casey Enigma* (Cork: Mercier Press, 1980).

Ó hAodha, Micheál, *The Abbey—Then and Now* (Dublin: The Abbey Theatre, 1969).

O'Casey, Sean, *Autobiographies* (London: Macmillan, 1963). 2 vols.

-------, *Selected Plays of Sean O'Casey* (New York: George Braziller, 1954).

-------, *The Letters of Sean O'Casey 1910-1941*, ed. David Krause (New York: Macmillan, 1975). 4 vols.

-------, *The Letters of Sean O'Casey 1959-1964*, ed. David Krause (Washington: The Catholic University of America Press, 1992). 4 vols.

O'Connor, Frank, *The Art of the Theatre* (Dublin: Maurice Fridberg, 1947).

O'Grady, Standish, *'On The King's Threshold', Laying the foundations 1902-1904*, eds Robert Hogan, and James Kilroy (Dublin: Dolmen Press, 1976): 73-4.

O'Kelly, Donal, *'Asylum! Asylum!', New Plays from the Abbey Theatre, 1993-1995*, eds C. Fitz-Simon, and S. Sternlicht (Syracuse, New York: Syracuse University Press, 1996).

O'Kelly, Seumas, *The Shuiler's Child: A Tragedy in Two Acts* (Chicago: DePaul UP, 1971).

O'Neill, Michael J., *The Abbey at the Queen's: The Interregnum Years 1951-1966* (Nepean, Ontario: Borealis Press, 1999).

O'Neill, Michael, *Lennox Robinson* (New York: Twayne, 1964).

O'Toole, Fintan, 'Hidden Charges', *The Irish Times* 25 October 1994. Reprinted in O'Toole, Critical Moments.

-------, *Tom Murphy: The Politics of Magic*, rev. ed. (Dublin: New Island, 1987).

-------, 'Modernisation and Modernity', *Crane Bag* 9. 2 (1985).

-------, *Critical Moments: Fintan O'Toole on Modern Irish Theatre*, eds Julia Furay and Redmond O'Hanlon (Dublin: Carysfort Press, 2003).

-------, 'In Conversation with Redmond O'Hanlon', *Critical Moments*, 341-77.

O'Connor, Brian, ed., *The Adorno Reader* (Oxford: Blackwell Publishers, 2000).

O'Connor, Joseph, 'Theatre', *Magill* 7 March 1985.

O'Donnell, Mary, 'Blood sacrifice and faith under duress', *Sunday Tribune* 22 April 1990: B4.

O'Hanlon, Eamonn, 'Observe as a son of Ulster marches on Broadway', *Sunday People* 9 March 2003.

Ohsasa, Yoshio, *The History of Modern Japanese Drama: Taisho and Showa Era* (Tokyo: Hakusui-sha, 1986).

Ohyama, Ikuo, 'City and Living Problems', 'The Issues of Country and City', *Waseda Literature* (August 1916): 7-11.

Okada, Shin-ichiro, 'Beauty of City Perspective', 'The Issues of Country and City', *Waseda Literature* (August 1916): 12-15.

Olagun, Modupe, 'Dramatizing Atrocities: Plays by Wole Soyinka, Francis Imbuga, and George Seremba Recalling the Idi Amin Era', *Modern Drama* 5. 45. 3 (Fall 2002).

Oliver, Kelly, ed., *The Portable Kristeva* (New York: Columbia University Press, 1997).

Orr, Philip, Programme Notes, Lyric Theatre Programme (2003), 'Observe the Sons of Ulster': 11-12.

Peacock, Alan, ed., *The Achievement of Brian Friel* (Gerrards Cross: Colin Smythe, 1993).

Pfeil, Lawrence, Jr., 'A kiss before dying', *New York Blade* 7 March 2002: 49.

Pilkington, Lionel, *Theatre and the State in Twentieth-Century Ireland: Cultivating the People* (London and New York: Routledge, 2001).

Pine, Richard, 'Frank McGuinness: A Profile', *ILS* 10.1 (1991): 29-30.

-------, *The Diviner: The Art of Brian Friel* (Dublin: University College Dublin Press 1999).

Poizat, Michel, *La voix du diable. La jouissance lyrique sacrée* (Paris: Métailié 1991).

Rabaté, Jean-Michel, *James Joyce and the Politics of Egoism* (Cambridge: Cambridge University Press, 2001).

Richards, Shaun, ed., *The Cambridge Companion to Twentieth-Century Irish Drama* (Cambridge: Cambridge University Press, 2004).

-------, 'Throwing Theory at Ireland? The Field Day Theatre Company and Postcolonial Theatre Criticism', *Modern Drama* 5. 47. 4 (Winter 2004).

Robinson, Lennox, *Curtain Up: An Autobiography* (London: Michael Joseph, 1942).

-------, *Ireland's Abbey Theatre: A History, 1899-1951* (London: Sidgwick and Jackson, 1951).

-------, *Two Plays: Harvest; The Clancy Name* (Dublin: Maunsel & Company, Ltd., 1911): 1-61.

-------, ed., *The Irish Theatre: Lectures Delivered during the Abbey Theatre Festival* [...] 1938 (London: Macmillan, 1939).

Roche, Anthony, *Contemporary Irish Drama: From Beckett to McGuinness* (Dublin: Gill & Macmillan, 1994).

Russo, Mary, *The Female Grotesque: Risk, Excess and Modernity* (London: Routledge, 1994).

Ryan, Ray, ed., *Writing in the Irish Republic: Literature, Culture, Politics 1949-1999* (Basingstoke: Macmillan; New York: St Martin's Press, 2000).

Saddlemyer, Ann, ed., *Theatre Business: The Correspondence of the First Abbey Directors: William Butler Yeats, Lady Gregory and J.M. Synge* (Gerrards Cross: Colin Smythe, 1982).

Scarry, Elaine, *The Body in Pain: The Making and Unmaking of the World* (Oxford: Oxford University Press, 1985).

Schmitt, Olivier, 'A la recherche de la paix sur les rives de la Somme, résister à l'envahisseur allemand', *Le Monde* 24 Mai 1996: Culture 27.

Seremba, George, 'Napoleon of the Nile' (2004). Unpublished script.

-------, *Come Good Rain* (Winnipeg: Blizzard Publishing, 1993).

Sheridan, Kathy, 'Turning a Haven into a Home'. *The Irish Times* 14 August 2004: W5.

Simonson, Robert, 'Observe The Sons of Ulster march into the Newhouse', Playbill 6 February 2003, available at http://www.playbill.com.

Simonson, Robert, 'The Sons of Ulster father an opening at Lincoln Center', Playbill 24 February 2003, available at http://www.playbill.com.

Simpson, Alan, 'The Staging of O'Casey's Plays', *The Sean O'Casey Review* 5. 2 (1979): 131-56.

Singleton, Brian, 'Challenging Myth and Tradition', *Modern Drama* 43.2 (2000).

-------, 'Interculturalism', *The Oxford Encyclopaedia of Theatre and Performance*, ed. Dennis Kennedy, vol. 1 (Oxford: Oxford UniversityPress, 2003).

Smyth, Patrick, 'Stage drama provides relief from beef war', *The Irish Times* 14 June 1996: 10.

Soma, Gyofu, 'My View', 'The Issues of Country and City', *Waseda Literature* (August 1916): 18-20.

Sommer, Elyse, Review, Curtain Up, 2003, http://www.curtainup.com.

Spencer, Charles,' Pack up the troubles in an old kitbag', *Daily Telegraph* 22 August 1995.

Stackman, Will, 'Observe the Sons of Ulster Advancing on the Somme [sic]', 2002, http://www.aislesay.com.

Stembridge, Gerard, *That Was Then* (London: Methuen Drama, 2002).

Stewart, Victoria, *About O'Casey* (London: Faber and Faber, 2003).

Swander, Homer, 'Shields at the Abbey', *Eire-Ireland* 5. 2 (1970): 25-41.

Synge, John Millington, *'When The Moon Has Set in Long Room': Bulletin of the Friends of the Library*, ed. Mary C. King, Trinity College Dublin, Double Number 24-5 (Spring-Autumn 1982).

-------, *Collected works*,. 4 vols. (London: Oxford UP, 1962-1968).

Tereshchuk, David, '"Observe the Sons of Ulster" pulls no punches', The Wild Geese Today, 2004, http://www.thewildgeese.com.

Todd, Mary, 'Two versions of within the Gates', *Modern Drama* 10.4 (1968): 346-55.

Todorov, Tzvetan, *The Fantastic: a structural approach to the literary genre* (Ithaca: Cornell U.P., 1975).

Tompkins, Joanne, 'Space and the Geographies of Theatre: Introduction', *Modern Drama* 46 (2003): 537-41.

Trotter, Mary, *Ireland's National Theaters: Political Performance and the Origins of the Irish Dramatic Movement* (Syracuse, NY: Syracuse University Press, 2001).

Vogel, Elfin, 'Observe the Sons of Ulster Marching towards the Somme', *Das Boot, 2003,* http://www.dasboot.org.

Voltaire (1764, 1964), *Dictionnaire philosophique* (Paris: Garnier-Flammarion, 1764, 1964).

Waters, John, 'Alone again, naturally (Interview with Frank McGuinness)', *In Dublin* 14 May 1987: 18.

Watt, Stephen, et al, eds, *A Century of Irish Drama: Widening the Stage* (Bloomington: Indiana University Press, 2000).

Welch, Robert, *The Abbey Theatre 1899-1999: Form and Pressure* (Oxford: Oxford University Press, 1999).

Willett, John, *The Theatre of Bertolt Brecht* (Connecticut: New Directions, 1959).

Worth, Katharine, *The Irish Drama of Europe from Yeats to Beckett* (London: Athlone Press, 1978).

Wotton, George, *Thomas Hardy: Towards a Materialist Criticism* (Totowa: Barnes and Noble, 1985).

Yeats, W.B., *Essays and Introductions* (London: Macmillan, 1961).

-------, *Explorations* (London: Macmillan, 1962).

-------, *The Collected plays of W.B. Yeats* (New York: Macmillan, 1953; York: Cambridge University Press, 2001).

-------, *The Collected Works of W.B. Yeats* Volume III *Autobiographies*, eds, William O'Donnell, and Douglas N. Archibald (New York, Scribner, 1999).

-------, *Uncollected Prose*, eds, John P. Frayne, and Colton Johnson, vol. 2 (London: Macmillan, 1975).

Biographies

Joan FitzPatrick Dean is Curators' Teaching Professor of English at University of Missouri-Kansas City, where she teaches dramatic literature and film. She was Fulbright Scholar and Visiting Professor at the National University of Ireland-Galway. Her books include *Dancing at Lughnasa* (Cork University Press, 2003) and *Riot And Great Anger: Stage Censorship in Twentieth-Century Ireland* (University of Wisconsin Press, 2004).

Lisa Fitzpatrick lectures in drama at the University of Ulster at Magee. She was awarded her PhD from the Graduate Drama Centre at the University of Toronto. Her main research interests are contemporary Irish theatre, women's writing, Canadian theatre, and postcolonial theatre.

Mika Funahashi was educated at Aoyama Gakuin University and currently lectures at several colleges in Tokyo, Japan. She has published essays on Marina Carr both in Japanese and English and translated *The Mai* for its Japanese premier by Tokyo Engeki Ensembre in October 2005.

Jason King is a graduate of McGill University (BA), Simon Fraser University (MA), and the National University of Ireland, Maynooth (PhD). He has lectured at National University of Ireland, Maynooth, and National University of Ireland, Cork, and currently teaches at the Centre for Canadian Irish Studies, Concordia, Montreal. His research interests focus on the literary culture of the Irish diaspora, the Irish in Canada, and the literature of social change in contemporary Ireland reflecting its transformation from an emigrant-sending to an immigrant-receiving society. He has published numerous articles about Irish diasporic writing in journals and edited collections on both sides of the Atlantic, half of which focus on Irish-Canadian literature and the literary culture of the Irish in Quebec.

Mary C. King is Visiting Professor of Cultural Studies at National College of Ireland, Dublin and author of *The Drama of JM Synge*. She has written, lectured and broadcast widely on Irish literature and Irish Theatre. She worked recently with Druid Theatre, Galway, preparing for the Druid-Synge Cycle of Synge's plays. She also lectured on Synge, Marina Carr, and Martin McDonagh, and led the Synge seminars, at the revived Synge Summer School in Wicklow, in 2005.

Chiaki Kojima is a PhD candidate of the University of Tokyo and a doctor at Cork University hospital. Working on her dissertation entitled, 'From Irish Drama to Japanese New Drama', she has published a number of articles on the subject. She was awarded a Sasagawa Scientific Research Grant.

Mária Kurdi is Professor in the Department of English Literatures and Cultures at the University of Pécs, Hungary. Her main fields of teaching and research are Irish literature and English-speaking drama. Her publications include two books on contemporary Irish drama, a collection of interviews with Irish playwrights, and an anthology of excerpts from critical material for the study of Irish literature in Hungary.

Helen Lojek is Professor of English at Boise State University, Idaho, where she teaches American literature and contemporary English language drama. Articles on Brian Friel, Frank McGuinness, Anne Devlin and the Charabanc Theatre Company have appeared in such journals as *Contemporary Literature, Modern Drama,* and *Irish University Review*. Her most recent publications are *Contexts for Frank McGuinness's Drama* (CUA, 2004) and *The Theatre of Frank McGuinness: Stages of Mutability* (Carysfort Press, 2002).

Patrick Lonergan lectures in English at National University of Ireland, Galway, and is an Ireland Representative for the International Association for the Study of Irish Literature. He writes about theatre in the west of Ireland for *The Irish Times*, and is reviews editor of *irish theatre magazine*. He has lectured on Irish drama at a variety of venues, including the Edinburgh International Festival, the Royal Irish Academy, and the Notre Dame Irish Seminar. He is currently working on a book on *Irish Theatre and Globalization*.

Donald E. Morse is University Professor of American, Irish, and English Literature at the University of Debrecen, Hungary, and Professor Emeritus of English and Rhetoric at Oakland University. He is the author of *The Novels of Kurt* Vonnegut and his previous books include *The Fantastic in World Literature and the Arts* (1987), *More Real than Reality: The Fantastic in Irish Literature and the Arts* (1991), and *The*

Celebration of the Fantastic (1992), all available from Greenwood Press. His most recent publication is *Brian Friel's Dramatic Artistry* (Carysfort Press, 2006) and *Anatomy of Science Fiction* (2006).

Christopher Murray is Emeritus Professor in the School of English and Drama, University College Dublin. A former editor of *Irish University Review* (1986-1997) and chair (2000-2003) of the International Association for the Study of Irish Literatures (IASIL), he is author of *Twentieth-Century Irish Drama: Mirror Up to Nation* (1997) and *Sean O'Casey Writer at Work: A Biography* (2004), and has edited *Brian Friel: Essays, Diaries, Interviews 1964-1999* (1999) and the RTE Thomas Davis Lectures for Samuel Beckett's centenary, *Beckett at 100, The Centenary Essays* (2006). He is currently editing *Selected Plays of George Shiels*.

Paul O'Brien lives in Dublin and is a writer and critic. His most recent work includes *Sean O'Casey and Hugh MacDiarmid: Politicians who couldn't help being writers* (2005), *Shelley and Catherine Nugent: Spirits of the Age* (2005), and *Shelley and Revolutionary Ireland* (2002).

Riana O'Dwyer is Senior Lecturer in the English Department at National University of Ireland, Galway. She has been Chairperson of the International Association for the Study of Irish Literatures [IASIL] since 2003 and was one of the organizers of IASIL Triennial Conference 2004 at Galway. She has lectured and published on Joyce, modern Irish drama, Irish studies, and Irish women novelists of the nineteenth century.

Alexandra Poulain is a senior lecturer at the University of Paris IV–Sorbonne, where she teaches English and Anglo-Irish literature and drama. She writes on modern and contemporary Irish drama and has translated plays by Colin Teevan, Frank McGuinness, Tom Murphy, and Thomas Kilroy into French.

Irina Ruppo graduated with a BA degree in English from Hebrew University Jerusalem (2002) and an M.Phil in Anglo-Irish Literature from Trinity College Dublin (2003). She is currently completing a PhD at National University of Ireland, Galway, on *Ibsen and the Irish Revival*.

Christa Velten-Mrowka graduated in philosophy and English and American literature at Johann Wolfgang Goethe University in Frankfurt, where she also studied with Horkheimer and Adorno. She taught English language and literature in Kronberg and Bad Homburg, near Frankfurt. She is the German translator of John Dewey, *Art as Experience* (with co-translators D. Sulzer and G. vom Hofe) and author of essays on O'Casey and Friel.

Index

Abbey Theatre, 1-27, 43-44, 46, 48-49, 56, 69-93, 105, 129, 170
Abe, Isoo, 54
Adorno, Theodor, 10, 95-106
Aisteoirí Átha Cliath, 21
Allgood, Sarah, 22, 74
Amin, Idi, 155, 158, 160
Anglo-Irish Agreement, 81, 82
Antoine, André, 11, 15
Archer, William, 34
Arnold, Matthew, 24, 31, 39
Artaud, Antonin, 76
Atkinson, Brooks, 77
Ayling, Ronald, 72, 74, 79

Balzac, Honoré de, 19
Barczewski, Stephanie, 67-68
Barnes, Ben, 2-3, 6, 15, 24-25, 67
Barone, Rosangela, 60, 67
Barry, Kevin, 83
Barry, Sebastian, 7, 22-23, 170, 173
   Hinterland, 170, 174, 176-178
   The House of Bernarda Alba (after Lorca), 22
   The Steward of Christendom, 173
Barthes, Roland, 172
Beckett, Samuel, 4, 14, 38, 46, 79, 104, 105, 139, 166
Behan, Brendan, 71
Belfast Newsletter, 91
Bentley, Eric, 22, 27, 77, 80
Berliner Ensemble, 77
Bharucha, Rustom, 157

Bloomsday, 1, 165
Blythe, Ernest, 15, 20-24, 27
Bond, Edward, 23
Bordo, Susan, 121-128
Boucicault, Dion, 3-6, 70, 105, 140
   The Colleen Bawn, 4
   The Shaughraun, 3- 6, 12, 25
Bowen, Elizabeth, 134, 140
Brecht, Bertolt, 71, 74-78, 80
Brown, Terence, 26, 133-134, 139-140

Cahill, Frank, 70
Carolan, Stuart, 14
Carr, Marina, 2, 9, 11, 23, 27, 128, 141-151, 170, 174-175
   Ariel, 11, 142, 146, 170, 174-178
   By the Bog of Cats..., 9, 27, 141-143, 148, 151
   Low in the Dark, 143
   On Raftery's Hill, 142, 144
   Portia Coughlan, 2, 141-144, 149
   The Mai, 9, 141-151
Castle, Gregory, 29, 36, 39, 61, 68
Celtic Literary Society, 41
Cerquoni, Enrica, 128, 145, 151
Charabanc Theatre Company, 8, 118
Chaudhuri, Una, 127
Chekhov, Anton, 14-15, 19, 55, 76
Chirac, Jacques, 86
Churchill, Winston, 134
Clarke, Austin, 24
Clarke, Jocelyn, 86, 92

Collini, Stefan, 67-68
Colum, Padraic, 8, 17, 41, 43-46
   Broken Soil, 44
   The Fiddler's House, 41, 44, 46
   The Miracle of the Corn, 44
Coole Park, 74
Corkery, Daniel, 172
Cousins, James, 44
Craig, Gordon, 76, 80
Crawley, Peter, 164
Cumann na nGaedheal, 41
Curtin, Deirdre, 171
Cusack, Cyril, 74, 79

Dantanus, Ulf, 100, 105
Dante, 32, 34
Darwin, Charles, 30-33, 36, 40
de Jongh, Nicholas, 85, 91
de Valera, Eamonn, 131-132
Dean, Joan FitzPatrick, 8, 26, 41, 138, 140
Deane, Seamus, 172, 179
Devlin, Anne
   After Easter, 124
Dickens, Charles, 70
Dickinson, Emily, 82
Digges, Dudley, 41
Dolan, Michael, 73-74
Dostoevsky, Fyodor, 19
Dowling, Joe, 15, 24-25, 27, 91
DruidSynge, 10, 29, 38, 68
Drury, Martin, 22
Dubbeljoint Theatre Company, 121
Dublin Drama League, 19, 21, 26, 49, 75-76, 80
Dublin Fringe Festival, 27
Dublin Theatre Festival, 38, 129, 133, 138
Duffy, Bernard, 70
Duke, Michael, 89, 92
Dürrenmatt, Friedrich, 175, 179

Edwards, Hilton, 19-20, 83, 91
Egoyan, Atom, 129, 139
Eliade, Mircea, 107, 116
Eliot, T.S., 99
Ellis-Fermor, Una, 14
Ervine, David, 85, 91

Fallon, Gabriel, 74-80
Fannin, Hilary, 11
Farrell, Bernard, 2
Father Ted, 7
Fay, Willie, 16
Fitzgerald, Barry, 74
Fitzgerald, Charles, 83-84, 91
Fitzpatrick, Lisa, 11, 169, 181
Fitz-Simon, Christopher, 12, 49, 56
Flannery, James W, 79, 96, 105
Fleming, Deborah, 66, 68
Foley, Imelda, 125, 128
Frankfurt School, 95
Frazier, Adrian, 16, 26, 42-43, 46
Freud, Sigmund, 35, 109
Fricker, Karen, 11, 89
Friel, Brian, 9-10, 15, 23, 83, 95-105, 122, 131, 140, 153-155, 161, 165, 172-173
   Dancing at Lughnasa, 15, 122, 153, 154-155
   Faith Healer, 100-105
   Give Me Your Answer, Do!, 98, 104
   Molly Sweeney, 101, 105
   Performances, 105
   Translations, 23, 83, 98, 131
Fugard, Athol, 166
Funahashi, Mika, 9, 141

Gaelic League, 16, 18, 20-21
Garvey, Maire, 43
Gate Theatre (Dublin), 14, 15, 19-20, 24-25, 75
Gate Theatre Studio (London), 76
Goethe, Johann Wolfgang von, 18, 33, 108
Goldsmith, Oliver, 14
Gomme, George Lawrence, 62, 68
Gonne, Maud, 41
Gorky, Maxim, 77
Gregory, Lady Augusta, 2, 4, 11, 15-17, 20-23, 26-27, 29, 39, 50, 61, 68, 70-74, 76, 79
   Cuchulain of Muirthemne, 17
   Spreading the News, 2
Grein, J.T., 15
Grene, Nicholas, 4, 12, 100, 105, 109, 116, 137, 139-140, 153

Griffith, Arthur, 43, 46
Guardian Newspaper, 11, 80, 84
Gwynn, Stephen, 44

Habermas, Jürgen, 171, 173-174, 178
Hamilton, Sheila, 84
Hampstead Theatre, 83
Hardy, Thomas, 8, 10, 59-68, 101-102, 104
   The Mayor of Casterbridge, 59-66
   The Return of the Native, 60
Hasegawa, Seiya, 54
Haughey, Charles, 174, 176
Hauptmann, Gerhart, 15, 17
Heaney, Seamus, 23, 27, 46, 169-170
   The Burial at Thebes, 15, 23, 27
Hill, Ian, 84, 89-92
Hitler, Adolf, 131-133
Hogan, Robert, 27, 43, 46, 56-57, 74, 79
Horniman, Annie, 16-17, 25, 46, 49
Howe, Stephen, 37, 40
Hughes, Declan, 169
   Shiver, 169
Hunt, Hugh, 15, 20, 25
Hutchinson, Ron, 83
Hyde, Douglas, 15-16, 20
Hynes, Garry, 15, 29, 38, 78

IASIL, 1-2, 6, 128, 140, 166, 183
Ibsen, Henrik, 14-19, 29-36, 55, 75
   Ghosts, 29-30, 37-38
Ichikawa II, Sadanji, 49
Independent Theatre (London), 15, 69
Inghinidhe na hÉireann, 41
Irigaray, Luce, 126, 128
Irish Homestead, 44
Irish Literary Theatre, 4, 6, 14-15, 41, 69
Irish Times, The, 12, 25, 27, 78, 83, 85, 91-92, 139-140, 161, 166

Japanese New Drama, 47, 57, 182
Jeffery, Keith, 82
John, Augustus, 76
Johnston, Denis, 76, 79-80
Johnston, Jennifer, 83

Jones, Marie, 8, 117-118, 127-128
   A Night in November, 118, 126
   The Hamster Wheel, 118
   Women on the Verge of HRT, 8, 117-24, 127
Jordan, Eamonn, 128, 130, 139, 154
Joyce, James, 11, 14-15, 26, 30, 34-35, 39, 46, 75
   The Day of the Rabblement, 14, 75
Jubainville, Professor Henri d'Arbois de, 34

Kasozi, A.B.K., 161
Kavanagh, John, 15
Kavanagh, Patrick, 1
Keane, Terry, 174
Kearney, Richard, 171, 173, 174
Kennelly, Brendan, 23, 139, 170, 179
Kettle, Thomas, 44, 84
Key, Ellen, 138
Kiberd, Declan, 62, 68, 100, 105, 134, 140, 153, 155, 161, 172
Kilroy, Thomas, 23, 27, 43, 46, 80, 102, 105
King, Jason, 11, 153, 166-167
King, Mary C., 10, 29, 40, 68
Kipling, Rudyard, 67
Knebel, Maria, 22, 79
Knowles, Ric, 159
Kojima, Chiaki, 8, 47
Kosok, Heinz, 71, 79
Kristeva, Julia, 120, 127, 171, 178, 179
Kuti, Elizabeth, 11

Lacan, Jacques, 30, 109
Lang, R.D., 60
Larkin, Jim, 70
Late Late Show, The, 3, 165
Lavelle, Honor, 43
Legendre, Pierre, 107, 116
Levitas, Ben, 16, 18, 29
Lincoln Center (New York), 87
Littlewood, Joan, 71
Llewellyn-Jones, Margaret, 123, 127
Lojek, Helen, 9, 81, 135, 139
Lonergan, Patrick, 1, 156
Long, Joseph, 86

Longley, Michael, 83, 91
Lorca, Federico Garcia, 22
Lyric Theatre (Belfast), 24, 83, 91, 92
Lysaght, Patricia, 123, 126-128

Mac Anna, Tomás, 15, 25
MacDonagh, Thomas, 21
MacLiammóir, Micheál, 19
Malone, Andrew, 53
Marlowe, Christopher, 108, 114
Martyn, Edward, 15-16, 20
Marx, Karl
    Das Kapital, 35
Mason, Patrick, 3-4, 15, 25-26, 85, 130, 145
Massey, Raymond, 76
Mathews, P.J., 16
Matsui, Shoyo, 8, 47-57
    Kesa and Morito, 49
McAuley, Gay, 118, 127
McCafferty, Owen, 7
McCann, Donal, 15
McColgan, John, 3, 5-6
McCormack, W.J., 29-30, 38, 60, 62, 67-68, 73-74
McDonagh, Martin
    The Pillowman, 46
McDonald, Ronan, 29
McGuinness, Frank, 2, 9, 23, 27, 38, 46, 81-92, 105, 129-140, 173
    Dolly West's Kitchen, 9, 129-140
    Innocence, 46
    Observe the Sons of Ulster Marching Towards the Somme, 81, 91-92, 130, 139
    Someone Who'll Watch Over Me, 92, 130, 135
McIntyre, Tom, 11

McMaster, Brian, 78
McMinn, Joe, 83
McMullan, Anna, 27, 117, 125, 127-128, 151
McPherson, Conor, 7
Meany, Helen, 6, 12
Medea, 145, 148, 170
Meehan, Paula, 2, 25
melodrama, 3-4, 72, 110

Melvin, Dorothea, 85, 91
Mercier, Paul, 2, 20, 25
Mercier, Vivian, 43, 46
Merriman, Victor, 162
Mikami, Hiroko, 131, 133, 139
Miller, Arthur, 13
    The Crucible, 13
Molière, 15, 18
Mooney, Ria, 22
Morash, Chris, 4, 11, 24, 27, 29, 87, 92
Morrison, Conall, 4
Morse, Donald, 9, 129
Moscow Arts Theatre, 69, 79
Moylan, Thomas, 70
Murphy, Cillian, 7
Murphy, Tom, 10, 23, 27, 107, 116, 139
    Bailegangaire, 109, 116
    The Gigli Concert, 2, 10, 25, 107, 108, 116
    The Morning After Optimism, 107
    The Sanctuary Lamp, 107
    Too Late for Logic, 107
Murray, Christopher, 7, 8, 10, 13, 72, 74, 79, 105, 130, 139
Myers, Kevin, 85, 91

National Literary Society, 41
Nemirovich-Danchenko, Vladimir Ivanovich, 15
New Ireland Forum, 81
Ní Chaoimh, Bairbre, 164, 166
Ní Dhuibhne, Eilis, 11, 149, 151
Nic Shiubhlaigh, Máire, 16, 26
Nietzsche, Friedrich, 10, 33-34, 95-97, 105
    Twilight of the Idols, 95
Nightingale, Benedict, 85, 91
Noh Drama, 47
Norman H.F., 44

O'Brien, Eugene, 25
O'Brien, Flann, 7
O'Brien, George, 74
O'Brien, Paul, 10, 69, 183
O'Casey, Sean, 4, 12, 27, 69, 78-80
    Cathleen Listens In, 75

Juno and the Paycock, 15, 20, 72-75
Purple Dust, 72, 78
Red Roses for Me, 72-73, 79
The Cooing of the Doves, 73
The Crimson in the Tricolour, 72-73
The Frost in the Flower, 70, 72
The Harvest Festival, 70, 73, 79
The Plough and the Stars, 20, 73-75, 78
The Shadow of a Gunman, 19, 69, 71, 73
The Silver Tassie, 20, 69, 70-72, 75-77
The Star Turns Red, 72
O'Connor, Fergus, 70
O'Connor, Frank, 77, 80
O'Donnell, Daniel, 119
O'Donnell, Mary, 84, 91
O'Hara, Joan, 22
O'Kelly, Donal, 154-161, 165-166
  Asylum! Asylum!, 154-166
O'Kelly, Seumas
  The Flame on the Hearth, 44
  The Matchmakers, 44
  The Shuiler's Child, 41, 44-46
O'Neill, Charlie
  Hurl, 154-155, 161, 164, 166
O'Neill, Eugene, 22
O'Neill, Michael J., 22, 80
O'Sullivan, Seamus, 44
O'Toole, Fintan, 25, 103, 113, 116, 129, 131, 139, 159, 162-163, 170, 179
Obote, Milton, 155, 158, 160
Ohsasa, Yoshio, 55, 57
Okada, Shin-ichiro, 54
Olagun, Modupe, 160
Ooyama, Ikuo, 54
Oresteia, 174-175
Orr, Philip, 89, 92
Owen, Wilfred, 82

Parker, Stewart, 5, 46, 139
  Heavenly Bodies, 5, 25, 46
Pater, Walter, 34
Pavis, Patrice, 157
Peacock Theatre (Dublin), 141, 162

Pilkington, Lionel, 16, 29, 81, 90
Pine, Richard, 139
Pinter, Harold, 23
Pirandello, Luigi, 19, 76
Poizat, Michel, 114, 116
postcolonialism, 171-172
postnationalism, 171-174
Poulain, Alexandra, 10, 86, 107
Progressive Unionist Party, 85

Quinn, Marie T., 41

Red Kettle Theatre Company, 84
Richards, Shaun, 12, 156, 166
Riverdance, 3, 5
Roberts, George, 44
Robinson, Lennox, 2, 8, 18, 21, 26-27, 47-48, 57, 72, 75, 80
  Drama at Inish, 2
  Harvest, 8, 48-57, 73
Robinson, Mary, 86, 165
Roche, Anthony, 100, 105, 139
Ross, Florence, 32
RTE (Radio Telefis Eireann), 6, 12, 85, 91, 92
Ruppo, Irina, 8, 59, 183
Russell, George (AE), 44, 75
Russo, Mary, 119, 124, 127

Scarry, Elaine, 145, 150-151
Schaubühne (Berlin), 78
Schauspielhaus (Zurich), 78
Schiller, Friedrich, 18, 33
Schopenhauer, Arthur, 34
Seremba, George, 153-167
  Come Good Rain, 154-166
Sewamono, 52
Shakespeare, William, 4, 18, 70, 83
Shaw, G.B., 15, 18, 48, 73, 76
Shelley, P.B., 70
Sheridan, Peter, 25
Sheridan, R.B.
  The Rivals, 13
Shimamura, Hogetsu, 47
Shiraishi, Jituzo, 54
Sihra, Melissa, 128
Simpson, Alan, 71, 79
Sinn Fein, 43, 72
Soma, Gyofu, 54

Sophocles, 14, 18, 23
Spenser, Charles, 91
Stafford, Maeliosa, 87
Stanislavsky, Konstantin, 69, 77
Steiner, George, 98
Stembridge, Gerard (Gerry), 14, 170
Stoppard, Tom, 23
Strindberg, August, 19, 55, 76
Sunday Tribune, 84, 91, 141
Synge, Alexander, 36
Synge, Barbara, 29, 38
Synge, J.M., 2, 4, 8, 10, 16-46, 49, 59-68, 95-96, 105, 137
  Deirdre of the Sorrows, 38
  In the Shadow of the Glen, 35, 37-38, 41-45
  Riders to the Sea, 35, 39, 60
  The Aran Islands, 30, 33, 36, 67
  The Playboy of the Western World, 2, 5, 7, 35, 37, 39, 42, 59, 61, 95
  The Tinker's Wedding, 42
  The Well of the Saints, 35, 42
  When the Moon Has Set, 29, 30, 34, 36-40

Taibhdhearc na Gaillimhe, 21, 23
Teevan, Colin, 170, 183
Theatre Guild (New York), 76
Theatre of Ireland, 43-46
Tierney, Michael, 133
Todd, Mary, 71, 79
Toller, Ernst, 19, 76-77

Tompkins, Joanne, 118, 127
Trinity College Dublin, 32, 40, 166
Trotter, Mary, 16

University College Dublin, 91

Vernon, Emma, 43
Voltaire, 112
Vonnegut, Kurt, 132

Walker, Frank, 43
Watt, Stephen, 4, 11-12
Weigel, Helene, 77
West, Michael, 23
Whitbread, J.W., 4
Wilde, Oscar, 96
Williams, Caroline, 117, 127
Wills, Clair, 132, 134
Woods, Vincent, 25, 44, 45
Worth, Katherine, 14

Yeats, W.B., 2, 4, 10, 14-31, 34-50, 57, 67-79, 83, 96, 105, 157
  Cathleen Ní Houlihan, 5, 16, 176
  On Baile's Strand, 17
  On the Boiler, 16, 39
  Purgatory, 2, 39
  The Countess Cathleen, 15
  The King's Threshold, 41-44, 46
  The Shadowy Waters, 17

Zakhava, Boris, 77

CARYSFORT PRESS

Carysfort Press was formed in the summer of 1998. It receives annual funding from the Arts Council.

The directors believe that drama is playing an ever-increasing role in today's society and that enjoyment of the theatre, both professional and amateur, currently plays a central part in Irish culture.

The Press aims to produce high quality publications which, though written and/or edited by academics, will be made accessible to a general readership. The organisation would also like to provide a forum for critical thinking in the Arts in Ireland, again keeping the needs and interests of the general public in view.

The company publishes contemporary Irish writing for and about the theatre.

Editorial and publishing inquiries to:

CARYSFORT PRESS Ltd
58 Woodfield, Scholarstown Road,
Rathfarnham, Dublin 16,
Republic of Ireland

T (353 1) 493 7383 F (353 1) 406 9815
e: info@carysfortpress.com
www.carysfortpress.com

NEW TITLES

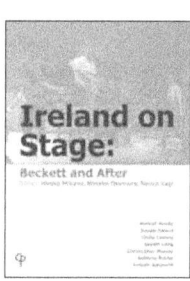

IRELAND ON STAGE: BECKETT AND AFTER
EDITORS: HIROKO MIKAMI, MINAKO OKAMURO, NAOKO YAGI

A collection of ten essays on contemporary Irish theatre. The focus is primarily on Irish playwrights and their works, both in text and on the stage, in the latter half of the twentieth century. The essays range from Samuel Beckett to Brian Friel, Frank McGuinness, Marina Carr, and Conor McPherson. There is frequent reference back to Wilde, Yeats, Synge, Shaw, O'Casey, and Joyce.

ISBN   978-1-904505-23-5
€20

GOETHE AND ANNA AMALIA: A FORBIDDEN LOVE?
BY ETTORE GHIBELLINO, TRANS. DAN FARRELLY

In this study Ghibellino sets out to show that the platonic relationship between Goethe and Charlotte von Stein – lady-in-waiting to Anna Amalia, the Dowager Duchess of Weimar – was used as part of a cover-up for Goethe's intense and prolonged love relationship with the Duchess Anna Amalia herself. The book attempts to uncover a hitherto closely-kept state secret. Readers convinced by the evidence supporting Ghibellino's hypothesis will see in it one of the very great love stories in European history – to rank with that of Dante and Beatrice, and Petrarch and Laura.

ISBN   978-1-904505-24-2
EAN   9781904505242
€25

EDNA O'BRIEN
'NEW CRITICAL PERSPECTIVES'
EDITED BY KATHRYN LAING
SINÉAD MOONEY AND MAUREEN O'CONNOR

The essays collected here illustrate some of the range, complexity, and interest of Edna O'Brien as a fiction writer and dramatist…They will contribute to a broader appreciation of her work and to an evolution of new critical approaches, as well as igniting more interest in the many unexplored areas of her considerable oeuvre.

ISBN 1-904505-20-1
€20

THE THEATRE OF MARTIN MCDONAGH
'A WORLD OF SAVAGE STORIES'
EDITED BY LILIAN CHAMBERS AND EAMONN JORDAN

The book is a vital response to the many challenges set by McDonagh for those involved in the production and reception of his work. Critics and commentators from around the world offer a diverse range of often provocative approaches. What is not surprising is the focus and commitment of the engagement, given the controversial and stimulating nature of the work.

ISBN 1-904505-19-8
€30

BRIAN FRIEL'S DRAMATIC ARTISTRY
'THE WORK HAS VALUE'
EDITED BY DONALD E. MORSE, CSILLA BERTHA, AND MÁRIA KURDI

Brian Friel's Dramatic Artistry presents a refreshingly broad range of voices: new work from some of the leading English-speaking authorities on Friel, and fascinating essays from scholars in Germany, Italy, Portugal, and Hungary. This book will deepen our knowledge and enjoyment of Friel's work.

ISBN 1-904505-17-1
€25

PLAYBOYS OF THE WESTERN WORLD
PRODUCTION HISTORIES
EDITED BY ADRIAN FRAZIER

'Playboys of the Western World is a model of contemporary performance studies.'

'The book is remarkably well-focused: half is a series of production histories of Playboy performances through the twentieth century in the UK, Northern Ireland, the USA, and Ireland. The remainder focuses on one contemporary performance, that of Druid Theatre, as directed by Garry Hynes. The various contemporary social issues that are addressed in relation to Synge's play and this performance of it give the volume an additional interest: it shows how the arts matter.' *Kevin Barry*

ISBN 1-904505-06-6
€20

NEW TITLES

OUT OF HISTORY
'ESSAYS ON THE WRITINGS OF SEBASTIAN BARRY'
EDITED WITH AN INTRODUCTION BY CHRISTINA HUNT MAHONY

The essays address Barry's engagement with the contemporary cultural debate in Ireland and also with issues that inform postcolonial criticial theory. The range and selection of contributors has ensured a high level of critical expression and an insightful assessment of Barry and his works.

ISBN 1-904505-18-X
€20

IRISH THEATRE ON TOUR
EDITED BY NICHOLAS GRENE AND CHRIS MORASH

'Touring has been at the strategic heart of Druid's artistic policy since the early eighties. Everyone has the right to see professional theatre in their own communities. Irish theatre on tour is a crucial part of Irish theatre as a whole'. *Garry Hynes*

ISBN 1-904505-13-9
€20

GEORGE FITZMAURICE:
'WILD IN HIS OWN WAY'
BIOGRAPHY OF AN ABBEY PLAYWRIGHT
BY FIONA BRENNAN
WITH A FOREWORD BY FINTAN O'TOOLE

Fiona Brennan's...introduction to his considerable output allows us a much greater appreciation and understanding of Fitzmaurice, the one remaining under-celebrated genius of twentieth-century Irish drama.
Conall Morrison

ISBN 1-904505-16-3
€20

THE POWER OF LAUGHTER
EDITED BY ERIC WEITZ

The collection draws on a wide range of perspectives and voices including critics, playwrights, directors and performers. The result is a series of fascinating and provocative debates about the myriad functions of comedy in contemporary Irish theatre. *Anna McMullan*

As Stan Laurel said, it takes only an onion to cry. Peel it and weep. Comedy is harder. These essays listen to the power of laughter. They hear the tough heart of Irish theatre – hard and wicked and funny. *Frank McGuinness*

ISBN 1-904505-05-8
€20

NEW TITLES

EAST OF EDEN
NEW ROMANIAN PLAYS
EDITED BY ANDREI MARINESCU

Four of the most promising Romanian playwrights, young and very young, are in this collection, each one with a specific way of seeing the Romanian reality, each one with a style of communicating an articulated artistic vision of the society we are living in.
Ion Caramitru, General Director Romanian National Theatre Bucharest

ISBN 1-904505-15-5
€10

SYNGE: A CELEBRATION
EDITED BY COLM TÓIBÍN

Sebastian Barry, Marina Carr, Anthony Cronin, Roddy Doyle, Anne Enright, Hugo Hamilton, Joseph O'Connor, Mary O'Malley, Fintan O'Toole, Colm Toibin, Vincent Woods.

ISBN 1-904505-14-7
€15 Paperback

POEMS 2000–2005
BY HUGH MAXTON

Poems 2000-2005 is a transitional collection written while the author – also known to be W. J. Mc Cormack, literary historian – was in the process of moving back from London to settle in rural Ireland.

ISBN 1-904505-12-0
€10

HAMLET
THE SHAKESPEAREAN DIRECTOR
BY MIKE WILCOCK

"This study of the Shakespearean director as viewed through various interpretations of HAMLET is a welcome addition to our understanding of how essential it is for a director to have a clear vision of a great play. It is an important study from which all of us who love Shakespeare and who understand the importance of continuing contemporary exploration may gain new insights."

From the Foreword, by Joe Dowling, Artistic Director, The Guthrie Theater, Minneapolis, MN

ISBN 1-904505-00-7
€20

NEW TITLES

GEORG BÜCHNER: WOYZECK
A NEW TRANSLATION BY DAN FARRELLY

The most up-to-date German scholarship of Thomas Michael Mayer and Burghard Dedner has finally made it possible to establish an authentic sequence of scenes. The widespread view that this play is a prime example of loose, open theatre is no longer sustainable. Directors and teachers are challenged to "read it again".

ISBN 1-904505-02-3
€10

MUSICS OF BELONGING:
THE POETRY OF MICHEAL O'SIADHAIL
EDITED BY MARC CABALL AND DAVID F. FORD

An overall account is given of O'Siadhail's life, his work and the reception of his poetry so far. There are close readings of some poems, analyses of his artistry in matching diverse content with both classical and innovative forms, and studies of recurrent themes such as love, death, language, music, and the shifts of modern life.

Paperback €25
ISBN 978-1-904505-22-8

Casebound €50
ISBN: 978-1-904505-21-1

CRITICAL MOMENTS
FINTAN O'TOOLE ON MODERN IRISH THEATRE
EDITED BY JULIA FURAY & REDMOND O'HANLON

This new book on the work of Fintan O'Toole, the internationally acclaimed theatre critic and cultural commentator, offers percussive analyses and assessments of the major plays and playwrights in the canon of modern Irish theatre. Fearless and provocative in his judgements, O'Toole is essential reading for anyone interested in criticism or in the current state of Irish theatre.

ISBN 1-904505-03-1
€20

THE THEATRE OF MARINA CARR
"BEFORE RULES WAS MADE" - EDITED BY ANNA MCMULLAN & CATHY LEENEY

As the first published collection of articles on the theatre of Marina Carr, this volume explores the world of Carr's theatrical imagination, the place of her plays in contemporary theatre in Ireland and abroad and the significance of her highly individual voice.

ISBN 0-9534-2577-0
€20

NEW TITLES

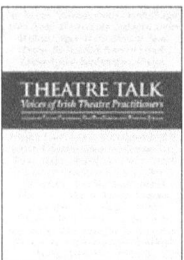

THEATRE TALK
VOICES OF IRISH THEATRE PRACTITIONERS
EDITED BY LILIAN CHAMBERS &
GER FITZGIBBON

"This book is the right approach - asking practitioners what they feel."
Sebastian Barry, Playwright

"...an invaluable and informative collection of interviews with those who make and shape the landscape of Irish Theatre."
Ben Barnes, Artistic Director of the Abbey Theatre

ISBN 0-9534-2576-2
€20

SACRED PLAY
SOUL JOURNEYS IN CONTEMPORARY
IRISH THEATRE BY ANNE F. O'REILLY

'Theatre as a space or container for sacred play allows audiences to glimpse mystery and to experience transformation. This book charts how Irish playwrights negotiate the labyrinth of the Irish soul and shows how their plays contribute to a poetics of Irish culture that enables a new imagining. Playwrights discussed are: McGuinness, Murphy, Friel, Le Marquand Hartigan, Burke Brogan, Harding, Meehan, Carr, Parker, Devlin, and Barry.'

ISBN 1-904505-07-4
€25

GOETHE AND SCHUBERT
ACROSS THE DIVIDE
EDITED BY LORRAINE BYRNE & DAN FARRELLY

Proceedings of the International Conference, 'Goethe and Schubert in Perspective and Performance', Trinity College Dublin, 2003. This volume includes essays by leading scholars – Barkhoff, Boyle, Byrne, Canisius, Dürr, Fischer, Hill, Kramer, Lamport, Lund, Meikle, Newbould, Norman McKay, White, Whitton, Wright, Youens – on Goethe's musicality and his relationship to Schubert; Schubert's contribution to sacred music and the Lied and his setting of Goethe's Singspiel, Claudine. A companion volume of this Singspiel (with piano reduction and English translation) is also available.

ISBN 1-904505-04-X
Goethe and Schubert: Across the Divide. €25

ISBN 0-9544290-0-1
Goethe and Schubert: 'Claudine von Villa Bella'. €14

GOETHE: MUSICAL POET, MUSICAL CATALYST
EDITED BY LORRAINE BYRNE

'Goethe was interested in, and acutely aware of, the place of music in human experience generally - and of its particular role in modern culture. Moreover, his own literary work - especially the poetry and Faust - inspired some of the major composers of the European tradition to produce some of their finest works.' *Martin Swales*

ISBN 1-904505-10-4
€30

NEW TITLES

THEATRE OF SOUND
RADIO AND THE DRAMATIC IMAGINATION
BY DERMOT RATTIGAN

An innovative study of the challenges that radio drama poses to the creative imagination of the writer, the production team, and the listener.

"A remarkably fine study of radio drama – everywhere informed by the writer's professional experience of such drama in the making…A new theoretical and analytical approach – informative, illuminating and at all times readable." *Richard Allen Cave*

ISBN 0-9534-2575-4
€20

TALKING ABOUT TOM MURPHY
EDITED BY NICHOLAS GRENE

Talking About Tom Murphy is shaped around the six plays in the landmark Abbey Theatre Murphy Season of 2001, assembling some of the best-known commentators on his work: Fintan O'Toole, Chris Morash, Lionel Pilkington, Alexandra Poulain, Shaun Richards, Nicholas Grene and Declan Kiberd.

ISBN 0-9534-2579-7
€15

THE THEATRE OF FRANK MCGUINNESS
STAGES OF MUTABILITY
EDITED BY HELEN LOJEK

The first edited collection of essays about internationally renowned Irish playwright Frank McGuinness focuses on both performance and text. Interpreters come to diverse conclusions, creating a vigorous dialogue that enriches understanding and reflects a strong consensus about the value of McGuinness's complex work.

ISBN 1-904505-01-5
€20

THE DRUNKARD
TOM MURPHY

'The Drunkard is a wonderfully eloquent play. Murphy's ear is finely attuned to the glories and absurdities of melodramatic exclamation, and even while he is wringing out its ludicrous overstatement, he is also making it sing.'
The Irish Times

ISBN 1-904505-09-0
€10

NEW TITLES

THREE CONGREGATIONAL MASSES
BY SEÓIRSE BODLEY,
EDITED BY LORRAINE BYRNE

'From the simpler congregational settings in the Mass of Peace and the Mass of Joy to the richer textures of the Mass of Glory, they are immediately attractive and accessible, and with a distinctively Irish melodic quality.' *Barra Boydell*

ISBN 1-904505-11-2
€15

THE IRISH HARP BOOK
BY SHEILA LARCHET CUTHBERT

This is a facsimile of the edition originally published by Mercier Press in 1993. There is a new preface by Sheila Larchet Cuthbert, and the biographical material has been updated. It is a collection of studies and exercises for the use of teachers and pupils of the Irish harp.

ISBN 1-904505-08-2
€35

BACK LIST

SEEN AND HEARD (REPRINT)
SIX NEW PLAYS BY IRISH WOMEN
EDITED WITH AN INTRODUCTION
BY CATHY LEENEY

A rich and funny, moving and theatrically exciting collection of plays by Mary Elizabeth Burke-Kennedy, Síofra Campbell, Emma Donoghue, Anne Le Marquand Hartigan, Michelle Read and Dolores Walshe.

ISBN 0-9534-2573-8
€20

UNDER THE CURSE
GOETHE'S "IPHIGENIE AUF TAURIS",
IN A NEW VERSION BY DAN FARRELLY

The Greek myth of Iphigenie grappling with the curse on the house of Atreus is brought vividly to life. This version is currently being used in Johannesburg to explore problems of ancestry, religion, and Black African women's spirituality.

ISBN 0-9534-2572-X
€10

THEATRE STUFF (REPRINT)
CRITICAL ESSAYS ON
CONTEMPORARY IRISH THEATRE
EDITED BY EAMONN JORDAN

Best selling essays on the successes and debates of contemporary Irish theatre at home and abroad.

Contributors include: Thomas Kilroy, Declan Hughes, Anna McMullan, Declan Kiberd, Deirdre Mulrooney, Fintan O'Toole, Christopher Murray, Caoimhe McAvinchey and Terry Eagleton.

ISBN 0-9534-2571-1
€20

URFAUST
A NEW VERSION OF GOETHE'S
EARLY "FAUST" IN BRECHTIAN MODE
BY DAN FARRELLY

This version is based on Brecht's irreverent and daring re-interpretation of the German classic.

"Urfaust is a kind of well-spring for German theatre… The love-story is the most daring and the most profound in German dramatic literature." *Brecht*

ISBN 0-9534257-0-3
€10

IN SEARCH OF THE SOUTH AFRICAN IPHIGENIE
BY ERIKA VON WIETERSHEIM
AND DAN FARRELLY

Discussions of Goethe's "Iphigenie auf Tauris" (Under the Curse) as relevant to women's issues in modern South Africa: women in family and public life; the force of women's spirituality; experience of personal relationships; attitudes to parents and ancestors; involvement with religion.

ISBN 0-9534-2578-9
€10

THE STARVING AND OCTOBER SONG
TWO CONTEMPORARY IRISH PLAYS
BY ANDREW HINDS

The Starving, set during and after the siege of Derry in 1689, is a moving and engrossing drama of the emotional journey of two men.

October Song, a superbly written family drama set in real time in pre-ceasefire Derry.

ISBN 0-9534-2574-6
€10

HOW TO ORDER
TRADE ORDERS DIRECTLY TO

CMD
Columba Mercier Distribution,
55A Spruce Avenue,
Stillorgan Industrial Park,
Blackrock,
Co. Dublin

T: (353 1) 294 2560
F: (353 1) 294 2564
E: cmd@columba.ie

*FOR SALES IN NORTH AMERICA
AND CANADA*

Dufour Editions Inc.,
124 Byers Road,
PO Box 7,
Chester Springs, PA 19425,
USA

T: 1-610-458-5005
F: 1-610-458-7103

www.ingramcontent.com/pod-product-compliance
Ingram Content Group UK Ltd.
Pitfield, Milton Keynes, MK11 3LW, UK
UKHW022000220326
11408UKWH00003B/405